SIGNIFICANCE OF INDO-RUSSIAN RELATIONS IN 21ST CENTURY

SIGNIFICANCE OF INDO-RUSSIAN RELATIONS IN 21ST CENTURY

Editor
V.D. CHOPRA

PUBLICATIONS

KALPAZ PUBLICATIONS

DELHI-110052

Significance of Indo-Russian Relations in 21st Century

Rs. 790

ISBN: 81-7835-647-3

Published in 2008 in India by
Kalpaz Publications
C-30, Satyawati Nagar,
Delhi-110052
E-mail: kalpaz@hotmail.com
Phone : 9212729499

Laser Type Setting by: Quick Media, Delhi
Printed at : Singal Print Media, Delhi

Contents

List of Contributors

1. Prof. V.P. Dutt	Former Pro-Vice Chancellor, Delhi University and former Member of Parliament; Leading Expert on International Affairs, an Author.
2. Prof. K.R. Singh	Former Professor, School of International Studies, Jawaharlal Nehru University, New Delhi; Expert on India's Foreign Policy.
3. Prof. P.L. Dash	Professor of Eurasian Studies at the Centre for Central Eurasian Studies, University of Mumbai; Expert on Russia.
4. Prof. V.D. Chopra	Former Chief Editor, *Patriot* (Daily) and *Link* (Weekly), Vice President International Institute for Asia - Pacific Studies, New Delhi and a well-known Author, expert on Indo-Russian Relations.
5. Mr. Manohar Singh Batra	Former Deputy Director General, All India Radio and expert on International Affairs particularly Russia, Afghanistan and UN.
6. Prof. B.K. Shrivastava	Former Professor, Centre for American Studies, Jawaharlal Nehru Universi'y, New Delhi and expert on Gulf Countries.
7. Brigadier (Retd.) Chandra B. Khanduri	Well-known Author in Military History and Strategy Expert in United Nations Peace Keeping Operations and Developments, and Defence Analyst.

8. Dr. Ranjan Kumar	Assistant Professor, Centre for Russian and Central Asian Studies, School of International Studies, Jawaharlal Nehru University; and an Expert on Russia.
9. Dr. Ranjana Mishra	Head, Department of History M.D. Shah Mahila College, SNDT University, Mumbai.
10. Dr. Nivedita Das Kundu	Associate Fellow, Institute for Defence Studies and Analyses, New Delhi.
11. Dr. Sanjay Deshpande	Lecturer in the Centre for Central Eurasian Studies, University of Mumbai.
12. Dr. Debidatta Aurobinda Mahapatra	Research Associate in the Centre for Central Eurasian Studies, University of Mumbai.
13. Dr. Kishore Kumar	Joint Secretary, Society for Indian Ocean Studies, New Delhi.
14. Prof. Kalim Bahadur	Former Professor, Jawaharlal Nehru University, New Delhi and an Expert on Pakistan, Afghanistan and Religious Fundamentalism and Terrorism.
15. Major General (Retd.) Afsir Karim	Security Expert and Editor, Aakrosh - Journal on Terrorism; Leading Expert on Terrorism and Security.

Introduction

This book is based on research papers by scholars and experts on 'Global and Regional Significance of Indo-Russian relations in the 21st Century'.

The study is a non-official and a voluntary intellectual exercise and has been conceptualized to give a fresh look to the Indo-Russian relations in the new historical conditions with an inter-disciplinary approach.

The scholars and experts who have contributed papers for this book are specialists in their areas of research. Though a large number of books have been written in the recent decades on Indo-Soviet and Indo-Russian relations, the merit of this book is that it critically examines and evaluates these relations on the basis of empirical data and statistics with an open mind and without any preconceived notions and ideological fixation in the new situation.

Statistics are indicators of processes taking place in social development if one goes by statistics; Asia-Pacific has already emerged as a region of the future. In fact some scholars have described the 21st century as the 'Asian Century'. This underlines that 'Centre of Gravity' of politics and economics has clearly shifted to Asia. That brings into focus as to why the attention of the major world powers is now riveted on this region. The statistics clearly show that if in the end of the last century Japan became a super economic power and penetrated into the economy of the United States, in the beginning of the 21st century, China and India have emerged as Asian Giants. To give one example, Indian entrepreneurs are buying over some of the major industries in the western world such as steel and motor car manufacturing industries. Americans, protected for two centuries by vast oceans, enriched by natural resources are facing new political and economic challenges. They are engaged in adjusting their political and economic policies to the new realties. This study has been confined to Indo-Russian relations.

It may be recalled here that in 1947 when India became an independent and sovereign state and the last British soldier left the shores of India, the decolonization in the world assumed a new dimension. India not only became the leader of the Afro-Asian nations, but also laid the foundation of Indo-Soviet friendship. This opened a new chapter of building relations with the Soviet Union.

In 1971 when India stepped out from the status of a backward agrarian state to the most developed nation among the developing countries, it marked the beginning of a new phase of Indo-Soviet relations.

This conclusion is reflected in the various papers in this book. Before we refer to these trends, it is necessary to examine the changes that are taking place in Russia.

After the disintegration of the Soviet Union and dismantling of its centrally controlled economy in the early 90's of the last century, the western world came to believe that Russia had been reduced to the status of a secondary power. There is no doubt that in the first two to three years under the leadership of Boris Yeltsin, Russia did receive a serious setback. However pride in Russian patriotism asserted itself and it recovered from the shock of the disintegration of the Soviet Union. It evolved its own model of democratic system and market economy. Nevertheless Russia created its own model of mixed economy in which public sector occupied a key position. Thus a period of resurgence of Russian economy and political stability began. In this connection one important factor about Russia's oil wealth needs to be underlined. According to some experts before the disintegration of the Soviet Union it had thirty percent of the known oil resources of the world. Now Russia has twenty percent of the known oil wealth of the world. Thus even today, Russia is one of the topmost countries as far as oil wealth is concerned and the Russian political leadership is using these oil resources to build the economy of their country. This has given stability to Russia's economy. It has begun to sell oil to the western countries. This has far reaching implications.

Moreover public and private sectors of India are negotiating with Russia for investments in the offshore oil explorations. There is yet another aspect which binds India and Russia together. Both these countries are witnessing a popular upsurge of national pride. The new generation of India transcending party barriers has a sense of pride in their country. This is rooted in the history of Indian national movement in which their forefathers participated. That the slogan Chak De India (raise India to a height) has gripped the minds of Indian youth is a manifestation of resurgence of patriotism.

Almost identical is the nationalist upsurge which Russia is witnessing. Russian youth recalls with pride how their forefathers with remarkable determination defended the integrity and unity of the country against Nazi invasion during the Second World War. Millions of Russian men and women laid down their lives in the struggle.

This upsurge of national pride both in India and Russia indicates that in the coming period the political leadership of both the countries will have to evolve a model of co-operation in a relationship keeping in the forefront the national interests of their respective lands.

This study shows that notwithstanding the fact that India is building new relationship with the United States, Indo-Russian relations continue to grow and flourish. This reflects multiplicity of India's foreign policy. Beside this it has to be kept in mind that both India and Russia are committed to multipolarism. This has been reiterated by the political leaders of both the countries. It is in this sense that one should estimate the global significance of Indo-Russian relations. However in this book a paper has been included on 'State of US Relations with Russia and Its Implications for India'. This shows linkage between bilateralism and multilateralism. It is for instance of a far reaching significance that India has not only close relations with Iran but is against any military action by the United States. This clearly illustrates the multi-polarity of India's foreign policy.

Another important aspect of this study is that it examines Indo-Russian defence co-operation. The study shows that India imports about 70 per cent of its military hardware from Russia and these components are used in some of the strategic areas of defence, though it is diversifying its military purchases, primarily to modernize its naval and air force services. It is at the same time importing Russian technology and equipment in certain sensitive areas. This is how Indo-Russian relations have become an important component of defence of India's security and sovereignty.

Russia exports to India a substantial portion of its military hardware. This according to one estimate comes to about 40 per cent of Russian production. The cold statistics clearly bring out how the military co-operation between India and Russia is in the larger interests of the two countries.

In this study the strategic relations between India and Russia have been analyzed. There are some scholars who are of the opinion that Indo-Russian relations have already assumed a strategic character. There are others who are of the view that these relations are on the threshold of assuming a strategic character. However, what clearly stands out is that arms deals have deeper implication than the commercial deals.

Indo-Russian co-operation in Science and Technology, particularly nuclear and space technology, is of far reaching importance than what appears. Soviet Union and now Russia have been making available to India their expert knowledge in these sensitive areas without any strings.

It may be mentioned here that Russia is one of the four countries of the world which have developed advanced technology and equipment for generation of nuclear energy. The other countries are United States, France and Japan. In fact multifaceted scientific co-operation has been thriving between India and Russia. The most important co-operation is in nuclear energy. As a culmination of this process Russia has reaffirmed its support for India acquiring peaceful nuclear technology. Russia has agreed to provide India four 1000 MW generating capacity nuclear reactors at the nuclear power plant in Kudankulam in Tamil Nadu and build more reactors at new sites. Memorandum of intent between the department of atomic energy of India and federal atomic energy of Russia has been signed.

It is also relevant to mention here that this study examines Indo-Russian economic co-operation between the two countries. It brings out the problems and potentialities which have unfolded themselves in this area. In fact it will not be incorrect to say that in this specific area there are still gaps which need to be filled. India for instance has lost the market for tea. However, some entrepreneurs in India are making serious attempts to tap the vast Russian market for tea.

In this study, four papers have been included on the rise of terrorism, religious fundamentalism and secessionism. Both India and now China are facing a new challenge to the unity and integrity of their countries. India, however, is facing a very complex situation in the sense that if Jammu and Kashmir and North Eastern region are facing the growing menace of terrorism, in the Hindi speaking belt Hindu revivalism is once again on the ascendancy. That being the situation it was felt necessary to critically examine historical roots of this development and give a look to the socio-economic and ideological basis of it. The study clearly shows that these dangers have their basis in the colonial past of this vast Afro-Asian region. What is more disturbing is that in the modern world, both terrorism and religious fundamentalism were used in the last decades of the 20th century for their narrow economic and strategic interests. This study also brings out that it will be wrong to identify these divisive tendencies with one religious community. It has different variants. This is graphically reflected in the various regions of African and Asian countries and in India too. That is why a paper has been included in this book on rise of Hindu revivalism, though it is not directly connected with the main theme of the book. The upshot of this matter is that when India is emerging as a global power in Asia, it has to grapple with these problems. Russia has evolved its own strategy which has been criticized by some of the western powers. From whatever angle you look at it, when Asia has emerged as the focal point of our planet, all the multicultural, multi-religious and multiethnic societies have no other option but to evolve a common coherent policy. The cooperation between India and Russia on this specific question provides a model for it. Therein lies the significance of commonality of approach between these two countries.

Let us now look at the evolution of Indo-Russian relations historically. However, before we undertake this exercise, it will not be out of place to mention that Indo-Russian relations have a unique character. It goes without saying that there is no conflict of interest between the two countries. There is for instance no boundary dispute. On the contrary both the academics and political elite have always been taking keen interest in the developments in each other's country. This is illustrated by some of the facts of history before the October Revolution. Russian scholars took deep interest in India. Russia, for instance, was one of the first countries which translated Rig-Veda, Ramayana and Mahabharata. Again, Russian scholars translated some of the outstanding literary books of India such as Kalidas's 'Shukantla' and Rabindra Nath Tagore's *Gitanjali*. It is also pertinent to mention here that Russian scholars have compiled history of India in two volumes beginning with the period when India was the cradle of human civilization to the modern era. Again, when India witnessed its first war of Independence in 1857, Russian media gave a day to day coverage to it and in one of the editorials of a leading newspaper, it was predicted that "this is the end of the colonial rule in India". When India won its independence in 1947, the Russian media described it as the beginning of the end of colonialism in the world.

Without going into further details some important facts need to be recapitulated. For instance the 1962 'Sino-Indian Armed Conflict' was described by the Soviet leaders as 'an unfortunate conflict between our brother and friend'. Again in 1965 when armed conflict between India and Pakistan took place, Khemkarn (Amritsar) became the graveyard of 'Patton Tanks' and India captured large areas of Pakistan. It was the Soviet leaders who invited Indian and Pakistani leaders to Tashkent and an agreement between the two countries look place. One of the leading scholars has contributed a paper in this book analyzing Indo-Soviet, Indo-Russian relations evolved during the last sixty years. This paper has emphasized the multidimensional character of these relations and how the Indo-Russian relations in the 21st century will become a key factor in the changing equations among the various countries.

This book is the product of intellectual inputs of a former Pro-Vice Chancellor of Delhi University, scholars from Jawahar Lal Nehru University, New Delhi, scholars from University of Mumbai, scholars from research institutes, two retired army officers who are strategic experts, one outstanding media expert and about half a dozen young scholars, who are doing research work on Russia. Some of the scholars who have contributed papers in this book are not personally known to me. In my search to identify scholars and researchers I came to know about them and they generously agreed to cooperate with me. This indeed was a rewarding experience. In this sense this book is a product of both experienced and young scholars.

I must also express my gratitude to Mr. Manohar Singh Batra for his help and co-operation in compiling this creative book. He not only made valuable suggestions, but also revised the entire manuscript.

Finally, I hope that this book will make a useful contribution to the thought structures of scholars, academics and India's foreign policy makers.

V. D. CHOPRA

1

India-Russia Relations : Regional and Global Significance

V.P. Dutt

Indo-Russian relations have multi-dimensional implications. The bilateral relationship is the core (as we shall see), but its significance on the regional and in the global power dynamics is no less important from the Indian point of view. They have helped in maintaining a certain equilibrium in the region, their contribution to the changeover in Afghanistan in the last two decades has been considerable and has provided a measure of rectification in the global balance of forces. They have demonstrated the absence of any serious national irritant in their mutual relations and very substantial complementarities in their viewpoints on world issues. Their goals are not too dissimilar and their need for each other is quite palpable.

We must first take a look at the world situation, the Russian perspective and then the Indian perspective. It was only a few years ago that America stood at the pinnacle of its power, emerging as the lone superpower in the world, towering over all other countries in military power, its economic power still hugely attractive, even though two other economic powerhouses - European Union and Japan - had somewhat dimmed its luster. No less, America's "soft power" (a term popularized by Joseph Nye) was acknowledged even by its critics. America was a "city on the hill", a land of opportunities. America had no peer. Some members of the European Union occasionally carped at it, but could offer no alternative to American power and position in the world.

By contrast, the only rival it had, the Soviet Union suddenly collapsed in sordid dissolution and its successor state, Russia, shorn of many of its earlier constituents, was gasping for breath and revival. Of course Russia was still a large landmass straddling across the two continents of Europe and Asia and it still had massive nuclear weapon power to destroy the earth, but it was an impoverished and bedraggled Russia that had to look to the West for help and sustenance.

Boris Yeltsin, who had virtually seized power from Mikhail Gorbochev and had become President of the Russian Republic, pathetically tried to assert equality for Russia with other big powers but had no political or economic muscle to back it up with. Russia's economic policies were taken over by foreign advisors who, in utter disregard of Russian background and conditions, gave it the full capitalist treatment. The results were disastrous. Russian production slid precipitously. A mafia economy arose. John Kenneth Galbraith was constrained to say that never was Russia so badly advised as by the foreign advisors. Yeltsin was too weak, his knowledge of economic affairs insufficient, and his state of health increasingly dubious.

Yeltsin made sporadic efforts to play big in international fora, particularly in his talks with the U.S. president, Bill Clinton. He would rave and rant as vividly described by Clinton's aide, Strobe Talbot, and then cave in. Clinton indulged him, humouring him, politely sidestepping his grandstanding, ignoring his occasional inebriated condition but having his way at the end when Yeltsin would sign more or less on the dotted line. It was an unnatural situation, but there it was. Russia had become a client state of the West, occasionally humoured as a big power to assuage its amour proper. More of a condescending gesture than anything else.

Yeltsin's failing health and addictions obliged him to nominate a successor. He surprised every one by nominating Vladimir Putin. Putin, almost the opposite of Yeltsin in most ways quickly set about the task of putting Russia's house in order, to bring some stability into a chaotic situation. Putin gradually tightened his grip on the administration, brought about normalcy and stability, but also pushed Russia on the road towards rapid economic growth. He made shrewd political and economic use of Russia's huge energy resources. In any case, the net result of Putin's efforts has been that Russia has become with China, India and Brazil, one of the fastest growing economies of the world. Russia became once again a factor to be reckoned with.

Almost inevitably, along with other developments that we shall discuss in a while, this changed the architecture of the international system and power relations in the world. This is perhaps one of the principal reasons for the increasing irritability in the relations between Russia and the West. An assertive and stronger Russia on the international scene requires new adjustments from the West which it finds painful to make. This is not to endorse everything that Putin has done or is doing. It is for the Russian people to decide about their form of government and their leadership. But as Putin said recently during the current spat with Britain, "Russia is not a banana republic". The fact for analysis from our point of view is the rise of Russia again as a major power.

The revival of Russia coincided with other major developments in global economics and politics, particularly the rise of China - and later of India. Economically it became a much more diversified world. Asia-Pacific in its breeder sense was the hub of a great deal of new economic activity. Along with existing economic power houses of the European Union and Japan, economic pluralism was already a significant characteristic of the new era in the globalized world. In terms of purchasing power parity, China was the third largest economy and India the fourth. Even otherwise China had already outstripped Britain's economy and was approaching the volume of the German economy. The economies of other East Asian and Southeast Asian countries were also doing quite well.

All this was necessarily going to impact the global power structure. Particularly the rise of Russia, China and India could alter the context and the substance of international discourse. All these countries had one major common objective - promoting multipolarity and democratization of international system. Russia, China and India had no intention of building a new power bloc or to get entangled in any military alliance. They had their own separate relations with the U.S. which none of them was going to imperil. But they could help reduce the rigours of one-power dominance. Moreover, the U.S. had itself invited some diminution in its global reach and ability to decisively influence the course of international relations because of military overreach, especially the military misadventure in Iraq. We use the words "some diminutions" advisedly, for the US was still more powerful and had more influence on world affairs than any other country.

Indo-Russian relations are a part and parcel of the new architecture of international relations and have both a regional and global dimension. The core has to be the bilateral relationship which we consider first as it has a direct bearing on the regional situation.

Undoubtedly the Putin era led to the reestablishment of a special relationship although more in line with contemporary realities. As we have noted earlier, India and Russia had no legacy of any emotional conflict, no territorial dispute, no race for parity with each other, no fear of dominance by the other, no serious differences on international issues and, more significantly, a commonality of approach and convergence of interests in the regions surrounding India, the joint advocacy of a multi-polar world and negotiated settlement of issues that divided the world.

Putin described himself as the best friend of India in the international community and within Russia and he described India as "a long-term partner and ally". He did not consider Moscow's relations with other countries to be an alternative to friendship with India. Fighting terrorism was a common objective and there should be no double standards (a clear reference to the militants in Kashmir and in Chechenya who were being portrayed as freedom fighters). There was verified information, he told the Indian Parliamentarians, that the same organizations — even the same individuals - were responsible for terrorist acts from the Philippines to Kosovo, Kashmir to Afghanistan and the northern Caucasus.

Russia's relationships with India came to be governed by the so-called Delhi Declaration signed in New Delhi. Stressing their dedication to the common ideals of peace, democracy, the rule of law, human rights and fundamental freedoms, non-violence and secularism, they recognized their special responsibilities being among the largest multi-ethnic, multi-lingual and multi-religious states in strengthening international peace and security and "democratization of International relations". They reaffirmed their strategic relationship and called for progressive reduction of nuclear weapon with the ultimate aim of their total elimination. More significantly, they undertook to inform each other of any foreign policy initiatives in the international arena and not to participate in any military, political or other alliances directed against the other side or to conclude any treaties, agreements and understanding that infringed upon the independence, sovereignty, territorial integrity or national security interests of the other side. Of course, they stressed that their relationship was not directed against any other country.

Herein lay the regional and global significance of Indo-Russian relations. They were not just nominal but active partners in the fight against terrorism and also undertook to inform each other about any significant international initiative they took. Much of the terrorism that India faced came from across the border with Pakistan which was unequivocally condemned by Russia. Russia raised this issue at the international fora also. Putin came down quite hard on terrorism in his talks with the US president and quizzed George Bush on Pakistan's role during their meeting in St. Petersburg in November 2001. While he supported General Musharraf, he asked Bush, "what can happen with armies armed with weapons that exist in Pakistan, including weapons of mass destruction. "We should not forget about this", he was quoted to have said. He was also reported to have referred to the Pakistani military leadership as "a junta with nukes".

It was in keeping with the spirit of the Delhi Declaration that the Russian President kept Prime Minister Vajpayee in the loop about General Musharraf's visit to Moscow in February 2003. He telephoned Vajpayee before the visit and after the visit to keep him apprised of the talks. If Musharraf had any hopes of diluting Indo-Russian relationship, he must have been disappointed. Of course Russia would want to normalize its relations with Pakistan and it did so, but it was made quite apparent that this would not be at the expense of the special relationship with India.

Signifying both the regional and international significance of India-Russia relations is their extraordinary defence, energy and geopolitical relationship. As against Chinese and U.S. military aid to Pakistan, India's defence relationship with Russia enabled it to keep the military edge in the subcontinent. It is no secret that China made good Pakistan's military losses both after the 1965 and the 1971 wars against India. This is of course without taking into account the assistance that China gave for Pakistan's acquisition of nuclear weapons and missile capability. The United States has also poured billions in aid to Pakistan's military. Even today it is passing over $ 1 million a month to the military for the fight against terrorism.

India's defence relations with Russia constitute the most important component of their relationship. We have already spelt out some of the details in some of Mr. V.D. Chopra's earlier books. But completing the picture we might note that the then Defence Minister Pranab Mukherjee visiting Moscow in November 2005 in preparation for the Putin-Manmohan Singh summit, while chairing India-Russia joint defence group, affirmed that Russia would remain India's largest and most secure source of defence hardware.

The ongoing deals with Russia totaled nearly $ 9 billion. A 10-year defence cooperation agreement between India and Russia until 2010 included more than 200 projects worth $ 20 billion. New avenues were explored. Russia agreed to share the technology for an advanced naval vassal (ATV) and an air defence vassal. The ATV was an indigenous project for the development of nuclear submarines.

We may refer to two characteristics of these defence ties. One was that in most cases the agreement provided for the manufacturing within the country of the high-tech arms being purchased by India. The second related to joint research and production of some high-class weapons.

For a while there were certain glitches over the Soviet anxiety about the protection of intellectual property rights, as the Russians were supplying India their latest state-of-the-art weaponry that had not even yet been inducted into the Soviet army. These glitches were, however, resolved at the Putin-Manmohan Singh summit in 2005. The Indian Prime Minister announced after their talks that they had identified the medium-range transport aircraft and the generation of fighter aircraft as two such projects for joint research and development. After the Brahamos, this will be the second such project to be jointly produced by the two countries.

It is only fair to note that India has been diversifying its sources of defence supplies. There is a strong defence line with Israel which has already become the second largest defence supplier to India. France too has a robust defence relationship with India. India has occasionally turned to Swedish, British and other firms. Now the United States too is eyeing the Indian market. It would be natural if Russia felt some concern if it slipped somewhat in the Indian arms market. But Russia appears to have accepted the fact that India would be meeting its needs from various sources. It feels confident that its niche is secure for many coming years. Equally Russia, unlike USA, France and UK, has not supplied any military hardware to Pakistan and has made it clear that it would not take any step in this regard likely to affect Indian interests. The regional significance of it is too obvious to need elaboration.

Of course, India cannot be complacent in this regard, as there are indications that not always do India's perceptions coincide with those of Russia in regard to certain military supplies, not necessarily directly by Russia. A case in point was the supply of Chinese-produced jet fighters equipped with Russian engines.

Russia and China had reached an agreement in April 2007 on joint assembly of JF-17 fighters powered by Russia's RD-93 engines and their marketing in third countries. The planes, according to the Russian media, would reportedly be sold to Pakistan and some countries of Asia and Africa with whom the Chinese were supposed to have traditionally strong positions. According to the Russian media President Putin personally supervised the Chinese deal which opened the way to China's acquisition of 100 RD-93 engines worth $ 238 million with the right to re-export the planes.

India had strongly objected to the supply of Russian engines for re-export of planes to Pakistan and the original Russian contract had banned any re-export of the engines. But the media quoted Kremlin sources as saying that the deal did not hurt Indian interests. That might be so, but obviously India cannot lower its vigil.

Having said that the perspective must be kept that Russia's defence ties with India have been both invaluable and unsubstitutable and that Russia has not been a supplier of military hardware to Pakistan in any meaningful sense - the kind that USA and China have been for Islamabad.

Equally, if not more significant, was Russia's partnership with India on the civilian use of nuclear energy. Nuclear energy would become over time the lifeline of India's energy supplies for its fast expanding economy. Russia had already set up nuclear power reactors at Kundankulam. This cooperation got incrementally enhanced in 2007—there were indications in 2005 itself that the two countries would be engaging in intensive talks to fortify this cooperation. In May 2005, Manmohan Singh met Vladimir Putin on the sidelines of the Victory Day celebrations and the two decided to begin working on a more comprehensive framework for civilian nuclear cooperation. Manmohan Singh assured Putin that India would be tightening its nuclear materials export controls and the safeguards of the nuclear reactors and subsequently Parliament passed new legislation in this regard. It is interesting to note what Putin told Manmohan Singh "while there are many guests in Moscow, there is only one India," Putin said, according to Indian Prime Minister's security advisor, M.K. Narayanan.

This decision led to new agreement on nuclear cooperation when the Russian President visited India in January 2007. A joint statement on the subject on 25 January stated that India and Russia as States possessing advanced nuclear technologies underlined the need to further develop cooperation in promoting the use of nuclear energy for peaceful purposes "in accordance with their respective international obligations and national legislations". They believed that nuclear energy would provide "an indispensable source of energy to future generations". To help India realize its goal of promoting nuclear power and achieving energy security in a sustainable manner, Russia decided to construct 4 additional power units at Kundankulam with India undertaking that the reactor facilities and the nuclear fuel supplied by Russia would remain under the IAEA safeguards during the entire period of their actual use.

Russia also undertook to work with the participating governments of the Nuclear Suppliers Group (NSG) to create conditions through amendments to its guidelines to facilitate expansion of civilian nuclear energy cooperation with India. Russia was entirely supportive of the 123 nuclear deal being worked out between India and the U.S. Russia was bound by its commitments to the international body to restrict nuclear fuel supplies unless sanctioned by the NSG. It believed that an Indo-US deal on nuclear civilian cooperation was a sin-qua-non for a meaningful future cooperation in this field between India and Russia. Once the agreement was legally done with the U.S. and once the NSG made the necessary exception for India, Russia's cooperation with India in the civilian nuclear power generation field could be raised to new levels. Such cooperation would have an important bearing on the global scene.

Before considering further the regional and international significance of Indo-Russian relations, we may note that India's economic sinews were being partly lubricated by Russia's energy supplies. Russia is emerging as a major supplier of traditional and non-renewable energy resources in a world where a great many countries are hunting around for the supply of or securing the supply of fuels. In this situation Russia's partnership in the non-nuclear energy field also has a significance that goes beyond the bilateral relationship. India's active involvement in developing Russia's energy sources started many years ago when ONGC VIDESH acquired a 20 per cent share in one of the largest oilfields in Russia's Far East-Sakhalin and in one of India's largest investment in an oilfield. By 2007 Sakhalin-I is expected to provide 700,000 barrels of oil and 200 million cubic feet of gas to India.

Already in 2005 Russia had been telling India that it regarded India as a strategic partner in the energy field too, and was interested in securing Indian investments in deploying its energy resources. The then Petroleum Minister, Mani Shankar Aiyer had held out the prospect of the Indian investments climbing up to some $ 25 billion in Russia's oil and gas industry in the coming few years, "what we are saying is, Gazprom has a huge amount of gas and we have the money". India was also acquiring equity stake in ex-Yukos unit, Yogansk which had been producing nearly 12 per cent of the country's natural oil output.

Coming back to the regional dimension, what is noticeable is the complementarity in approach and policies of the two countries from the days of the Soviets to present day Russia. Over time the demise of the Soviet Union did not result in any spectacular course change by Russia in this region primarily because the interests did not change. Only if we take the wider region, has there been a remarkable change by Russia in Russia's relations with China and that is all to the good of India's interests. The notable transformation in Sino-Russian relations has been beneficial to India, as we shall see in just a while.

Afghanistan is another area in which the regional significance of India-Russia relations is apparent. The lines of the two countries have been running parallel to each other for a long time. The U.S. extended assistance to all anti-Soviet elements fighting the Soviet army indirectly through General Zia-ul-Haq and the ISI and directly through the CIA. The Soviets were obliged to withdraw, but the indiscriminate nature of this arms aid and the volume of it led eventually to the rise and the empowerment of the Taliban led by Mulla Omar, and their associate Al Qaeda led by Osama bin Laden. Both Russia (under Putin) and India realized the dangerous import of these developments and the threat of terrorism emanating from Kabul and the religious extremists. As is well known, Afghanistan became one of the breeding grounds (apart from Pakistan) for the training and export of terrorists and terrorism to India, Russia and, as was witnessed later, the entire world.

Quite early as the 21st century was ushered in, India and Russia were coordinating their policies in the region. Away from the public glare, they were shoring up the Northern Alliance, providing it with material assistance, economic and military, Russia's probably larger than that of India. India also played host, again keeping it away from public glare, to the families of a number of Northern Alliance leaders, who were fearful of their lives. Even Hamid Karzai had studied in Simla.

The assistance from Russia and India was of some significance in bolstering up the Northern Alliance which was engaged in fighting the Taliban in the northern areas of Afghanistan, before the Al Qaeda attack on USA changed the international situation. When the U.S. decided to attack and displace the Taliban, even though reluctantly, it had to turn to the Northern Alliance which was a ready and handy instrument to move on towards Kabul and overthrow the Taliban. Even after the capture of Kabul, when the contours and composition of a new government were being decided, it was the coordinated Russian and Indian opposition that prevented Taliban elements from being included in the new dispensation, even though Washington seemed to be willing for such inclusion on the insistence of Musharraf.

India and Russia kept in close consultation through a joint group they had set up for coordinating policy on Afghanistan. If only Washington had persisted with the campaign to eliminate Al Qaeda and its leadership in Afghanistan with all its means and in cooperation with the international community, the menace of global terrorism would not have assumed its current proportions. Instead, the U.S. administration frittered away the opportunity and concentrated on dethroning Saddam Hussain on fictitious grounds, giving new life and vigour to the Al Qaeda terrorists and derailing the international coalition against terrorism.

The reemergence of the Taliban and heightened activity by the Al Qaeda in the tribal belt of Pakistan poses a grave danger to Afghanistan, India, Russia and to Pakistan itself.

The U.S. is now more alive to the danger emanating from the activities of the Taliban and Al Qaeda basing itself in Quetta and the tribal areas of Pakistan. The Americans are now mounting pressure on Pakistan to step up the war against jehadis in their territory and have also raised the level of the allied operations in Afghanistan as the resurgence of the Taliban and the Al Qaeda is highly deleterious for the regional balance and for the interests of all those countries including the U.S. and the international community. The need for Russia and India to remain coordinated is even more patent. Their cooperation would have a beneficial impact on the emerging situation in that region.

Russia and India are both rising powers. In fact Russia is a re-rising power, it already had many of the attributes associated with a big power, not just the possession of an atomic weapon arsenal that could destroy the world, but also a highly educated citizenry and a very well-developed scientific community. Russia has been building a geopolitical relationship with India, just as it was building a geopolitical relationship with China. Perhaps there is a larger element of trust with India than with China. It was essentially through Russian efforts that India, China and Russia held a summit of their own on the sidelines of the G8 in St. Petersburg in 2006.

Of course these relationships were not intended to constitute any kind of military alliance, or an alliance directed against the United States or any other country. Russia had its own relationship with USA, so did China and so did India, and neither of these was going to get that relationship embroiled in their mutual relations. Moreover it was fanciful to imagine that any country or any combination of countries could substitute for the relations with the United States.

India-Russia strategic partnership was beneficial to both countries in meeting the challenges of economic development, terrorism, the emerging energy crisis, uses of nuclear power, and unilateralism involved in the current structure of world politics.

The objectives of the two countries were stated boldly and meaningfully in the joint statement issued by President Vladimir Putin and Prime Minister Manmohan Singh on 25 January 2007 during the former's visit as chief guest on India's Republic Day. India and Russia undertook to "work towards the establishment of a multi-polar world order based on the principles of the rule of law, sovereign equality, territorial integrity and non-interference in the internal affairs of States". The strengthening of the UN in maintaining peace and security and increasing the efficiency and authority of the UN "form important elements of India-Russia cooperation at the international level". India and Russia stressed the need to implement the process of UN reforms so as to reflect contemporary realities and Russia reiterated its support to India "as a deserving and strong candidate for the permanent membership in an expanded UN Security Council".

Their stand on terrorism was also unequivocal. They recognized terrorism as one of the gravest threats to international peace and security and affirmed that there was no justification for any act of terrorism, irrespective of motivations, wherever and by whosoever committed. They were also convinced that terrorism "cannot and should not be associated with any nationality, religious, cultural or ethnic group". They also expressed their concern over the dangers in the spread of terrorist organizations and expressed their determination to counter these threats, while calling for a dialogue among civilizations and cultures.

Their thinking and policy on Afghanistan, Iran and Iraq were strongly close to each other. They shared their concern over the fast deteriorating situation and the growing threat by the Taliban and other extremist forces in Afghanistan and were clear in their determination to continue helping an independent and democratic Afghanistan. On Iran both sides wanted a solution through political and diplomate means while underscoring the need for more active and transparent cooperation of Iran with the IAEA in order to resolve outstanding verification issues.

Undoubtedly a new situation is unfolding itself as regards India's foreign relations. India and USA are endeavouring to establish a new relationship, discarding the acrimony of the last half century, recognizing the importance of each other and in a way recognizing the realities of the contemporary world that only cooperation secures peace. This is not the occasion to analyse the 123 agreement, its pros and cons. Quite apart from it, there is no doubt that many new avenues of cooperation between the two countries will be becoming available. This would be all to the good. The priorities are always determined by the country's requirements.

However, it must be kept in mind that while opening new options, we must not ignore our existing friendships, particularly those with whom we have extraordinary complementarity of interests. It does not serve any Indian interests to support any U.S.-inspired move to contain and hurt Russia. As a veteran Indian journalist has put it,.. "the imperative is to enter the new phase of international relations with eyes wide open, armed with the knowledge that it will require all the resources of good diplomacy to pursue closer relations with the United States, while keeping the non-aligned mindset intact", and I might add, while keeping the close relations with Russia intact.

2

Indo-Russian Relations : From Friendship to Strategic Partnership

K.R. Singh

Defining Norms of International Relations

Indians have a weakness to emotionalize even foreign relations as is reflected in terms like friendship, war to the finish (*aar par ki ladai*) etc. Consequently when regional and international environment alters radically, we are unable to adjust our emotional vision and tend to look at bilateral and multilateral relations through the old vision. This results in a disjointed response and expectations that are not based upon ground realities.

Bilateral relations, to be properly analysed, need to be placed in their broader canvas of time and space. One needs to take into account constantly changing environment; domestic, regional and global, and the overall impact upon foreign relations of both the parties. There is no doubt that one has witnessed a fluidity in domestic as also regional and global environment of both the countries—India and Russia—since 1990 that has left the imprint upon their bilateral relations.

The end of the Cold War brought about a major restructuring of international order. The old order, based upon two major alliance systems; the NATO and its supporters and the Warsaw Pact, gave way to what can be called a unipolar system under the leadership of USA. The non-aligned movement (NAM) that was a feeble response of some states in the South to ward off pressures from either bloc during the first two decades of the Cold War soon lost its *raison d'etre* when more and more developing countries began to side with the US-led coalition, especially following the Soviet military intervention in Afghanistan. By the time the USSR was willing to call it quits, the NAM was already fading out as a movement of global significance though countries like India continued to pursue their policy of non-alignment.

For some time majority of the states accepted the sole leadership of USA. That status was, however, soon challenged not only by Russia and China but also by a set of West European powers like France and Germany. While USA sought to retain its hold over NATO and to use it as a tool of its world leadership, it found that it could not rely upon all the NATO members to actively support its unilateralist agenda. Thus, the concept of reliable and dependable 'alliance' system was weakened. New formulations were offered to serve specific purposes. They included the 'coalition of the willing' as in the case of Afghanistan since 2001 and Iraq since 2003, 'interest partnership' as in proliferation security initiative (PSI) and war on terrorism, SLOC protection etc. New terms like group (G-7) and organization (Shanghai Cooperation Organization) were also added as an alternate to alliance. A term like 'strategic partner' was introduced to underline closer bilateral relations. Sometimes, this strategic partnership was further qualified by adding terms like economic, technology, energy etc. These innovations in bilateral, regional and multilateral relations offered state actors multiple options to define their role in the fast changing world order. Indo-Russian relations also reflected these changes since the end of the Cold War.

Imprint of Cold War era

Though world order has undergone restructuring since the end of the Cold War, it is not easy to erase the imprint of five decade long Cold War era, and patterns of relations and perceptions that had been generated. Though the situation might have altered, people continue to compare and contrast the performance of international actors in the light of their past (Cold War) role. Hence, a brief resume of factors that helped to formulate Delhi's foreign relations and those of Moscow, as also those factors that brought them close will be useful in putting relations between these two capitals in proper perspective.

Despite its leading role in the context of decolonization, Afro-Asian solidarity, non-aligned movement and South-South cooperation, India lacked a major input in its foreign relations. It lacked the firm support of a major power that could offer diplomatic support at international level, help promote economic growth and technological progress as also help it in creating a viable defence capability at an affordable price. Its rivalry with Pakistan and China and opposition to US-led alliance system had virtually isolated India at regional and international levels. Since India was opposed to the policy of alliance, it needed 'friends' that could offer help without demanding alliance membership in return. Indo-Soviet relations need to be seen as a product of that environment. It flourished since it helped both the countries to develop close relations without demanding allegiance or subservience. Even the strategic agreement of 1971 was termed as Friendship Treaty.

USSR too needed 'friends'. Its experience with ideological partners was not happy especially after its break with China and Albania in early sixties. Its Warsaw Pact 'allies' in Eastern Europe were proving to be increasingly unreliable, largely due to historical facts. In the post-Cold War period they even turned hostile and joined the NATO. The change in Moscow's perception was slow. Its policy during the Stalin era was ideologically rigid. It rejected overtures even from India. Things, however, changed since the Khrushchev era with the 20th Party Congress endorsing the policy of cultivating friendship with non-aligned states. They were neither enemies nor allies but were 'friends' - a new designation in international relations during the Cold War era. That enabled Moscow to develop close ties with several developing states like Egypt, Syria, Iraq, India, Indonesia etc. While Moscow's friendship with states like Egypt, Iraq, Indonesia withered away, it got further cemented over the decades *vis-a-vis* India.

Moscow's 'friendship' with Delhi evolved gradually. While 1955 marked the beginning of that relationship, relations were still formal in 1965. The *Annual Report* of the Ministry of External Affairs, 1965-1966, while dealing with the bilateral relationship with USSR during that year said that the year was noteworthy for its development of 'improved' political, cultural and economic relations. It also added that the Soviet stand on Kashmir remained unchanged and that Soviet Union had offered its 'good offices' for Indo-Pak meeting in Tashkent.[1] By 1971-72, the perception had altered dramatically. The *Report* of 1971-1972, while commenting upon the Indo-Soviet Treaty of 1971 (the so-called Friendship Treaty) said that the important aspect of the treaty was the 'credible assurance' that in the event of an attack or a threat thereof, the two sides shall immediately enter into mutual consultation in order to remove such a threat and to take appropriate effective measures to ensure peace and security of their countries. Thus, it was in essence a bilateral security arrangement just short of an alliance. Indian Minister of External Affairs, in his statement in the Lok

Sabha on August 9, 1971 on the subject, called it a Treaty of Peace Against War.[2]

Moscow helped India in setting up heavy industries, in exploiting natural resources like oil and gas as well as in strengthening scientific and technological base. Bilateral trade expanded under rupee-rouble arrangement. That also facilitated defence-related cooperation. It will not be wrong to say that after mid-sixties most of the military-related equipment acquired by India came from USSR or some Warsaw Pact state. Over the decades, India proved to be a very responsible user of Russian defence equipment. That prompted Moscow to allow transfer of advanced weapon-related technology to India. That trust of the Cold War era remains true even now despite the pinpricks from some motivated parties. Most of these variables were going to face serious stress since the end of the eighties and more so during the first half of the nineties when USSR was disintegrating.

Restructuring of New International Order

The correlation of forces during the Cold War, based primarily upon a clash of ideology between capitalism and socialism, and led by two Super Powers, USA and USSR, was loaded in favour of US-led alliance. While the Western Bloc continued to stick together, the Socialist Bloc suffered a series of setbacks due to internal divide. On the eastern front, China, a major country professing socialism, not only developed serious ideological differences with the Soviet Union, after 1971-72 it virtually joined hands with the West to confront USSR. On the European front, Moscow's efforts to cultivate the Warsaw Pact allies too failed. They were attracted more towards the European model than the Socialist model. Even in USSR there was a resurgence of ethnic loyalty not only in Central Asia and the Caucasus but also in the 'European' areas like Ukraine, Belarus and along the Baltic coast.

USSR would still have survived as a Super Power but for the fact that the faith in the system was being seriously questioned by many of the young elite. A society that was not used to 'free' thinking got intoxicated under the impetus of *glasnost* (openness - mass media) and *perestroika* (restructuring - social, economic and political). Instead of acting as flood-gates designed to release surplus water, they undermined the dam itself. By the end of 1991 there was no Soviet Union. Demise of the Warsaw Pact and the subsequent east-ward expansion of the NATO as also the disintegration of the ex-Tsarist Empire were the logical outcome of the trends set in motion since the end of the eighties. These developments had global repercussions. They helped in the restructuring of the world order by giving a boost to political, economic and social 'liberalism' besides further consolidating the leadership of USA as the sole Super Power.

Impact upon India

India was not only affected by these developments at international level, but was also facing major internal challenges since the late eighties. At regional and even international level it was facing increasing isolation. It was confronted with financial crisis especially in foreign currency and had to restructure (liberalize) its economy. For that it needed Western approbation. The Congress Party was fast losing its hold and the country was being subjected to pulls and pressures of coalition politics. Foreign policy was also influenced by these developments. India's over-reliance upon USSR was being increasingly questioned, especially when Moscow could not deliver equipment and spares because of the collapse of the centralized Soviet structure.

USSR/RF: Perception of the New Elite

The matter was further compounded due to the changed priorities among the new elite in Moscow at that time who wanted to rewrite Moscow's relations with its erstwhile friends as also enemies. The shift was visible even during Gorbachev's leadership when the 27th Party Congress downgraded Soviet Union's relations with the South and supported greater interaction with the North. Its influence was felt much more during the early years of leadership of Boris Yeltsin. Thus, Moscow began to shake off its Cold War legacy of Socialism and hitched its wagon to Western-style free-market economy. The new policy also affected relations between Delhi and Moscow. Earlier 'friendship' began to be replaced by a new ethos in which India began to be treated as any other trading partner. The new elite's demand that bilateral economic transactions be confined to hard currency as also controversy over exchange rate of rupee vs rouble made matters worse. Never in the history their bilateral relations since 1955 had reached such a low watermark as between 1990-92. In a way, that was one major factor that prompted India to diversify its political, economic and military relationship.

Changing Global Perception of Moscow

Indo-Soviet/Russian Federation relations were affected by the rapidly altering perception of the role that Moscow was expected to play in the changing new environment. It is, therefore, important to do a quick survey of Moscow's foreign policy since 1990 if not earlier. Graham F. Fuller, commenting upon the last days of the Soviet foreign policy, said that ever since the collapse of its ideology the Soviet Union had been in a state of confusion about what constituted its national interests. Communism had provided the USSR with a global vision. It postulated a theoretical interest in every political conflict in the world that might historically advance international communism. It, likewise, postulated the need to check, whenever possible, Western and specially American interests. He added that the *glasnost* and *perestroika* delivered the *coup d'grace* to Marxism-Leninism as the guiding principle of foreign policy. The Soviet ship was left rudderless. How were national interests abroad to be charted after the global ideological fixation dropped away. Moscow, after 1989, started into a vague and idealistic formulation of 'new thinking', a conceptual *tabula rasa* with no useful precedents to guide actual future policy.[3]

The new thinking that often amounted to bending backwards to accommodate the view of US-led coalition, was amply reflected in the unrestrained support given by Soviet Foreign Minister, Eduard Shevardnadze, in the context of Kuwaiti crisis when Moscow voted on the dotted line even on Security Council Resolution 678 of November 30, 1990 that legitimized military action against Iraq as also ceasefire Resolution 687 of April 3, 1991 that legitimized the subsequent coercive policy of the US-led coalition against Iraq.

Moscow had yet to reconcile itself not only with the loss of its hold over Eastern Europe but also of the loss of what constituted parts of the Russian empire. As Ronald Dannreuther had commented, the new leadership was trying to adjust an imperial mentality to a post-imperial capability. Russia needed to learn how to lose an empire and find a new role in regional and international affairs.[4] According to Alwin Z. Rubinstein, shedding an empire after 450 years was a traumatic experience. Russia had retreated into its heartland.[5]

The new elites in Moscow had believed or were made to believe that once they broke away from the past, all the doors would be opened to them for socio-economic and political integration with the West. Soon, the reality of realpolitik dawned upon them. Even the disintegrated Russia was too large and potentially powerful a state to be allowed to revive and thus emerge as a potential challenge to the global hegemony of US-led coalition. The socio-economic condition of many citizens of ex-USSR/Russia had worsened after the collapse of state-supported social welfare system. The situation had worsened to such an extent that even India offered rupees fifteen crores in humanitarian assistance that included baby food, rice, medicines etc.[6] Not only were promises of economic support not forthcoming but efforts were made to further erode Moscow's position along its entire periphery from the Baltic Sea, East Europe, the Caucasus and extending upto Central Asia. That undermined the power base of the pro-West elite and created an environment that helped in correcting the tilt. That indirectly helped improve Indo-Russian relations.

Change in policy was reflected in the coming into prominence of a different set of elite. Kozyrev, who was associated with the pro-West tilt was replaced by leaders like Yevgeny Primakov. Moscow had no desire to confront or reject the West, yet it needed a theoretical framework to contest the then existing unipolar world order. Primakov was credited with promoting the concept of multipolar as against unipolar world order. It enabled Russia to play the role of an independent centre of power and influence as well as to develop, diversify and multiply contacts and partnership with other world powers. It also enabled Moscow to strike a right balance between the East and the West.

Gerhard Simon, while analyzing the role of Primakov, underlined the following factors. By pursuing one-sided links with the West, Russia would lose its independent profile. USA was neither a foe nor an ally. A certain distance would reconstitute one of the requirements for an independent role on international stage. CIS was for Russia's interest and safeguarded Russia's position as a leading power. Russia must seek new partners in the East, and policy towards West and East must balance each other so as to avoid any one-sided dependence.[7]

Putin: Russia Reasserts its Role

The newly formed state was in chaos with more than twenty parties and blocs contesting for power. President Yeltsin, who was increasingly seen as unable to control the situation, suddenly resigned as the President on December 31, 1999. Vladimir Putin, a former Colonel in the Soviet Committee for State Security (K.G.B.), who was gradually making space for himself in Russian politics, was appointed as acting president by the Duma. Putin, however, obtained 52.9 percent votes in the presidential election in March 2000. His nearest rival had obtained only 29.2 percent votes. Putin was formally installed as President on May 7, 2000.

Russia needed a strong leader and Putin proved himself to be the one. His first priority was to bring order out of the chaos that was due to scramble for power among various groups and to check economic corruption due to the policies of various 'oligarchs' who had got control of valuable national resources including oil and gas. They also manipulated the media and were largely supported by elements abroad especially in the West. Putin also had to recreate the Russian armed forces and restore the morale of the fighting men who had been unable to handle the problem in Chechnya. Simultaneously, he had to handle the foreign policy. Obviously, the process of domestic consolidation had the priority. Only after that goal had been attained could Putin reassert Russia's position in international arena.

The primary challenge before the political elite of the new state was to redefine the strategic role of the new state following the drastic curtailment of its previous physical space as also defence capabilities. Some sought to offer Russian Federation a fortress Russia status. Robert Legvold wrote, "Although it would involve geographical retrenchment, fortress Russia is not isolationist. Nor does it require to give up great power aspirations. On the contrary, Russia would still exert every effort to make itself a country of consequence.[8] The concept of 'fortress' would give the image of a state under siege. Hence it was a negative concept and would have restricted the strategic vision of a new state.

There is no doubt that policy makers in Moscow were trying hard to work out a framework of a new concept that would help redefine Russia's new strategy. That was reflected in Foreign Policy Concept of the Russian Federation as approved by President V. Putin on June 28, 2000.[9] That document reasserted Russia's position as a great power and one of the most influential centres of the modern world. It said that Russian Federation's foreign policy was pre-determined by the geopolitical position of Russia as one of the largest Eurasian powers. Thus, it emphasized Russia's role as a part of Europe as also of Asia. The concept rejected the unipolar world order and expressed desire to achieve a multipolar system of international relations as also to strengthen international institutions like the UN. The document also noted that the Near Abroad, especially the southern periphery, would remain the focus of its policy. It underlined the need for strengthening economic relations not only with West but also with China and India. Moscow also hoped to develop close cooperation with the European community and thus encourage the concept of a multipolar world order.

Russia has also played its energy cards very effectively to get the maximum economic and political mileage. It has blocked American efforts to divert bulk of oil and gas of the Caspian Sea region away from Russia. Also, Putin has succeeded in regaining effective state control over key oil and gas infrastructure that had earlier been cornered by self-seeking oligarchs. Rise in the global price of oil and gas as also increase in production of energy resources has strengthened Russian economy. That also helped to strengthen Putin's position.

Russian policy of opening up the oil and gas reserves of Siberia and along the Pacific coast to foreign energy companies will make Russia a major supplier of energy resources to the Asia-Pacific region. Russia has world's largest known gas reserves amounting to about 47 trillion cubic metres (tcm). Natural gas and CNG are going to be as important as crude oil in the near future. Of the total known gas reserves that amounted to 175 tcm in 2003, Russia (47.0 tcm), Iran (26.7 tcm) and Qatar (25.8 tcm) together have 57.3 per cent of total global reserves. Reportedly some major exporters of natural gas, that include Russia, are contemplating the formation of an organization of gas exporting countries, on the line of the OPEC. If that materializes, Russia will emerge as a key actor in global energy scene. Since India is going to be a major importer of oil and gas, these developments are bound to affect Indo-Russian relations in the years to come.

Indo-Russian Relations : Reaffirming Continuity

Ties between Delhi and Moscow were too deep to be uprooted even by the major restructuring of global environment as also by drastic grass-root transformation in the Soviet/Russian society. As A. Kislov and A. Frolov had noted, India's policy towards Russia contains a very large measure of continuity.[10] The first indication of the revival in ties between Delhi and Moscow was the visit of

Indian Foreign Minister to Moscow in November 1991 and his meeting with President Yeltsin. It was followed by the visit of Prime Minister P.V. Narasimha Rao in January 1992 followed by the visit of President Yeltsin to Delhi on January 27-29, 1993. The new Indo-Russian Treaty, that replaced the 1971 Treaty (20-year period), was signed during that visit as also other agreements like the one dealing with rupee-rouble exchange rate. The new treaty lacked the security-related clauses of 1971 treaty.

Though the new treaty lacked the earlier ethos of the 'Friendship Treaty' of 1971, yet it was the beginning of a new relationship between India and the Russian Federation. The *Annual Report* of the Ministry of External Affairs of 1992-1993 noted that the visit of President Yeltsin, "laid a foundation for future friendship and close interaction between India and Russian Federation."[11]

The next major step was taken during the visit of Prime Minister Narasimha Rao—June 27 to July 2, 1994. The Moscow Declaration underlined the common interests, mostly of domestic concern, of both the states. It touched upon the need for protection of interest of pluralistic states and reflected the common approach to problems faced by multi-ethnic states. It also reflected the common concern of both the states towards the danger of religious extremism as also policy of fanning aggressive inter-ethnic and inter-religious hatred.

The mood of a new entente was reflected in the assessment by the Ministry of External Affairs of India. Its *Annual Report* for 1996-1997 said, "Based on continuity, trust and confidence, relations with Russian Federation are an important foreign policy priority for India. With post-Cold War transitional difficulties now left well behind, India's relations with Russia are progressing well in almost all areas of bilateral cooperation including trade and economy, science and technology, culture and defence. There is recognition both in India and Russia of the strategic dimension of Indo-Russian relations. Both countries share similar perception on many international issues."[12]

Years since mid-nineties, that reflected the imprint of the multipolar global approach of Yevgeny Primakov, saw a boost in bilateral programmes that had stagnated since 1990-1991, particularly in the field of science, technology, space and defence. India was facing serious problems in the field of defence. In that context the visit of Igor Rodionev, Defence Minister of Russia, to Delhi in October 1996 was a major landmark since it was the first visit at that level since 1990. It helped streamline the supply of defence equipment as well as in smoothening the path for new acquisitions like three Talwar-class frigates, Su-30 aircraft, BrahMos missile, new main battle tanks etc. These steps were important for India's security since India, despite its new pro-West policy, was still denied Western military-related technology.

Indo-Russian Relations: Putin era

There is no doubt that President Putin lent a greater depth to Indo-Russian relations. The Declaration of Strategic Partnership, issued during his visit to Delhi in October 2001 underlined the point that the strategic partnership was time-tested and was marked by continuing trust and mutual understanding. It had elevated the multifaceted ties between the two countries to a qualitatively new and higher level, and had laid the foundation for further development in Indo-Russian relations.[13] Bases of Indo-Russian ties were further underlined during the visit of Prime Minister Vajpayee. In the joint statement with President Putin on November 6, 2001 both sides affirmed their commitment to promote an equitable multipolar world order based on the principles of law and equity, territorial integrity and non-interference in domestic affairs. The joint statement also stressed the need for reform in the UN, including expansion of the Security Council.

Indo-Russian cooperation during the Putin era has continued to strengthen despite the change of regime in New Delhi and the increasing tilt towards USA and Japan. Cooperation in the field of energy is not restricted only to the exploration and exploitation of oil and gas along the Pacific Coast but includes nuclear field as reflected in the construction of nuclear reactors by Russia. Russian cooperation in defence is on course despite some criticism about delay in delivery schedule of the aircraft carrier as also malfunctioning of old ex-Soviet defence equipment. India is a big spender on defence and is estimated to spend more than $30 bn over the next five years. For some, downgrading Russian cooperation can be a means to promote the interests of other suppliers. But no other arms producer has shown the willingness to develop jointly the next generation weapon systems like the fifth generation MiG-35 series of aircraft or the more sophisticated version of missiles or PGMs. It shows the mutual trust and confidence in each other's scientific and technological capabilities.

By contrast, others are willing to sell their technology that is being replaced but not share their new technology with India. Despite all the show of 'partnership' USA is willing to share the technology of old aircraft like F-16 and F-18 but not the new F-22. Also, Indian defence capability today and for years to come will be so deeply interlinked with that of the ex-Soviet Union/Russian Federation, that it will be difficult to find an alternative and reliable replacement in that sector.

Indo-Russian Relations; From Friendship to Strategic Partnership

As noted earlier, the term friendship was invented in the context of international relations to bypass the constraints of alliance-based relations. Use of that term ended when bilateral relations deteriorated as in the case of Egypt, or with the end of the Cold War. New terms were needed to define new patterns of relationships. This transformation was clearly visible when the *Annual Report, 1999-2000*, of the Ministry of External Affairs, New Delhi, sought to define Indo-Russian relations. It said that relations between India and the Russian Federation have been historically close, friendly and time-tested. One of the priorities of the Ministry would be to strengthen our time-tested relations. "We have sought to raise the level of our bilateral ties to that of a strategic partnership." It added that a Declaration on Strategic Partnership was to be signed between the two countries during the next Summit meeting.[14] That declaration was formally signed during the visit of President Putin to Delhi in October 2001.

Indo-Russian relations have retained the warmth even after the change of regime in New Delhi except that under the prime-ministership of Dr. Manmohan Singh, India has tried to push economic agenda in the forefront of its bilateral relations with Russia as well. According to the *Annual Report* of 2006-2007, promoting economic and commercial cooperation is now a "priority for both countries".[15] The continued high level of bilateral interaction was reflected in visits by President Dr. A.P.J. Abdul Kalam to Russia in May 2005 and visit by President Putin to India as the Chief Guest at the Republic Day celebrations in January 2007.

Areas of Common Concern

The concept of strategic partnership denotes that India and Russia have multiple common interests and that they would like to pool their resources for optimum results. These common interests are global or international, regional as also bilateral. In the context of international system both are working towards strengthening multipolar world order as also international institutions like the United Nations. Recognizing that India has emerged as a major international actor, Russia has offered its support for India's candidature for permanent membership of the Security Council. This was reiterated by Russian Foreign Minister, Igor Ivanov, during the joint press conference on the occasion of the visit of India's Foreign Minister Jaswant Singh to Moscow in May 1999.[16]

India and Russia also have their regional priorities. Extended South-West Asia in general and Central Asia in particular has emerged as an area of mutual concern at least on three points. The first is to contain the growth of radical Islam in the region and more particularly in Afghanistan. According to the *Annual Report* of 1996-1997, interaction on developments in the region lying between the borders of India and Russia have been found to be beneficial and contacts are being maintained on the evolving situation in Afghanistan.[17] The growing strength of the Taliban and its links with radical Islamic groups were already causing concern by mid-nineties. That continues to be an area of common concern even now. Other issues of common concern revolve around the need to develop regional energy-based resources and finally to stabilize Central Asia so that it can function as a link between Russia and India via the Indian Ocean.

In this context the role of China assumes significance since China too is interested in two areas of common concern in the region viz. threat posed by groups professing radical version of Islam and energy. Can bilateral relations be given a trilateral shape? Steps are being taken to formulate triangular links between China, India and Russia. The initiative has come from Russia and the primary focus is on economic cooperation. There are proposals to induct Brazil in the near future. The three countries have held meetings at the level of Foreign Ministers.

It is possible that this trilateral interest partnership, with focus on economy, might strengthen further in the years to come but one doubts if China can be a strategic partner of India like Russia is. India has a long history of friendship with Russia. The same cannot be said about Sino-Indian relations. Despite efforts to iron out differences impression persists that China has not given up its old policy of trying to isolate India in India's own space of strategic concern. Hence, while India and Russia can develop bilateral strategic partnership, the time is not yet ripe for a trilateral strategic partnership between India, Russia and China. Also, India, while strengthening its strategic partnership with Russia, is also keeping its options open *vis-a-vis* USA and Japan in the context of balancing the possible pressure from China and its regional supporters in India's immediate strategic space.

India and Russia have always had close cooperation in matters like military-technical cooperation, atomic energy, space etc. The importance given to this aspect is clear from the fact that generally a Deputy Prime Minister is in charge of that subject. Several bilateral exchanges are made to update cooperation in these fields. India has an ambitious space programme that includes even reaching the moon (*Chandrayan*). Russia can be a major partner, specially when Indian scientists have proven their capability in this field. Another dimension of space-based technology is related to improving precision guidance of munitions specially at a longer range.

Defence-related technology as also trade has been a major component of bilateral relations since the sixties. There is no exaggeration that ex-Soviet/Russian equipments have been the backbone of India's defence preparedness. That will continue to be so in future as well despite efforts to diversify supplies.

As per data given in the *Military Balance, 2005-2006*, Indian Army depends heavily upon ex-Soviet/Russian equipment. They constitute 75 percent of its main battle tank (T-72 and T-90), hundred percent of the armoured infantry fighting vehicles (BMP-I and II), about fifty percent of heavy artillery and all the SAMs and most of the anti-tank missiles. Except for the ageing aircraft carrier INS Virat, and the recently acquired large amphibious ship (LPD), that was being decommissioned by USA, and four German submarines most of the modern fighting ships of the Navy are either acquired from Soviet Union/Russia or constructed in India with major equipments from there. India has ordered the new aircraft carrier INS Vikramaditya from Russia as also naval version of MiG-29 aircraft that will operate from that aircraft carrier as also the one that India proposes to build in Kochi. Most of the warships that are being built also carry Russian equipment. There are unconfirmed reports that Russians are helping India build its indigeneous nuclear-powered submarine.

The Air Force is equally dependent upon ex-Soviet Union/ Russian equipment. That includes almost 80 percent of its frontline combat aircraft. More modern aircraft like Su-30 are being acquired or built under license in India. Experts believe that Su-30 is equal in performance to the best American aircraft like F-15 and F-18, and far superior to much talked about F-16. Almost all the medium and heavy-lift helicopters as also attack helicopters, medium and heavy transport aircraft, SAMs, AAMs etc are also of Russian origin.

Not only have the Russians given to India their latest military equipment, they have also shown willingness to offer India participation in the development of their new weapons like the fifth generation fighter that reportedly has stealth technology, scramjet power plant, PGMs, missiles etc. BrahMos missile has demonstrated the advantage of Indo-Russian joint venture in high-tech weapon technology. More such joint ventures can be taken up. Now that both states have shown willingness to open defence-related technology for private-sector participation, there is scope for involving private sector particularly in the context of information technology and precision guidance system that involves input of specialized manpower and technology.

Conclusion

The new geopolitical environment as also multiple levels of bilateral and multilateral interaction have opened new vistas for defining bilateral relations. They offer India and Russia options to diversify their interest partnership as also to raise the level of their bilateral relations to that of strategic partnership without simultaneously compromising their other bilateral and multilateral interest partnerships. Thus, neither Russia nor India need to put their bilateral ties into the strait jacket of alliance relations. Both can evolve their own pattern of partnership with others without allowing that to come into conflict with the foundation of their bilateral relations.

There is no reason to doubt that both Russia and India will take advantage of the new environment to further strengthen their bilateral relations. USSR lost its status as a Super Power but Russia has been able to regain its status as a great power whose views can no longer be dismissed. If India too wants to play the role of a partner in the great power league, it also must learn to think and behave like one. India must realize that to be an actor in a multi-polar global order, it must be willing to play the role at least of a regional power even if that hurts the feelings of some elements in and around India who would prefer India to be a weak and humble state locked up in the confines of the sub-continent now renamed South Asia. Hence, the success of Indo-Russian strategic partnership will also depend upon India's willingness and courage to acquire the role and, therefore, responsibility of a great power in the Indian Ocean region. Can India do so ?

References

1. Government of India, Ministry of External Affairs, *Report, 1965-1966,* New Delhi, 1966, p. 44. (Henceforth cited as MEA Report).
2. MEA, *Report, 1971-1972.* New Delhi, 1972, p. 68.
3. Fuller, Graham F., "Moscow and the Gulf War", *Foreign Affairs,* 70(2), Spring 1991, p. 56.
4. Dannereuther, Roland, "Russia, Central Asia and the Persian Gulf", *Survival,* 35(4), Winter 1993-94, p. 95.
5. Rubeinstein, Allvin Z., "Russia in search of a New role: Changing Geopolitical Compulsions in Central Asia", *World Affairs* (New Delhi), 1(2), April-June 1997, p. 63.
6 MEA, *Report 1991-1992,* New Delhi, 1992, p. 39.
7. Simon, Gerhard, "Russia's Identity and International Politics", *Aussenpolitik,* 48(3), 1997, p. 253.
8. Legvold, Robert, "Russia's Unformed Foreign Policy", *Foreign Affairs,* 80(5), September-October 2001, p. 63.
9. Text, *Strategic Digest,* 30(9), September 2000, pp. 1247-56.
10. Kislov, A. and Frolov, A., "Russia and the World Arms Market', *International Affairs* (Moscow), 49(4), 2003, p. 148.
11. MEA, *Annual Report,* 1992-1993, New Delhi, 1993, p. 62.
12. MEA, *Annual Report,* 1996-1997, New Delhi, 1997, p. 55-56.
13. *Strategic Digest,* 31(11), November 2001, p. 1475.
14. MEA, *Annual Report,* 1999-2000, New Delhi, 2000, p. 52.
15. MEA, *Annual Report,* 2006-2007, New Delhi, 2007, p. 37.
16. MEA, *Annual Report,* 1999-2000, New Delhi, 2000, p. 53.
17. MEA, *Annual Report,* 1996-1997, New Delhi, 1997, p. 56.

3

India and Russia : The Threshold of Partnership

P.L. Dash

Introduction

The year 2007 is unlike any other year in the annals of Indo-Russian ties. Sixty years ago, on 13 April, 1947, India and the former Soviet Union had established their diplomatic relations. India was then not independent and the former USSR was limping back to normalcy from the ruins of the II World War. However, both countries were optimistically nurturing hopes of a palmy future: India about achieving independence and making fresh forays into building democracy; and the USSR hoping to build a world socialist system. China, as a major player in the international system, was still far off. Socialist China came into being only in 1949. That period has changed. The forward march of history over the past sixty years has predetermined that these three great countries - Russia, India and China - are likely to play a defining role in the scheme of things to come in Eurasia. Their tryst with destiny began with their resurgence and economic development nearly two decades ago; and their rendezvous with defining the world order has just begun with the dawn of the millennium.

Lo and Behold! Sixteen years have passed so quickly after the Soviet sunset! Sixteen fruitful years of incredible changes have overwhelmed the world. These sixteen years have witnessed a total transformation of the entire contour of international relations. What was earlier known as Cold War rivalry is no longer a conceivable proposition. The great east-west divide has suddenly evaporated. Through these sixteen years, many new countries have occupied their distinct places in the world map. Some of them have become major actors in international politics; while others have become the pawns in the hands of the sole super power - the United

States. These sixteen years are mute witness to the process of change in the very concept of superpower. New phenomena such as war on international terrorism, joint efforts to combat such nagging menaces as drugs and narcotic trafficking, arms and money laundering and illegal human trafficking have affected the health of so many countries. Through these sixteen years, some dictatorships have gone while others have appeared. In the periphery of India, Russia and China – three potent powers of the 21st century - Iraq is in the throes of a civil war, Iran is turbulent on the threshold of its going nuclear. Afghanistan is no better. Of course, a country that produces 89 percent of the world's opium cannot hope to live better. Only one more country - Myanmar - shares 7 percent of the world opium output, while the rest of the world just has 4 percent share of opium production.[1] Pakistan has been swaying between domestic upheaval and international pressures to deal with a resurgent Taliban against whom it is officially fighting and unofficially collaborating. The Kashmir problem overshadows as much the social fabric of that state as Chechnya has been overshadowing that of Russia. Oil prices have so skyrocketed that it has pushed the entire world into doldrums of speculation. Resurgent and militant Islam across the southern underbelly of the Russian Federation right from Chechnya through Dagestan to the countries of Central Asia is a discernibly destabilizing phenomenon. It seems the whole region contiguous to India, Russia and China are located in the periphery of a politically volatile and economically fragile countries the sum total of what Zbigniew Brezinsky called the 'Global Balkan.'[2]

In this overall context of a rapidly changing and highly volatile regional scenario, Russia and India have been trying to come out of the post-Soviet lull in their relationship, essaying to give a tangible shape to bilateral ties in various fields and putting their efforts together to rebuild what was once a model relationship between two asymmetrical socio-economic systems. Close collaboration between these two countries is a significant parameter of emerging relations in Eurasia. The added advantage of embracing China into a trilateral forum of Russia-India and China further accentuates the emerging scenario with possible cooperation. The fact that India's relationship with the United States has been brightening up for the past few years provide a further fillip to bilateral, trilateral and multilateral ties without any ideological baggage. The mantra of the epoch, it seems, is mutual advantage, greater cooperation for the upkeep of interests of all those countries participating on the platform of cooperation.

An Overview

The decade following the establishment of diplomatic relationship witnessed rapid increase in bilateral interactions. Exchange of visit at the apex level was the hallmark of this decade – a decade that was turbulent in Cold War block politics. This was the decade that witnessed too the genesis and initial growth of India's non-alignment from conceptualization to implementation. The Indo-Soviet relations of the 1950s could safely be divided into two phases: until the death of Joseph Stalin in 1953, when it was cool, and following Stalin's demise, when it assumed economic and political significance. India was the arena where the distinct lines of Cold War divide were drawn; and Nehru was the cynosure of all eyes, with his non-alignment flagship aligning and mobilizing the newly liberated countries into a solid anti-imperialist block. With both Pakistan and China tilting towards the western block, the Soviet Union had staked enough in befriending Nehru. The visit of Jawaharlal Nehru to Moscow in June 1955 and the return visit by Nikita Khrushchev and Nikolai Bulganin to India and other South Asian countries in December the selfsame year were clearly intended to woo and befriend each other on the face of mounting block politics. India as the major country of the subcontinent suited the Soviet scheme of things like no other country in the region. After all the interest was mutual; so were bilateral relations.

It is interesting to note that in the immediate aftermath of Stalin's death, the two countries began talk on building a steel plant in Bhilai in the autumn of 1953. At a time when the western countries were hesitant to extend any help to India build public sector enterprises, the Soviet Union readily agreed to provide India with financial and technical support to construct a steel plant; and an agreement to that effect was signed on February 2,1955. Then followed massive flow of funds and expertise to build the monuments of immortal friendship in concrete and steel. Of all the loans and financial support that the Soviet Union had extended to India between the 1950s and 1970s, "49.8 percent went to finance its metallurgy, 17.8 percent to its oil production and refining, 9 percent to heavy machine building and 5 percent to mining industry.[3] The very division of the pattern of help extended to India along metallurgy, energy, mining and machine building implied the importance of core priority sectors of the economy that would lay a solid foundation for future development of the country. The steel plants in Bhilai and Bokaro, the hydroelectric power plants at various scenic hill locales across India to make herself self-reliant in energy supply, numerous other enterprises built across the country, and that too all in the public sector, were the symbol of a friendship never earlier seen in history of bilateral relations.

The following decade was equally tumultuous. India was the victim of two attacks – one from China in 1962 and the other from Pakistan in 1965. The aftermath of both the wars was devastating, debilitating and destabilizing. It was in the aftermath of the 1965 war leading to Soviet mediated peace deal at Tashkent, when Lal Bahadur Shastri suddenly died that brought Soviet Union under Leonid Brezhnev and India under Indira Gandhi further closer to each other. On the face of China slowly tilting towards the US, Brezhnev doggedly decided to side with India. As a result, along the charted priority course of helping India in power, oil and steel sectors, massive Soviet investments were made in various projects in India. The mutually agreed Rupee - Rouble exchange arrangement precisely originated in these years from 1968 to take care of technology and arms transfers to India. The agreements implied that without bothering for hard currency reserves, India was free to pay the former USSR all her accumulated debt in a barter arrangement through Indian merchandise. This arrangement continued to serve its purpose until after the Soviet collapse.

Those were the golden years of Indo-Soviet bilateralism that evidenced a decisive strategic Soviet tilt towards India in the early 1970s. One could recall the calculated genocide perpetrated by the Pakistani military in East Pakistan and the resultant influx of millions of refugees right across the border crossing over to Indian territory. It was on the face of these mounting difficulties that Leonid Brezhnev had decided to throw his stoic support behind Indira Gandhi to face the impending challenge. Since March,1971, while Pakistan was getting ready for a war with India, the Soviet Union and India were seriously preparing to sign a Treaty of Peace, Friendship and Cooperation that finally materialized on 9 August,1971. The treaty was a defining moment in bilateral relations that had obvious multilateral impact on the unfolding situation in South Asia around 1971. The Soviet concerns were not adequately addressed by Pakistan or the US. There was a discernible attitudinal difference between what the Soviet Union and India wished to achieve and what Pakistan and the US wanted to uphold in East Pakistan.[4] Finally the Indo-Soviet Treaty became a precursor to stability in East Pakistan when Mujibur Rehman assumed power in Dacca. The rest is history. But the role played by the Soviet Union and India for the birth of Bangladesh was contrary to the role played by Pakistan and the US. The former was incredibly cataclysmic and while the latter received all moral denigration and political vituperation. This fact is firmly etched in history. Veteran Indian diplomat, KPS Menon had succinctly put it: "instead of a Washington, a Roosevelt, a Lincoln or even an Eisenhower, the USA had Richard Nixon."[5] While the credit for handling smoothly the birth of Bangladesh goes to Leonid Brezhnev and Indira Gandhi, the apathy of Nixon to India's position relative to the sub-continental affairs in South Asia had brought India and the Soviet Union closer to each other than ever earlier.[6]

From then on, throughout the decade that followed, there was no occasion to look back. Despite the fact that the monopoly of Congress rule has had an unexpected electoral demise, the relations between the two countries flowered and flourished. The forward march of Indo-Russian relations became an all encompassing phenomenon. Neither the post-emergency exit of Indira Gandhi from power, nor the advent of Morarji Desai in the office of Prime Minister of India could impact on the time tested nature of these ties. Desai's successors – Charan Singh, Chandra Shekhar and V.P. Singh and Brezhnev's successors – Yuri Andropov and Konstantin Chernenko in the post-Brezhnev Russia could do precious little to change the course of Indo-Russian bilateral relations. Instead, all of them were agile and agog to ensure more continuity than any tangible change. All these years both countries were on the threshold of swift transformations in the conduct of international relations.

The 1980s were a time of further sweeping changes and innovative ideas. While Gorbachev launched his twin policy of Perestroika and Glasnost, Rajiv Gandhi was envisioning to pilot India to progress and prosperity in the 21st century. It was these two leaders who first began talking about the twentyfirst century, when the century itself had still fifteen years to pass by. Throwing open to debate and implementation idea after idea, both Mikhail Gorbachev and Rajiv Gandhi were covertly widening the scope of Indo-Russian relations. Meetings between the two leaders were as regular as mutual exchange of visits between the two countries.

Whether it was the initiative of the Delhi Six[7] or to achieve a comprehensive security system in a world free of nuclear weapons, India and the Soviet Union were unanimous in their endeavors right up to the time of Soviet collapse in December, 1991. Despite the trade and commercial relations facing the downswing, both countries were constantly pursuing energetic tasks of visionaries and sounding optimistic about the future.

The post-Soviet lull in Indo-Russian relations was a testing time for bilateral ties. A host of problems such as India's Rupee debt to Russia, the Rupee-Rouble exchange rate, faltering bilateral trade, Yeltsin's preference to occident over the orient and his lack of understanding of the real essence of Indo-Russian relations were the roadblocks in mutual ties that impeded the process until the advent of Evgeny Primakov at the helm of affairs in 1996, first as Russian Foreign Minister and then as Prime Minister of Russia. Academician Primakov's coming to power is a distinct line in time and space of Yeltsin regime that bifurcates the entire Yeltsin epoch into two clear phases: the nonchalant phase of overlooking India initially; and the active phase of befriending India anew. The relations then and since have once again resumed their earlier tempo and particularly through the Putin years they have regained the earlier aura. In April, 2007, when both countries celebrated the 60th year of their diplomatic relations, one could safely assume that bilateral interactions are on the right path, upswing and flamboyant to take on the future challenges whenever and wherever they come.

Strategic Partners

The declaration of Indo-Russian Strategic Partnership is an action plan in the changing uni-polar context of the contemporary world. It implies that both countries are ready to face the unfolding challenges of the new, emerging world together. The declaration does not put any encumbrances on either party to sign similar such partnership with any other country. That's why India has signed partnership agreements with the US too. It allows both countries to choose their partners without any ideological baggage and shed the stereotype notions of the past differences. From the vantage point of a broad platform both countries are looking forward to implement the ideas of strategic partnership in various areas of cooperation. Put into effect on Putin's maiden official visit to India in October, 2000, the declaration on strategic partnership is a pointer to the versatile areas of cooperation in the years to come.

The strategic partnership agreement is truly an elevation of the 1971 agreement on Peace, Friendship and Cooperation in the changing context of post-Cold War international relations. In 1971 the situation was so very different. The South Asian continent was beclouded by a war–like situation that culminated into conflagration in December that year. The Nixon administration was pursuing a clear anti-India stance by persuading Pakistan to wage a war on India, and at the same time, provoking China to threaten India.[8] The US naval ship "Enterprise", popularly known then as the 7th fleet, was moving from the Indian Ocean menacingly to the waters of the Arabian Sea. In the backdrop of all these developments, the Soviet Union was siding with friendly India morally, technologically and militarily to ward off any threat and to ensure peace in the subcontinent. It was then that the famous treaty of friendship and cooperation had been signed. The situation is strikingly different today. The US has been trying to befriend India. Its largest nuclear powered aircraft carrier "Nimitz" has anchored on the port of Chennai on a friendly visit and its crews are doing community services in the streets of Chennai. And an Indo-US nuclear deal is being hotly debated to be signed. China, however, has been making all-out efforts to build strategic facilities at Gwadar in Pakistan and access warm waters of the Persian Gulf. While other powers continue to use Pakistan as pawn on the regional chessboard of international politics to make it serve a conduit of their military and strategic presence, Indo-Russian relations have assumed added strategic significance. The Indo-Russian closeness is further accentuated by Chinese endeavors to access Bangladesh and Myanmar and thereby encircle India from Gwadar in the west and Myanmar and Chittagong in the east. Such strategic Chinese motives are intended to counter and curtail India's strategic drive northward in the direction of Central Asia and Russia. Thus the US military presence in the Indian neighborhood and Chinese efforts to dominate the region are ground enough for India and Russia to strike a regional balance; and they have timely done so.

Aside from the varied range of military technological cooperation that both countries have charted out to follow, there are concrete evidences to suggest greater cooperation. On 16 October, 2005, India and Russia conducted their first ever joint exercises in the Rajasthan desert. Participated by Russian Defence Minister, Sergei Ivanov and attended by India's Chief of Services, this was a joint anti-terrorist and counter insurgency exercise controlled from the Mahajan firing range in the Thar desert. The exercises were successful, but a seemingly near fatal accident stole aura of the event. A Russian made AN-32 aircraft, participating in the exercises, suddenly dropped from the air a vehicle carrying anti-tank missile launchers, dangerously close to the pavilion, where VIPs, including Sergei Ivanov were seated. The incident was so unexpected that Air Chief Marshall, S.P.Tyagi and GOC, Southwestern Command, Lt. General Nagrajan ran for cover. Maintaining his cool through the incident, the Army Chief, J.J.Singh and the Russian Defence Minister, Ivanov came to the rescue of the visibly agitated Air Marshall Tyagi and pacified him by saying that such accidents do take place in "changing wind conditions."[9] While top military brass of both countries had pacified an excited media, speaking to the NDTV news channel in English, Ivanov later told that it was a novel experience for the Russian paratroopers to exercise in desert conditions, which would stand a good deal in their anti-insurgency training.

With the limited space of an article, only one instance from out of the numerous examples of Indo-Russian military cooperation can be cited in favour of the Mikoyan and Gurevich fighters, popularly known as MiG. The MiG Corporation of Russia and the Indian Air Force share over four decades of mutual relations. Despite series of serious accusations that MiGs have been frequently crashing because of their antiquated avionic techniques, and that they have outlived their utility for the Indian Air Force, the Government of India has decided to overlook the popular sobriquet of 'Flying Coffins' given to MiG by the Indian media, and once again chosen in June 2007 the most advanced of the series, MiG-35 for procurement. This is a revised version of multi-role fighter, MiG - 29, which is already in the Indian Air Force inventory.[10] Various generations of MiG have remained the core of India's combative force for over four decades. Now more than 550 MiG-21, MiG-23/27, MiG -25, MiG-29 aircrafts are there in the Indian Air Force inventory. Besides, MiG-29K aircrafts will constitute the core of fighter aircrafts on board Marshall Gorshkov. The Russian specialists have helped Indian experts at the Hindustan Aeronautics Limited located across India for licensed manufacture of spares parts, as well as for repairing, upgrading and maintaining the aircrafts.[11] In addition to the various generations of MiGs and helicopters, the ultramodern Sukhoi fighters are also in Indian Air Force inventory; and together they constitute the mainstay of combat. The Indo-Russian strategic partnership is a versatile, all-encompassing program that embraces 130 projects with emphasis on applied component of research. Therefore, within the ambit of that partnership, military technological cooperation is just one major aspect of the complex range of issues involved in bilateral ties.

However, given India's defence overdependence on Russia, the pervasive presence of Russia in all three segments of the Indian armed forces is obvious. It is this overdependence that needs diversification. In the years to come, as India grows in stature as an economic powerhouse, the current phase of overdependence will slowly dissipate to pave way for others to play a role in India's weapons basket. That impliedly conveys a clear message to all that, should Russia like to continue to maintain widespread presence in the field of military technological cooperation with India in the Air Force, Army and Navy, it has to take recourse to a competitive market at play along with other players, who are afield with their military stuff to sell.

The other major aspect is Indo-Russian energy cooperation. Through the Soviet years, India was buying Soviet oil in order to meet her energy requirements. After the Soviet collapse, there has been certain tangible disruptions in the swap arrangement the Soviet Union had with Iraq to supply oil to India. While alternative avenues are being explored to overcome these disruptions, sustained economic growth of over seven percent a year have put India in an energy hungry position to seek alternative supplies to meet her energy needs, growing every year almost at a higher speed than her economic growth. Russia, as a major energy giant of the world, is capable of meeting India's energy requirements. In this strategic area of energy cooperation, aside from the numerous hydroelectric power plants that have been built with Soviet/Russian collaboration, two vital areas of cooperation are emerging in the post-Soviet phase: India's involvement in the Sakhalin-1 project and the Soviet help to expand the nuclear plant at Kudankulam in Tamil Nadu. From this cooperation, what emerges is the complex approach to address India's energy needs from conventional oil supply to hydro, hydel as well as nuclear power stations, and Russia is invariably involved in most major collaborative energy projects in India. Gasprom has been participating in the gas exploration in the Bay of Bengal shelf. Such Russian companies as Stroitransgaz and Zarubezhneft have been actively taking part in various Indian energy projects.[12]

The real intention of the strategic partnership deal is to follow the principle of an old adage "A friend in need is a friend in deed". India and Russia have followed this adage more than adequately to prove their proximity to each other. The sheer breadth of bilateral relations is too impressive to detail in a short article. Yet it is one relationship that has been singled out by successive generations of leaders and this led to prove a tangible point of irreplaceable nature; some sort of an immortality that Indo-Russian relations live in perpetuity. What began with the journey of a merchant from the Russian city of Tver over four hundred years ago has gradually undergone a paradigm shift in the contemporary context: from a buyer-seller relationship, it has ascended through mutual cooperation, joint ventures, joint production to the strategic level of mutual partners. The joint production of supersonic cruise missiles – BrahMos – is a shining instance of partnering Brahmaputra and Moscow rivers together and export it to the world as a model of mutual friendship.

Some Critical Areas

One concrete area where both countries have huge advantage of cooperation is the emerging field of information technology. Russian attention to this emerging area of cooperation was evident, when president Putin chose to visit Infosys at Bangalore to see for himself the model of an IT complex that has earned for itself the credo of being a software giant. India's cutting edge image in information technology is an asset and Russia knows this adequately enough to take advantage of this advancement. The pervasive applicability of information technology in everyday life and in every sphere from weather forecasting to space research could stand a good deal help Russia better learn the management techniques of IT into its daily ethos of a knowledge driven society.

The Russians, particularly its critically thinking elite, consider the Indian IT miracle "a historical product of smart cooperation between the state, national enterprise and intellectual elite of the country".[13] The Russian IT industry is not at its nascent best, picking up very slowly but with an ambition to be reckoned one day as a big player in the world. Hopes are hopes, but realities are different. The Information Technology sector in Russia accounted for just 5.3 percent of the country's GDP in 2005, compared to 2 percent in 2000; almost one percent growth every year. With this pace of progress, Russia would be far away from being a world player in near future. Cooperation with India in this sphere would substantially help Russian IT industry to sustain itself, compete with others and reckon as an IT major in the world. Russia and India have been traditionally acknowledged for their seminal contributions to the world of Mathematics. Since computer science in general and IT in particular have a strong base of applied mathematics, joint research activities in developing frontier areas of information technology ought to be undertaken. After all in a globalizing world, nothing, and absolutely no achievement can be viewed in isolation.

India of 2007 is a transformed country. Beginning 1990s, it has been constantly changing. India of today remains totally incomprehensible, if one tries to understand her with a mindset of the 1960s or 1970s. The phenomenal growth of the IT sector in India has earned for it a deserving place to portray the country as a "knowledge economy". India has used its very base of skilled manpower to occupy a deserving place in the IT world. Russia has both – human and natural resources in plenty. It is a huge country that straddles across eleven time zones and its depth in science and technology is difficult to fathom. Efforts are already afoot to have IT parks in Moscow. While an IT park in Moscow can be construed as a pilot project for this purpose, other cities in Russia can also have such parks. This would not be too difficult because Russia has fewer cities - just 13 in total - with more than a million population and 13 IT parks for a country of Russia's size and population is not too much.

The imperatives of a rapprochement in the IT sectors of Russia and India is an essential prerequisite to follow in the years to come. Russian researcher, Andrey Volodin, citing World Bank sources writes: that "by 2020, seven of the most powerful economic systems of the world would be located in the East".[14] And the world's largest democracy, India, will be one among them. Therefore the inevitability of companionship of the world's largest democracy and the most domineering power in information technology will drive home a point to the world's nascent democracy and inceptive IT power – Russia and India together to work for mutual benefit in areas of common interests. This is an unavoidable proposition that both countries cannot afford to escape. With the opening up of Russia to the world market and liberalization of the Indian economy, Indian private sector business has evinced keen interest in recent years to expand business with the Russian Federation. Such efforts have been facing many a roadblock over the past one and a half decades. These impediments ought to be cleared off the way in view of the current, low Indo-Russian annual trade turn over: just over $2.5 billion with Russia against $15 billion with China and $30 billion with the US.[15]

The Indo-Russian defence cooperation has entered a critical phase in view of the competitive advantage proffered by globalization. Where matters are likely to change is in the area of India's overdependence on the Russian Federation for weapons, military hardware and spare supplies. If earlier India depended over 70 percent on the Soviet Union, in the new environment it cannot afford to do so. The post-Soviet experience of procuring spare parts for Soviet made weaponry has been traumatic for India. It is from this experience that India has learnt the lessons of putting its eggs in different baskets. And withdrawal of state patronage coupled with advent of globalization has provided the opportunities to look to a diversified source of spare supplies. Although it would take years to overcome the overdependence, a beginning has already been made. However, Russian weaponry still comes to India at a cheaper price compared to weapons from USA, UK, Israel or France. Thus quality products, their competitive edge, reliability and battle worthiness are some of the features that would sustain Russia as a prime weapons supplier to India. The shenanigans of age-old friendship would of course always matter as a trusted partner.

Another critical area of bilateral cooperation has been space research and exploration. In this vast area of interaction both countries have over a four plus decades of standing. Soon after Yuri Gagarin's first ever successful space mission in 1961, he visited India as an official guest of Jawaharlal Nehru. The warm welcome he received from Jawaharlal Nehru in Delhi and from the Indian people at other places he traveled within India set the background tone for the future Indo-Russian cooperation in space. From there began the journey to the unexplored space. And ever since those years, from Aryabhatt to Rakesh Sharma to Chandipur missile testing facilities in Balasore, the imprints of Russian collaboration in India's space research are laudably visible everywhere. It is one area where close interaction among the scientists of both countries, particularly between Glavkosmos and ISRO, is a regular feature. Since Russia has achieved commendable success in frontier areas of space research and the field has immense applicability to national security interest of both countries, space research remains a critical area of joint ventures and collaboration. The gamut of.

Indo-Russian relations is too broad to detail in one article, even in a book. Innumerable books have been penned by many authors. Yet few bilateral relations in the annals of history are as enduring as the one between Russia and India. This enduring legacy is an asset that would guide both countries to pass through the testing times as they did during the immediate aftermath of Soviet disintegration.

Conclusions

The twentyfirst century is different in many respects from the twentieth century. The Cold War bipolarity is passé. What has emerged is a globalizing world and slowly democratizing polity in those countries where democracy was markedly absent. In such a situation Indo-Russian relations have entered into the very competitive phase of relationship with inherent complexities of changing times. For example, India's relations with the United States is a significant factor to impact Indo-Russian ties simply because relations are likely to blossom in those areas where India has had close relations with Russia for many decades. On the economic front, the prospects for Indo-US trade and commerce have brightened up and Foreign Direct Investment inflow to India is on the upswing. On the political and diplomatic front, the imperatives of encountering a world laden with the fear of terror has brought the US and India closer to each other than ever before, leading to bilateral information sharing, conducting joint military exercises and holding apex level parleys regularly on burning and emerging issues of mutual interest. On the energy front, the Indo-US civilian nuclear deal is in the offing. On the issue of cooperation in the international arena, Indo-US commonality is more visible now than it was through the Cold War years. Thousands of Indian students are heading to the US universities for their higher education, while hundreds are heading to Russia in post-Soviet years.

While the Indo-US closeness in recent years has never cast a shadow on the revived tempo of Indo-Russian ties, what it has made clear is that the emerging, triangular Indo-US and Indo-Russian ties cannot remain anymore bilateral; it cannot be insulated from the US influence. These triangular ties have put India at the centre of attraction for both the US and Russia. And the stronger India grows in the upcoming years, the better will be the prospects for relations with both Russia and the USA. Thus all these three countries plus China are in a bind of complex relations to be evolved over the next few decades. The bind of these four countries plus

Japan would impact upon the merging ethos of mutual bilateral and multilateral relations with an incredible equanimity thus far not seen in the annals of relationship among nations. No country likes to respect a weak nation and accord it a place in the shape of things to come. As India grows stronger; so would grow its respect. This respect would bring dignity and dignity will thrust responsibility. Preparedness to handle these responsibilities will not exactly be a litmus test, will not necessarily be a rival action against one another, but surely, it would demand from all countries greater cooperation on a varied range of issues for which both India and Russia must stand prepared to breast the upcoming waves. The fight against international terrorism in the aftermath of 9/11 is a good reckoner in this regard. Similar instances, although at a narrower level, are surfacing to combat menaces such as drugs and narcotic trafficking, money laundering, human trafficking and small arms smuggling.

As Indo-Russian relations transit from a thoroughly state controlled partnership to the decontrolled, competitive milieu, the state will continue to remain an active player in strategic areas of collaboration, hold to itself the bridle of relationship as the main regulatory agent of bilateralism and leave the rest to the market forces to determine the salience of not only trade and commerce, but also a whole range of other issues where market forces dominate the scenario to benefit the state. Precisely, the export patronage of the state from the Indian side, import patronage from the Russian side and vice versa has evaporated. State is no longer the sole agent to control Indo-Russian bilateral relations; it has been effectively and partly replaced by market forces, non-state actors, NGOs, private agencies and enterprises and a plethora of other agencies in a competitive environment to ensure the smooth functioning of bilateral ties. Countries must adapt to the changing situation and act in a fashion that would be beneficial to their national interests.

References

1. Atul Thakur, On a Global Trip, The Times of India, 27 June, 2007, p. 17.
2. Zbigniew Brzezinski, The Hegemonic Quicksand, The National Interest, Winter 2003-2004, p. 6.
3. Russia and India: From Past into the Future, Sixtieth Anniversary of Diplomatic Relations, 1947- 2007, RIA Novosti and Russian Embassy in New Delhi, 2007, p. 46.
4. R.K. Jain, Soviet South Asian Relations, 1947-1978, Vol. 1, Radiant Publishers, New Delhi, pp. 105-107 (Documents Nos. 40-41).

5. K.P.S. Menon, The Indo-Soviet Treaty, Vikas Publishing House, New Delhi, 1971, p. 18.

6. P.L. Dash, Indira Gandhi and Soviet Union, Prachi Prakashan, New Delhi, 1988, p. 180.

7. Delhi Six was an initiative for achieving disarmament and a nuclear free world. Signatories to the initiative were Presidents of Argentina, Mexico, Tanzania and Prime Ministers of India, Greece and Sweden. Under the auspices of India, it was for the first time that leaders of Europe, Asia, Africa and Latin America expressed concerns over the issues of disarmament. Please refer to "Initiative of Delhi Six and the Soviet Position", Novosti Press Agency, Moscow, 1987.

8. The Times of India, 2 July, 2007.

9. Meenal Dubey, IAF Drops a Vehicle on VIPs, Nearly, The Hindustan Times, 17 October, 2005, p. 1.

10. MiG-35: The Best for India, New Theme, Vol. VII, No. 5, September-October, 2006, pp.10-12.

11. MiG Corporation on Indian Market, Aerospace Herald, No.1, January-February, 2005, pp. 6-7.

12. Vyacheslav Trubnikov, Not a Brother; but a Trusted Friend, Hezavesimaya Gazeta, 17 August, 2004.

13. Natalia Skorokhodova, Advanced India and Backward Russia (From Experience of Information Technology Development), Russian Analytica, Vol. 9, 2006, p. 40.

14. Andrey Volodin, Vostochnaya Model, Razvitiya: Ochenka Politicheskoi Effectivnosti, Apologiya, (A Monthly Humanities Digest) No. 7, September, 2005, p. 29.

15. Andrey Volodin, India-Russia-China in Free Geometry of World Politics, Apologiya, No. 9, 2006, p. 33.

4

Significance of Indo-Russian Relations—Regional and International—In the 21st Century

V.D. Chopra

Introduction

Any study of significance of Indo-Russian relations in the 21st century has to take into account certain important changes, which are taking place in the economy of the two countries and their role in the international polity. If statistics are any indicators, India has already entered a new phase in its economic development and moving forward to become a developed nation though as yet in its initial stages. This stands as a complete contrast to the economic development of India in the late 60s and early 70s of the last century, when Indo-Soviet relations had touched a new high. At that stage India was stepping out from a backward agrarian economy to a most developed nation among the developing countries. At that time Soviet Union was recognised as a super power both in the economic and military terms. Now Indo-Russian relations are evolving in a new historical condition and time tested Indo-Russian relations are developing once again rapidly. In this connection it may be mentioned that after the disintegration of the Soviet Union, Indo-Soviet relations received a temporary setback. Now the recent trends show that these relations are once again growing and deepening with new dimensions and are assuming a multidimensional character both nationally and internationally.

There is yet another aspect, which needs to be underlined. In a period of globalisation, according to some scholars, the work has assumed the character of a cosmic ship in which all the countries are its constituents. If this characterisation is correct, the bilateral relations between India and Russia have become a key factor in preserving the existence of this cosmic ship. In other words

Indo-Russian relations have a very significant role to play in preserving this cosmic ship. This in simple language means that Indo-Russian relations are a vital factor in maintaining world peace and building economic relations among the various countries on the principle of equity and parity.

It is pertinent to state here that in making an assessment of the role of Indo-Russian relations in the world polity, Indo-Russian relations have become a key factor in the world politics today.

Quite apart from this aspect it needs to be stressed that in the first decade of 21st century, Asia has become the centre of gravity of the world economy. In this development two Asian giants China and India are going to play a strategic role in the development of the economy of the world as a whole and that in the recent period that the attention of the most developed countries is now concentrated on these two countries.

India Emerging World Power

It should be mentioned that Indian capitalism is growing faster than ever before. As a matter of fact a section of top Indian capitalists have begun to penetrate into the economies of other countries including the developed nations. According to one estimate, during the next one decade, India will either match or takeover Japan in the pace of economic development, notwithstanding the fact that India has yet to go a long way in building a welfare state and elevating the conditions of life of the poorest strata of population. Nonetheless the hard reality is that Indian capitalism has begun to exhibit its maturity and now is poised to compete with the capitalists of the developed nations. This development is of far-reaching importance. Moreover, it brings into focus the increasingly independent character of Indian capitalism. It is no more subservient to the capitalists of the developed countries. "The Organisation for Economic Cooperation and Development (OECD), the elite club of developed countries, has observed in a report that India created more jobs than China, Brazil and Russia between 2000 and 2005 with 11.3 million net new jobs every year in India against 7 million in China, 2.7 million in Brazil and 7,00,000 in Russia. But then, if economics was only about absolute numbers, the world would be a lot easier place to live in. There is little doubt that in the time window highlighted, India has emerged as a key driver in a worldview involving the four developing Brazil, Russia, India and China (BRIC) nations that offer both competitors and customers to rich nations.

However, China had begun generating high growth and matching jobs long before India, which struggled for about a decade since economic reforms began in 1991 before it showed signs of sustainable growth, over which some question marks still hang. The number of new jobs created by India in the first half of this decade is creditable, but pales in front of the needs of a country that has one billion plus people." (Editorial of *Hindustan Times,* 21 June 2007).

It is relevant to recall that after the independence, Jawaharlal Nehru with the help of leading economists evolved a model of industrialising the country. He conceived that a backward agrarian country dominated by colonial rulers for centuries could not become a modern industrialised nation state without the help of Indian and foreign capital. He invited the foreign capital from Western countries and United States to help India in its attempt to industrialise itself. But there was no response to it. The situation in India at that stage was almost identical with that of the Soviet Union after the October Revolution. Lenin clearly spelt out the new economic policy, in which he visualised that foreign capital should be invited to industrialise the country. By and large Soviet Union had to tap its international resources, though it managed to get some technologies. Nehru on the other hand did not face this problem to that extent for two reasons. Firstly, during the colonial rule, because of certain historical reasons, Indian capitalism had started developing and set up industries in the various parts of the country. Most of these capitalists supported the national movement led by the Indian National Congress. Secondly, Nehru had another option open to him. He turned to the Soviet Union for help in industrialising the country. As a result of this, India entered into various agreements with the Soviet Union. Under these agreements India was given long-term loans on a nominal interest and technology. Indira Gandhi and Rajiv Gandhi pursued this policy of Nehru. Most of the public sector undertakings were built and expanded in the 60s and 70s with the Soviet financial and technical assistance. Significantly some of these public sector undertakings have become pride of India. These public sector undertakings also promoted the growth of the private capital. In this sense in the 60s and 70s India stepped out from a backward agrarian country to the stage of a most developed-developing country. However, if this policy laid the basis for industrialisation of the country since the 90s of the last century with the new policy of liberalisation and promotion of private capital both Indian and foreign, India in the beginning of the 21st century is step by step emerging as a world economic power, though it has yet to go a long way to become a developed modern nation state. Nevertheless this has created objective conditions for India to become a world power. This has its own bearing on India's relations with other countries, Russia in particular. Indo-Russian relations are now being constructed in the internal changing situation in our country and Russia on the one hand and globalisation of the world economy on the other.

Resurgent Russia

On the other hand Russian nationalism has started asserting itself with a remarkable determination during the last decade. Russia today is recognised as one of the five big economic powers of the world because it has begun to harness its oil resources. According to one estimate, Russia perhaps has the richest oil resources in the world and now Russians have begun to export oil to European countries, which has its own politico-economic implications.

It may be recalled here that Uzbekistan, the most populous Central Asian state, has joined the Russian-led Eurasian Economic Community that is a customs union comprising Belarus, Kazakhstan, Kyrgyzstan and Tajikistan. Belarus was once a part of Soviet Union. Alarmed at the eastward expansion of North Atlantic Treaty Organisation (NATO) and US interests in acquiring energy and strategic reserves in Central Asia, the Russians got together with the Chinese to counter US advances. The Russian-Chinese relationship is marked by competition for resources and influence and cooperation against Western inroads. The border issue is now settled and there have been military exercises and increased Russian arms sales and energy commitments to China. Forty-five percent of Russian arms have been to China, at the rate of $ 2 billion annually. The first-ever joint military exercise of the Collective Security Treaty Organisation (Russia, Belarus, Armenia, Kazakhstan, Kyrgyzstan and Tajikistan) and the Shanghai Cooperation Organisation (SCO) was held in 2007 in Russia's Volga-Urals Area. It was the President of Russian Federation, Vladimir Vladimirovich Putin who decided to consolidate Russia's vital assets of energy and strategic minerals. Gazprom, which today is estimated to control a third of the world's natural gas reserves, plans to become the world's largest energy company, once it diversifies into oil production. The argument is very simple -

Western companies will not get access to Russian energy resources unless Russian industry gets similar access to European markets. Gazprom and Gaz de France have signed a deal for supply of Russian gas to France until 2030. The Italians and the Austrians have agreed to similar deals with Gazprom that allow the Russian giant to strengthen its presence in Europe and integrate into the global economy. The Russian State owned company, Rosneft, plans to enter the Chinese market for retail in petrol and petroleum products. Pipelines into China would be built by Russians and not by Western companies. The Russians have become more active in Turkmenistan and seem to be beating off competition from the US, the European Union (EU), China and Iran as the new regime seeks to strengthen its ties with Gazprom. The fear in the West would be that these long-term bilateral arrangements would knock out the spot market mechanism at the New York and London stock exchanges, while also undermining the production sharing arrangements that had benefited Western oil conglomerates. The Russians are back in business and US advances have been halted. Putin gets no popularity points in Washington for this but he does in Moscow, which is important.

The other consolidation, of aircraft design and production, which includes MiG, Sukhoi, Illyushin and other aircrafts, into the State controlled United Aircraft Corporation should be of interest to India. After all, Russia remains India's biggest source of armament supplies. Putin's visit in January 2007 was an opportunity to sort out the defence production support problem while encouraging Russians to participate in India's energy sector development. Consolidation in the Russian nuclear industry would be next and Russia would be keen to see how the Indo-US nuclear deal proceeds, as this would be an opportunity to invest in India.

This means that Russia, as the next major energy power will be assertive and self-confident. It has enough petrocurrency that will enable it to take merit-based decisions on supplies of energy to buyers, not only from Europe, the US but also China and other Asian consumers, India included. This shows new vistas of Indo-Russian economic cooperation are opening. (V. Sood, *Hindustan Times*. 18 January 2007).

This reflects how Russia has emerged as a world power after the disintegration of the Soviet Union, if economic statistics and its foreign policy contours are any indications.

After a disastrous decade under the former President, Boris Yeltsin, Russia is on the way to economic revival. In the past few years, it has registered the highest growth rates in half a century. The economic stagnation, which it suffered in the 90s was even worse than during World War II. During 1940-1946, Soviet industrial production fell 4 percent. In 1990-1999 the fall was almost 60 percent, while the GDP fell 54 percent. The trend has further grown in the recent years. But Russia has already registered GDP at more than 8 percent. Russia's oil and gas industry has been the driving force that pulled the economy from the mire of the preceding decade. It is also interesting to mention here that Russia is the world's largest raw diamond producer. It is entering into an agreement with India for cutting and polishing diamonds. India has a well-developed technology in this area. If Indo-Russian cooperation in this field takes shape, this will create new vistas of economic cooperation between the two countries.

Externally Russia has begun to assert itself to defend its independence and sovereignty, particularly, in Central Asia and in the neighbouring countries which were once part of the Soviet Union. Above all, its relations with China have entered quantitatively a new phase.

It is germane to identify here that at the end of the 20th century and with the emergence of a unipolar world on the one hand, and rise of religious fundamentalism and terrorism on the other, new structures for regional cooperation have emerged. Slowly though steadily these structures have begun to exercise increasing weight in shaping international and regional relations. One such structure is Shanghai Agreement among Russia, China, and three Central Asian Republics (CARs) – Kazakhstan, Kyrgyzstan and Tajikistan. This has been recently described as Shanghai Forum in the political parlance.

There is no doubt that Shanghai Five started taking concrete shape after normalisation of relations between Russia and China. It is important to mention here that the Soviet-China border agreement in the eastern sector was signed in May 1991, and the Sino-Russian agreement on the western sector of the border on the five Principles of Peaceful Coexistence in December 1992. This process has gained momentum over the years as confirmed by high-level meetings between leaders of the two countries. The two countries have committed themselves to no first use of nuclear weapons and not to target nuclear-armed missiles against each other. This trend is being underlined to make out how the evolution of Sino-Russian relations in recent years is of far reaching importance.

In the field of economic development Russia had evolved its own model of 'mixed economy' in a period of globalisation of the world economy. In this sense its model of transition from a centrally planned economy, called socialist economy to capitalist economy has its own specific features. The two outstanding features of this market economy are the role of the public sector in strategic areas and welfare of the people, the wage earners and pensioners. Russia has discarded the old policy of the Yeltsin period of blindly dismantling the public sector in handing them over to new emerging big business houses. It is striking a balance between the public and private sectors. Above all, while encouraging foreign investments, it is building an independent economy, which no more is dependent on the World Bank and International Monitary Fund. Though, it will be naive to draw a hasty conclusion from this new trend in the Russian economic policy, it has begun to yield positive results. If the analyses are correct it shows that the new model of Russian economic development may place it in a strategic position in the world economy and that too in a period when the most developed nation in the world, the US is in the grip of a severe economic crisis. It is facing a dangerous deficit and nearly 60 lakhs people are unemployed. This implies that while one should not over-estimate the Russian model of economic development, it will be equally incorrect to ignore it.

Another significant development, which is taking place in Russia, is consolidation of its unity and integrity. Threat to political stability in a large number of multi-religious, multicultural and multiethnic societies across the world has become a real challenge today. It is high time the Indian intelligentsia drew appropriate lessons from what is happening to the Russian Federation, which was the backbone of the erstwhile Soviet Union - a super power - and even today is one of the biggest military powers of the world. Any student of social science who has an open mind would agree that growing menace of organised terrorism is looming large on the horizon and has surfaced itself in a large number of countries, which are grappling with the difficult task of building a nation state based on secularism, democracy and social justice. After the disintegration of the Soviet Union, in Russia a new drug mafia and a class of smugglers have emerged, which appears to be linked with the terrorists. One thing is certain that there is a nexus between narcotic smugglers and terrorists and some politicians are part of this chain including in Central Asia, Russia and Pakistan.

Indo-Russian Relations - Prospects and Problems

The main dimension of the present world order, particularly after the collapse of the Soviet Union, rise of the internalised market economy, which in economic idioms is called globalisation of the world economy and growth of political globalisation and above all exposition of the theory that now an era of limited sovereignty of each country under the supervision of the sole superpower - USA - are some of the main features of the new world order. This characterisation of the present international order may look to be too sweeping. However, if one goes by recent developments, political, economic and military, one tends to come to the conclusion that this assessment is nearer to the reality than what appears on the surface. It is apposite to indicate here that the three 'wars' launched by the transnational elite so far (Iraq, Yugoslavia, Afghanistan) have been aimed at securing the stability of the new world order in economic and political dimensions by crushing any perceived threats against it.

As against this, parallel developments are taking place in the various parts of the world in Asia and Eurasia. The chief among them are Indo-Russian, Sino-Russian and Sino-Indian relationship. In this triangular relationship, each one of them stands on a different footing with their own specific characteristics. Sino-Russian and Indo-Russian relations stand at higher level than Sino-Indian relations. Nevertheless, in the totality of the situation, these relations between these three countries are developing and deepening. If there are no conflicts and irritants between India and Russia, all the disputes between Russia and China have been resolved and their relations are developing and deepening, notwithstanding the recent claim of China on Arunachal Pradesh, which is an integral part of India. However, Sino-Indian relations are revealing new trends including solution of long standing border disputes between them. Similar trends are unfolding themselves in other parts of the world.

Indo-Russian Relations since 28 January 1993, when Treaty on Friendship and Cooperation between the two countries was signed has been deepening and developing and now is touching a new height in all the spheres - political, strategic and economic. To say this does not mean that one should minimise the circumstances due to which the friendship of the two countries has been deep-rooted for more than a century. Before the disintegration of the Soviet Union, Indo-Soviet relations had their own unique character and one need not go into it at this juncture as these relations have become a part and psyche of the two peoples and are a part of history.

What is new is that after a temporary pause in the process of the development of relations between these two countries, it once again started unfolding new contours in the beginning of 90s of last century. It should be mentioned here that the evolution of Indo-Russian relations has their own specific features in the sense that these two countries never witnessed any conflict, irritant and clash of interests. On the contrary, if Indian freedom struggle evinced keen interest in Russian people's struggle to build a new social order; Russian leaders morally and politically gave unflinching support to the Indian peoples' struggle for freedom. After India became an independent and sovereign state by overthrowing colonial rule, these relations were elevated to a higher level. What is most remarkable is that even after the disintegration of the Soviet Union, these relations are being restructured on a model, which has no parallel in history. Therefore, any examination of Indo-Russian relations has not only to take into account this historic fact but also should examine objectively the new trends in Indo-Russian relations in the beginning of the 21st century and on the basis of that assess the future prospects of these relations.

Russian President Vladimir Putin was the chief guest on Republic Day on 26 January 2007. This in itself brings into focus the significance of Indo-Russian relations in the 21st century. "Close engagement between the two countries is based on the proximity of fundamental national interests and rests upon centuries old history of peaceful and mutually beneficial contacts between India and Russia. The strength of these bonds has been tested many times in critical situations. India has always been, without any reservations, Russia's closest and most reliable friend, strategic partner and ally. Of principle importance is the general consensus existing in the two countries on the necessity of further enhancing their cooperation both bilaterally and in the international arena".

Seen in this background is a reference to the New Delhi Joint Declaration by the Indian Prime Minister, Dr. Manmohan Singh and the Russian President, Vladimir Putin in the beginning of December 2004. On the eve of Russian President's visit to India, Prime Minister Dr. Manmohan Singh made a pregnant formulation in an interview to Rossiiskaya Gazeta, "this visit will become a new landmark in the history of our relations. Great progress has been made in our political and strategic relations and we will develop it further, without letting it stop. We should think of the prospects of our strategic partnership. Our commercial and economic relations should be deepened and the optimal environment for mutual investments in the economies of both countries should be created. India and Russia are two large, fast growing economies with extensive base for further development. Along with the traditional spheres of trade we would like to promote high technology sector, i.e. information technology, biotechnology, banking and financial services. Energy sector is a very important component of our cooperation. We are looking forward to expanding our cooperation in peaceful uses of the nuclear energy and exploration of space. I hope Mr. Putin and I will exchange views on the crucial regional and world problems".

India and Russia took the unusual step of referring to their trilateral cooperation with China in a joint declaration signed by Manmohan Singh and Putin. While 'joint declarations' are normally confined to bilateral dealings, the document said, "the sides note with satisfaction that trilateral meetings at the Foreign Ministers' level of India, China and Russia have been taking place regularly. These meetings have been useful in promoting understanding and exploring areas of possible cooperation at a trilateral and at an international level". The trilateral meetings have also reflected a strong concern against terrorism anywhere and in any form. The two sides expressed their conviction, which could also result in social and economic development amongst the three countries", it added. This brings out clearly that Indo-Russian, Sino-Russian and Sino-Indian relations have begun to crystallise into a new triangle in the international relations at a time when unipolarism dominates the world politics. This can be aptly described as a nucleus for multipolarism. For the first time on an official level, the importance of a triangular relationship among the world's three major powers, the two biggest Asian powers and one Eurasian power has been spelt out. This in itself is of far reaching importance.

Let us look at this development from another angle. Indo-Russian bilateral relations are beginning to assume a new character in all the spheres. For instance, the 10th session of the Indo-Russian Inter-Governmental Commission on Trade, Economic, Scientific, Technological and Cultural (IRIGC) was held in New Delhi on 18 and 19 November 2004. Some important decisions taken during this session included holding of an Indo-Russian Round Table on Information Technology, which was held in Bangalore (1 and 2 December 2004), Indo-Russian Energy Meet in New Delhi (15 January 2005). Later, Canara Bank and State Bank of India signed agreements with two Russian banks to facilitate trade and mutual bank guarantees. Other areas of cooperation include projects for development of software products and also Indian assistance in the establishment of software parks in Russia, cooperation between Russian company, Sudoimport and Magnum International Trading for construction of auxiliary fleet ships in India and the development of the Indo-Russian Joint Venture Company to produce Titanium Dioxide in Orissa. India and Russia have identified energy, IT, banking, communications, and biotechnology as new areas of growth. Special emphasis is being given in expanding cooperation in thermal, hydro and nuclear energy for power production. Both the countries also supported development of cooperation between India and Russia with the purpose of participation of Indian and Russian companies in new oil and gas fields in Russia and third countries. Moreover, Petrotech would pave way for more Indo-Russian joint ventures along the hydrocarbon value chain. One of the major collaborators with India in oil and gas sector, Russia participated Petrotech in a big way. The conference has been held on the emerging option of 'gas hydrates' and 'deep water exploration'. Apart from petroleum and natural gas companies, the conference was attended by associated sectors such as shipping, road transport, power, engineering and financial institutions.

India and Russia historically had very strong trade ties. In fact, one important aspect of the old Indo-Soviet friendship was a special bilateral trade and economic relationship. However, after the disintegration of the Soviet Union, the economic relations between the two countries registered a steep decline. This period coincided with the transformation of Russia from a centrally planned to a market economy amid series of economic and financial crisis, as already mentioned earlier. The situation was further compounded by other factors, such as collapse of the socialist system in Russia and in other East European states. With globalisation of economy and introduction of economic reforms in India, these further compounded the situation. This led to a mutual decrease in the trade relations between the two countries. Besides this, the political establishment of Russia embarked on an economic path under the leadership of Boris Yeltsin, which intensified the internal economic crisis. However, Russian patriotism asserted itself and the new Russian leadership evolved its own model of mixed economy and began to build its economic relations with its old economic partners such as India in the new historical conditions, as already mentioned in this article. Under the leadership of Vladimir Putin, Russia began to carve out its own position in the world economy. Russia is now once again emerging as a world economic power as stated in some of the chapters of this book. The crux of the problem is that both India and Russia are evolving new policies for strengthening these economic relations in the larger national interests of both the countries. It is in this setting that new trends in economic relations between the two countries need to be examined.

Indo-Russian commerce, which had declined in the decade following the dissolution of the former Soviet Union, shows signs of renewal. There are commissions in place to oversee the economic revival, in which the Russian and Indian leaderships have invested considerable political will.

With their economy moving into a higher, more profitable gear, Russian businesses are viewing the Indian market with renewed interest, as are their Indian counterparts, whose presence in Russia becomes more visible by the day.

Russia has significant technology to offer, at prices that are better suited to Indian pockets than those on offer from the West. Russian science and technology are world class, as Indian buyers are discovering.

India is a large and long-term market for Russia's defence exports and exports of oil and hydrocarbons. Russia has security and trading interests in the northern reaches of the Indian Ocean. A friendly India straddling the Indian Ocean rim is — and will be — a strategic asset to the Russian leadership. Russia, like India, has a plural civil society. It is, therefore, concerned about preserving its multi-dimensional national identity, an interest, which India shares in terms of its national consolidation. While Russia has adjusted to its diminished international stature, it believes in the creation of a multi-polar world order.

Russia has proved to be a reliable partner in the transfer of sophisticated technologies of use to India — despite the expanding restrictive regimes sought to be imposed on transfer of such technologies. Russia is not only a large expanding market for Indian exports across the board — from raw materials to finished products — but is also a market for Indian investment and joint collaboration projects.

There is also a progressive concretisation of these interests in bilateral relations. Russia and India have managed the transition from economic and technological interaction conducted under governmental arrangements to the conduct of these relations by private sectors. A wide range of inter-State and inter-departmental agreements have been put in place over the last one decade in a number of specialised spheres. These are implemented and monitored by a Russia-India inter-governmental commission on trade, economics, scientific and technological cooperation.

Russian companies are now participating in the construction of nuclear and hydel-power plants, highways, modernisation and construction of steel plants, mining, oil and gas exploration in the Arabian Sea and the Bay of Bengal, as well as in the Northeastern states. Russian companies are also involved in aluminium production, modernisation of railways, construction of water desalination plants and subways in India.

This study shows after the disintegration of the Soviet Union, Indo-Russian relations have been elevated once again to new heights. The moral of this trend is that Indo-Russian strategic partnership has begun to assume a new economic content and if this trend develops Indo-Russian relations, it will become a major stimulus in building a multipolar world. In this connection one important factor should be kept in the forefront. Russia is one of the biggest oil producing countries in the world and it has begun to wield this instrument to carve out a significant role in the political economy of the world, as underlined earlier.

"Russia has embarked on a new geopolitical game, playing its energy card to reclaim global clout. Its vast energy reserves and control over the markets in the former Soviet Union are to be leveraged to turn Russia into a superpower. As global energy demand soars, the Russian President, Vladimir Putin, wants to position Russia as a key broker in the international market and use oil and gas exports as instruments to speed up the country's economic revival and enhance its geopolitical weight."

After dropping nearly 50 percent from the Soviet era peak, Russia's oil output has soared again to exceed 450 million tonnes together with gas condensates by the end of the 2004 making it the world's second largest producer behind only Saudi Arabia. Total oil reserves are a state secret in Russia, but the former Energy Minister, Yuri Shafranik estimates that Russia may have 44 billion tonnes of oil, more than Saudi Arabia does. Russia currently exports over 6.5 million barrels a day, taking crude oil and product together and plans to boost exports to about 9 million barrels a day by the end of the decade - roughly equal to Saudi Arabia's current exports by the end of present decade. It may be reiterated that Russian exports of oil to West Europe are increasing and it has its own political implications, because West Europe is becoming dependent on Russian oil.

In the last decade, Indian economy had also undergone a structural transformation in the aftermath of economic reforms. In the light of the transformation in both the economies, the trade basket of the two partners deserves a close re-examination in order to explore the possibilities of enhanced bilateral trade that has been languishing at US $ 1.3 billion currently as compared to US $ 5 billion in 1991.

With both countries struggling to define their relations with other major players on the global stage in a situation where the rules of international politics are in a state of flux and where the terms of the economic interaction between nations are being re-set, this summit between the Indian and Russian leaderships was of significance for the affirmation of continuity and mutual reassurance that it symbolised. What has added substance to it is the reinforcement of the faith that there is a real convergence of perspectives on issues as wide-ranging as the phenomenon of terrorism, ensuring the security of nuclear weapon stockpiles in a world facing a new assortment of threats and challenges, the conservation and promotion of multipolarity in global politics. Besides this it underlined the need for both the countries to make adjustments in the course of globalisation, and on issues specific to South, Central and West Asia. Russia's belief that India can and should make a substantial contribution to the evolution of a strong global consensus on these issues was revealed in its open support of the Indian campaign for a permanent seat in the United Nations Security Council.

Both Russia and India are victims of violence fuelled by fundamentalist ideology and it is natural that the two countries should strengthen their cooperation on the issue for mutual benefit. The terrorist movements in various countries are not localised problems, but feed each other through ideological and material support flowing across international borders. India and Russia have emphasised that the open societies of their countries "have been vulnerable to the threats posed by globalisation of terror, including new manifestations of linkage between terrorism and weapons of mass destruction".

There is yet another aspect of this study. It examines regional importance of Indo-Russian relations. These relations from the long-term point of view will influence the developments in this entire region. If Indo-Russian relations have a special significance in the Asia-Pacific region, the emerging triangular cooperation between India and Russia, Russia and China and India and China is of far reaching importance. Above all, there is commonality of interests between India and Russia in the Central Asia. These three components of Indo-Russian relations, if they continue to develop and deepen, will mould the course of events in this entire region. The study brings out sharply, the regional and international significance of Indo-Russian relations.

Finally, in the arena of bilateral relations between India and Russia, strategic cooperation between the two countries growing defence cooperation and their naval cooperation in Indian Ocean region should not be underestimated in the larger national interests of the two countries for peace and security. However, this study shows that in the sphere of economic cooperation, there is a big lag. The two countries are making an effort to address the deficiency in bilateral trade, which stands in such marked contrast to the very wholesome relationship they share in almost every other sphere.

Indo-Russian, Sino-Russian, Sino-Indian Triangle ?

Never before in the post Cold War period, American hegemony over the world what is called unipolarism has faced challenges from the various directions – the Arab world, Asia and even in some European countries - as now in the last years of the first decade of the present century. It is in the context of this development that Indo-Russian, Sino-Russian and Sino-Indian relations need to be given a fresh look.

Recent developments have once again underlined that regional forums have begun to exercise considerable weight in the international politics. Indo-Russian, Sino-Russian and Sino-Indian relations have begun to unfold a new trend. If this triangle firms up, it will stimulate the process of multipolarism, which will be of far reaching significance as already mentioned. This shows how a wind of change has begun to blow in the Asia-Pacific region. Indo-Russia, Sino-Russia and Sino-India relations are undergoing important changes. This reflects, there is a great need to ensure the smooth management of intra-state relationship in the Asia-Pacific region, so that this region is not subjected to destabilising tendencies.

Indo-Russian Relations

We have in detail examined the new trends in Indo-Russian relations. These trends need not be recapitulated except for the fact that Indo-Russian relations in the world polity have become a very important factor.

Sino-Russian Relations

Sino-Russian relations have been improving steadily and now have become an important factor. The process of the solution of the border dispute between the two countries began in the end of 1980s when a Joint Border Commission was set up. In 1994, the two sides agreed on no-first-use of nuclear weapons against each other. The two countries also de-targeted the missiles directed against each other and an agreement to this effect was signed when Chinese President Jiang Zemin visited Russia in September 1994. Further, in April 1997, an accord on mutual reduction of forces was signed in Moscow by Russia, China and the three Central Asian states - Kazakhstan, Kyrgyzstan and Tajikistan. Moreover, the successful conclusion of the border agreement between the two sides, during May 1991 on the Eastern Sector and September 1994 on the Western Sector removed a major irritant. In December 1999, it was announced that the border dispute has been finally settled as we have already mentioned in this article. Though there are some residual issues, these will be settled in future.

Economic cooperation between the two countries is undergoing basic changes. In 1999, the trade volume between the two countries was $ 5.72 billion, up 4.4. per cent from that in 1998. The trade volume of the first four months of 2001 was $ 2.5 billion, up 20.1 per cent from the same period of 2000. Russian imports from China have increased by 70 per cent, helping to balance bilateral trade. In 2000, China ranked the sixth among Russian trade partners. Trade between Russia and China is estimated to have reached $ 10 billion in 2001. The trade between the countries is rapidly expanding and Russian market is flooded with Chinese manufactured consumer goods.

The purpose of Putin's visit to China in July 2001 was to make plans for the long-term development of bilateral relations. There is a convergence of views between the two countries to protecting their common turf. This is amply reflected in the 20 years treaty of friendship initialled in Moscow at the end of Chinese President's visit to Russia in 2001. Putin and Jiang worked together to set up a new security forum towards offsetting Islamist threats to the Central Asian Republics.

After the December 2002 Putin's visit to Beijing, the relations between the two nations have taken a new turn. Both countries are now committed to building a multipolar world.

Over the past decade, the two nations have made significant progress towards building a relationship of strategic cooperation. This is based on the principle of building a cooperative bilateral relationship while maintaining an independent foreign policy.

China and Russia are both increasingly uncomfortable with the growing U.S. power. In the joint statement issued after the visit, they agreed that the main mechanism to safeguard world peace should be United Nations and that its role in solving international disputes should be increased. The Chinese and Russian concern arises from the growing U.S. unilateralism in global politics backed by its increasing military power.

A carefully drafted statement by the two countries has welcomed the proposal for a nuclear free zone in the Korean Peninsula.

There are clear manifestations of new trends in Sino-Russian relations.

Sino-Indian Relations

Now let us examine the evolution of Sino-Indian relations in the recent years, which constitute the third side of the emerging triangle.

It has to be taken into account that China and India are the largest and the most populated countries on our planet, which are described as the Asian giants. They are on their way to becoming economic models in the world.

Sino-Indian relations remained at a low level after the 1962 conflict till Indira Gandhi took the first step to upgrade the diplomatic relations between the two countries. Rajiv Gandhi's visit to Beijing in December 1988 marked a turning point in the evolution of the relations between the two countries. This was followed by a visit to India in 1991 by Chinese Premier Li Peng, and by P.V. Narasimha Rao to China in 1993. These visits brought in a large measure of political and military stability to a completely normalised pattern of India-China relationship. After that, several important visits have been exchanged. President K.R. Narayanan's visits to China in June 2000 and the visit of the Chinese President Jiang Zemin to India for instance are events of great significance. Since then regular visits of top leaders of the two countries have been taking place. This reflects how the two countries have put the past aside and are now constructing their relations in mutual interests of both the nations. Let us leave this at that and examine the content of the new relationship.

Firstly, China is facing Islamic militancy, which is fuelling separatism in the Xinjiang province inhabited by Uighur Muslims. The same problems are being faced by Russia in Chechnya. A similar scenario exists in Kazakhstan, Kyrgyzstan, Tajikistan and Uzbekistan. This situation has led to the formation of the "Shanghai Cooperation Organisation." The six nations have joined hands to fight the "three forces" - terrorism, separatism and extremism. This in turn has begun to influence positively Sino-Indian relations on the crucial issue of terrorism.

Secondly, China and India are engaged in economic development and modernisation. China is keen to participate in various projects for development of infrastructure in India. Indian goods and services have entered in the Chinese market. Chinese exports to India are rapidly increasing. There are more than a dozen Indian companies operating in the eastern part of Cnina. It should be kept in mind that the Chinese economy is the second largest economy in the world, next only to the U.S. in terms of purchasing power parity as estimated by the World Banks' criterion.

Thirdly, serious efforts are being made by both the countries to resolve the border disputes. This is confirmed by the fact that after recording their perceptions of the Line of Actual Control (LAC) along a 345 km "middle sector" stretch, India and China are gearing up for a similar exercise along their frontier in the Ladakh area. Both sides have defined their individual perceptions of the LAC along their border in Uttar Pradesh and recorded it on maps. There is a convergence of views on the LAC alignment along large portions in this sector. However, they differ on the lay of LAC in some segments. This confirms how efforts are being made to resolve their border dispute. As mentioned earlier in this article, China's claim on Arunachal Pradesh, which is an integral part of India, has created a new problem.

This does not mean that Sino-Indian relations are developing on the same model as Indo-Russian and Sino-Russian relations. India has serious reservations about supply of nuclear capable missiles by China to Pakistan.

If Sino-Indian border dispute is resolved, it will open new vistas of economic and political cooperation. It is suitable to state here that during the last few years, Sino-Indian border has remained more or less peaceful and no major border conflict has taken place.

The three countries have commonality of interests in fighting global terrorism and strengthening of politico-economic cooperation in the new historic conditions.

Convergence of political and economic interests of three countries India, Russia and China is bringing them closer to each other. If this triangular relationship continues to grow and deepen, it will become a decisive factor in this part of our planet. India and China are Asian giants and Russia is a powerful Eurasian nation. Nevertheless at the present stage the weakest link in this triangle is the relationship between India and China, though the leaders of the two countries are engaged in an exercise to keep their relations on an even keel and strive to resolve their differences on border dispute.

Conclusion

From whatever angle you look at Indo-Russian relations, these have begun to assume both regional and international importance. We have examined in this article the evolution of Indo-Russian relations after the disintegration of the Soviet Union and the fundamental economic changes, which are taking place in the two countries. We have also made a study of the regional importance of these relations in the context of triangle - Indo-Russian, Sino-Russian and Sino-Indian - to emphasise how this triangular relationship has begun to influence the three sides of this emerging model. This in itself is of global significance.

5

Sixty Years of India-Russia Cooperation

Manohar Singh Batra

When India became independent in 1947, Stalin's Soviet Union was quite indifferent to its interests, under the perception that the whole Indian subcontinent was an offshoot of capitalism. The Soviet leaders were of the view that India and Pakistan both were inclined towards the Anglo-American bloc. In pursuit of a policy of equidistance from these two newly freed countries, the Soviet delegate to the UN Security Council was absent at the time of voting when the Kashmir issue was discussed in 1948.

Pakistan's Prime Minister Liaquat Ali Khan visited Moscow in 1948 with an intent to establish friendly relations with the Soviet Union, but the relationship did not last very long. It was probably due to the fact that when Israel came into existence in 1948 with the blessings of the Soviet Union alongwith the western camp, Pakistan could not swallow it and huge demonstrations took place in Karachi, then capital of Pakistan. The Soviet annoyance to this was reflected in its refusal to participate in the International Economic Conference that was slated to be held in Karachi later in that year.

Very soon Pakistan cosied up to the United States of America and it offered a base to that country in the Gilgit area of the Pakistan occupied Kashmir. In that Cold War scenario any such concession to the US was an anathema to the Soviets, who considered it an act of hostility towards them. In 1949 the US offered military and economic assistance to Pakistan. Since the creation of Pakistan had the blessings of Britain, and the US was largely guided by that country towards the subcontinent, its policies towards Kashmir were influenced by the British preferences. Pakistan was sucked into military alliances like the South East Asia Treaty Organisation (SEATO) sponsored by the US in 1954 and the Central Treaty Organisation (CENTO) in 1955. The Soviet Union felt concerned over these developments and chose to increase its distance from Pakistan which came to be known as an active ally of the US-led opposite pole. Consequently it became closer to India.

In January 1952 speaking on Kashmir in the Security Council, the Soviet delegate, Jacob Malik observed that the plans put forward by UK and USA "instead of speaking a real settlement, were aimed at prolonging the dispute and converting Kashmir into a trust territory of the US and the UK under the pretext of giving it assistance through United Nations."

Towards the end of the Stalin period, USSR tried to develop trade relations with India. M.V. Nesterov, President of the Soviet Chamber of Commerce participated in the International Trade Fair at Bombay in January 1952. Speaking on the occasion he offered to supply machine tools, generators, agricultural machinery, electric equipment, fertilizers and foodgrains to this country. The Soviet support to India on the Kashmir issue in the Security Council was not given much importance by Prime Minister, Nehru as, perhaps, he did not want this issue to be a game between the two power blocs. *New York Times*, on January 21, 1952 wrote, "Indians fear Malik statement on Kashmir may complicate settlement of the dispute", that the "general feeling here is that India wants an early settlement of the long-standing issue before the UN and that the manner in which the Soviet delegate delivered his frontal attack against the West has hardly contributed towards that end."

The situation, however, changed a little later. On the one hand USA and Pakistan were coming much closer to each other, India was spearheading the non-aligned movement on the other. India was against all military alliances or any hegemonic action by any state. In one of his articles published in 'Studies in Indo-Soviet Relations' in 1986, T.N. Kaul wrote, "the essence of non-alignment is independence of non-aligned countries to judge each issue on its merits, without any previous commitment to one side or the other, as it affects the national interest of each non-aligned country, the legitimate interest of other non-aligned countries and the larger interest of peace, security and development throughout the world." In another article appearing in 'The Future of Commonwealth of Independent States' published in 1992, T.N. Kaul observed that this policy brought the two countries closer. There were other common factors in their approaches like disarmament, anti-colonialism and anti-racism and the concept of peaceful existence that influenced them.

In August 1953 the Soviet Premier Malenkov gave an indication that the relations between the Soviet Union and India were becoming stronger and their cultural ties were growing. He envisaged greater friendly cooperation between the two countries. The Soviets started encouraging the non-aligned nations to adopt a political programme that would help the Soviet strategic interests in the Third World. However, India while pursuing friendship with USSR, continued to defend its independence and the precepts of non-alignment. This policy brought the Soviet Union and the Indian Republic closer and the Soviets lent support to India on Kashmir in the meetings of the UN Security Council. Pandit Nehru visited the Soviet Union and a joint communique issued at the end of the tour emphasized that the best remedy of fear among small states was to adhere strictly to the principles of co-existence.

The first visit of the top Soviet leaders Nikita Khrushehev and Nikolai Bulganin to India in November-December 1955 was a big event for both the countries as it heralded a new era in Indo-Soviet relations. The Soviet leaders visited various important centres in this country and while in Srinagar they declared that if Indians from a hilltop in Kashmir called the Soviets for help, they would come immediately. This was a symbolic gesture of their feelings of friendship for India. In his banquet speech on November 20, 1955, Bulganin proclaimed that our relations were based on the well-known five principles declared alongwith Nehru in the month of June that year and the Soviet Union would strongly support these principles in its relations with other peace loving countries, who subscribed to these principles. Both the Soviet leaders reiterated their country's desire to adhere fervently to friendship with India through thick and thin and at all times. Krushchev repeatedly affirmed the Soviet support on Kashmir, which was one of the states of India whose future had been decided by the people of that state. Bulganin, addressing a press conference in New Delhi on December 14, 1955 remarked that during their visit of Kashmir they had seen the Kashmiris rejoice in their national liberation and their being an integral part of India. He expressed an apprehension that certain powers were making an attempt to separate Kashmir from India artificially and convert it into a foreign military base. But the people of Kashmir were emphatically opposed to these mischievous plans. According to Khrushchev the issue of accession of Kashmir to India had been irrevocably decided by the people of the state.

In February 1957, the Soviet Union applied its first veto on a resolution on Kashmir in the Security Council. The resolution had been sponsored by UK, USA, Australia and Cuba asking for use of a UN force to facilitate demilitarization to be followed by a plebiscite. The Security Council held that the use of such a force deserved consideration. And it authorised its president, Gunnar Jarring to visit India and Pakistan to bring about demilitarization. The Soviet delegate proposing amendments to the resolution argued that the people of Kashmir had settled the question themselves and now considered their territory an integral part of India. On February 20, 1957 the Soviet delegation vetoed the western-sponsored resolution on the plea that the resolution, as it stood, favoured Pakistan. In the opinion of the Soviet people, the delegate said that the people of Kashmir had already settled the question. On June 23, 1962 the Soviet representative again vetoed a resolution for holding a plebiscite in Kashmir, which was introduced by Ireland, supported by the British government.

Following the Chinese aggression against India in 1962, F. Kozlov, a Soviet leader, criticized the Chinese party at the Italian Communist Party Congress for playing with fire and endangering all the achievements of civilization. After the Indo-Pak war of 1965, Soviet Premier Kosygin offered to facilitate a meeting between President Ayub Khan of Pakistan and Prime Minister Lal Bahadur Shastri of India, at Tashkent to reach an agreement on the restoration of peace 'if both parties so desire'. That offer was accepted by both the countries. Kosygin attended the meeting on January 4, 1966 at the request of both the parties. The Tashkent Declaration was signed by Ayub and Shastri on January 10, 1966. Shastri profusely praised Kosygin for 'the great and noble role' played by him in holding these talks.

The Soviet leaders might have been of the view that the Kashmir problem was thrust on India and Pakistan. During the summit, Kosygin remarked "it should be recalled that the discord between India and Pakistan is the heritage of long dominations of colonialists who set enslaved peoples against each other." As a result of the summit, in the Soviet view, the Tashkent Declaration would improve relations between India and Pakistan on the one hand and further strengthen India's relationship with Russia on the other.

However, it was noticed that there was a slight shift in the Soviet policies towards Pakistan. In June 1966 a high level Pakistani military mission visited Moscow to explore the possibility of securing Soviet arms for that country. In response to India's warnings about any possible arm shipments to Pakistan, the Soviet leaders assured India that their policy on Kashmir had not changed. Inspite of these assurances, some senior Soviet naval officers led by an Admiral visited Pakistan in March 1968 to discuss the possibilities of cooperation between the two navies.

On the heels of this delegation, Kosygin himself paid a visit to Pakistan to strengthen relations between the two countries.Warmly reciprocating the Soviet leader's gesture, General Yahya Khan of Pakistan flew into Moscow in the first week of June 1968 to negotiate an agreement for the supply of Soviet arms to Pakistan. Within a day an agreement was announced and the delivery of tanks, artillery and the armed personnel carriers was begun. During his State visit to Moscow from July 8, 1968, India's President, Dr. Zakir Hussain raised the matter with the Soviet leadership and expressed this country's concern over the arms supply to Pakistan. But the Soviets did not pay any heed and India's Minister for External Affairs, Swaran Singh told the Parliament on April 9, 1969 that inspite of our stress on the danger implicit in the supply of arms to Pakistan, the Soviet policy continues to be to supply arms to Pakistan.

In late 1970 after a reappraisal by the Soviet leaders, they reverted to the policy of supporting India's stand on the Kashmir issue. This saw an abrupt end to the Soviet arms supply to Pakistan. On November 9, 1970 Swaran Singh informed the Parliament, "we are glad that the Soviet government have given consideration to our representations and have informed us that they have not supplied—and do not intend to supply - any military hardware to Pakistan in addition to that already supplied in the past."

The shift in USSR's policy on South Asia became evident during the events in East Pakistan. President Podgorny sent a letter to President Yahya Khan on April 2, 1971 urging him to take most urgent measures to stop the bloodshed and repression against the people of East Pakistan and to seek a peaceful political settlement. Swaran Singh met the Soviet Foreign Minister, Andrei Gromyko in Moscow in June 1971 and apprised him of the Pakistani war threats, the possible attitude of the US and the apprehension of the Chinese bid to exploit the situation in East Pakistan to its own advantage.

This led to a Treaty of Peace, Friendship and Cooperation between India and USSR signed on August 9, 1971. It dealt with the promotion of friendship, peace and security at bilateral and international levels. It emphasised mutual respect for each other's sovereignty irrespective of the ideological differences. It was signed for a period of twenty years as a legal basis of Indo-Soviet cooperation. The treaty consisted of 12 Articles and it provided that the contracting parties would consult each other in case of attack or threat thereof to remove such threat and to take appropriate effective measures to ensure peace and security of their countries. Under the Treaty, the Soviet Union extended credible assurances to India of Soviet assistance in case of attack by China or Pakistan.

As tension between India and Pakistan increased due to a reign of terror unleashed by the Pakistani army on the hapless Bengalis in East Pakistan and a deluge of refugees into the Indian territory, the Soviets issued enough warnings to the rulers of Pakistan over the repeated threats of war with India. Prime Minister Indira Gandhi paid a visit to Moscow in September 1971 to discuss the situation created by Pakistan. There was complete understanding between the top leadership of the two countries about the situation in the eastern wing of Pakistan, which demanded the earliest possible measures to reach a political solution.

When war broke out between India and Pakistan on December 3, 1971 the Soviet Union declared that it would not remain indifferent to the developments, especially when these were taking place in direct proximity to the borders of USSR and these involved the interests of its security. The Pakistani leaders were reminded of the dangerous course they were taking. All others were asked to stay away from the India-Pakistan conflict. USA introduced a resolution in the Security Council calling for a ceasefire, withdrawal of forces of India and Pakistan to their sides of the borders, posting of UN observers and for the use of the Secretary General's good offices. This was vetoed by the Soviet Union on December 5, 1971. The Chinese Ambassador at the United Nations, Huang Hua said during the debate that "India's aggression has taken place under the support of social-imperialism. It was a direct verbal Chinese attack on the Soviet Union. The Soviet Ambassador at the UN, Jacob Malik disposed it of as 'chatter, prattle and demagogy'. "

On December 6, 1971 USSR vetoed again an attempt of a UN ceasefire appeal. USA decided to send a taskforce of its Seventh Fleet, spearheaded by the nuclear-powered aircraft carrier, USS Enterprise to the Bay of Bengal. The Soviet Union made a quick counter move in the Indian Ocean area which acted as a deterrent.

About 93 thousand Pakistani forces surrendered to the Indian Army at Dacca on December 16, 1971 leading to the freedom of East Bengal from the Pakistani rule and the establishment of an independent country of Bangladesh.

On July 2, 1972 an agreement to resolve the Kashmir issue without any outside interference was signed by Indira Gandhi and Zulfiqar Ali Bhutto at Simla. It was hailed by the Soviet Union as a cornerstone of peace and cooperation between India and Pakistan. Under the Agreement India released the Pakistani prisoners of war who had surrendered in Bangladesh.

During the Janata Party rule, after the temporary eclipse of the Congress regime under Indira Gandhi, during 1977-80, the new Prime Minister Morarji Desai visited the Soviet Union twice and emphasised that the Soviet-Indian friendship had survived the test of time and that it was an important factor in the cause of peace and stability in Asia and the whole world. When Indira Gandhi returned to the helm in the government in 1980, there was a flurry of visits of the Indian and the Soviet leaders to each other's country. Brezhnev visited India in December 1980 at the head of a huge Soviet delegation. On her return visit to Moscow in September 1982, Indira Gandhi expressed her opinion that USSR should withdraw her forces from Afghanistan, which were introduced in 1979, but the Soviets omitted this from the joint communique.

The Indo-Soviet Joint Declaration issued at the conclusion of Mrs. Gandhi's visit expressed profound satisfaction at the results and noted that relations between the two countries were "characterised by respect and trust between the leaders and peoples and by the diversity of spheres and forms of cooperation." In his banquet speech on September 20, 1982, Brezhnev warned India against Pakistan's offer of a no-war pact. But in her speech at a reception the next day, Mrs. Gandhi reaffirmed India's intentions to reduce tensions with its neighbours, including China and Pakistan. It became obvious that there was not complete convergence between USSR and India on some of the global issues. While Brezhnev proposed in his banquet speech that the leading nations of NATO and the Warsaw Treaty should make a statement of their refusal to extend the sphere of activity of these alliances to Asia, Africa and Latin America, Mrs. Gandhi chose not to react to it at all. Nor did the joint declaration mention it.

Some sort of caution, if not mistrust, continued to persist in Indo-Soviet relations through the years 1982-84. However, the graph of their cooperation was going up. An agreement was reached between New Delhi and Moscow in the field of power generation. In March 1984 the Soviets sent Marshal Ustinov to India to finalise the deal for the supply of Mig 27 and Mig 29 planes.

After Indira Gandhi's assassination, the Soviet President Chernanko in his condolence message to the new Prime Minister, Rajiv Gandhi reaffirmed the Soviet resolve to strengthen relations of friendship with India. In turn Rajiv Gandhi assured the Soviet Premier Nikolai Tikhonov on November 2, 1984 that his government would continue the same policy as had been pursued by Jawaharlal Nehru and Mrs. Gandhi in strengthening friendly ties with the Soviet Union and other countries.

The repeated references to the desirability of continuing Nehru's and Indira Gandhi's foreign policy were in a way a reflection of their anxiety, as in the last days of Indira Gandhi's bilateral relations between India and the United States had begun to improve. Rajiv Gandhi paid an official visit to the USSR from May 21 to May 26, 1985 at the invitation of the Soviet leaders. They reiterated their resolve to continue to make consistent efforts to strengthen their mutual relations for the good of the peoples of the two countries and in the interest of universal peace. Gorbachev and Rajiv Gandhi concluded an agreement on guidelines for trade, economic, scientific and technical cooperation in the establishment of a number of specific projects in India, for further expansion and development of traditional mutually-beneficial contacts between the USSR and India. These agreements were designed to open broad horizons for interaction between the two great states bound by ties of sincere friendship. Both sides stressed the importance of ending arms race in the world and preventing it in space. The Soviet leaders expressed support for the initiatives of the heads of state and government of six countries aimed at the eventual exclusion of nuclear weapons from the life of mankind. It was noted that the USSR and India were against outside intervention in the internal affairs of South-West Asian countries and supported an immediate political settlement there through talks in order to protect the sovereign rights of the states in the region.

Both sides noted with satisfaction the growing role of the non-aligned movement in the common efforts to improve the world situation and in the struggle against imperialism, colonialism, neo-colonialism, racism and apartheid. Mikhail Gorbachev spoke highly of India's great contribution to the strengthening of the non-aligned movement and expressed the confidence that India would continue to contribute towards its further strength in the interest of peace and disarmament. Rajiv Gandhi appreciated the Soviet initiatives aimed at resolving the problems of disarmament and improving the international situation. He came back from USSR fully satisfied with the results of his visit. He was convinced that the Soviet Union had stood by India at every critical juncture and the Soviet help was of much substance and consequence in meeting certain critical situations. It was in national interest to continue warm relations with Moscow.

President Mikhail Gorbachev's return visit to New Delhi proved to be of great importance. After long and meaningful talks between Rajiv Gandhi and Gorbachev, a Delhi Declaration as a joint statement was issued, which endorsed Mahatma Gandhi's philosophy of non-violence as the desirable code of conduct by nations - not only internationally, but within the society itself. Making a statement in the Parliament, Rajiv Gandhi said that the USSR had "joined India in a common vision of a nuclear-weapons free and non-violent world" and that the Declaration had given expression to the ideas of Gandhi and Lenin. The significance of the document was enhanced as it was to be issued as an official document of the United Nations. The vision spelt out by the Delhi Declaration closely reflected the vision of Jawaharlal Nehru influenced by Gandhi.

India and USSR signed new agreements on economic and technical cooperation. They decided to reorient their cooperation in science and technology as joint research and joint production in many areas, including nuclear power, space technologies and high temperature physics. This was a far cry from the days when some academicians of the Soviet Union went to the extreme of describing Indian leaders such as Gandhi and Nehru as "bourgeois reformers" and even as "running dogs of Anglo-American imperialism." However, in the view of some scholars, the Delhi Declaration with its overtones of non-violence made us euphoric about prospects of ushering in a new millennium of peace and prosperity.

Rajiv Gandhi and Gorbachev exchanged four visits between 1985 and 1989. Indo-Soviet relations remained constant. Those even intensified in some aspects of defence and economic cooperation. Had India tried to disengage itself suddenly from the Soviet Union in matters of defence and economic relations, it would have affected its defence capabilities and economic progress. The volume of bilateral trade increased. Gorbachev increased rouble credit facilities for greater imports from India by the Soviet Union. In the sphere of defence, there was continuous flow of defence supplies. A nuclear-powered submarine was leased to the Indian Navy. Both leaders agreed to cooperate at the highest levels of policy-making on vital matters such as disarmament and development. They agreed to make peaceful coexistence the universal norm for international relations. Conflicts should be resolved peacefully without resorting to military means. They also agreed that human life should be recognised as supreme and non-violence should be the basis of community life. Inequality, oppression and discrimination were considered immoral and impermissible. Both leaders were of the view that outer space, oceans of the world and the ocean floor should be treated as a common heritage of mankind. There should be comprehensive international security arrangements, as international security is indivisible.

India and the USSR agreed that reducing the levels of conventional arms and armed forces would be an important contribution to the processes of general and complete disarmament. Rajiv Gandhi was convinced that the Indo-Soviet combined endeavour for ensuring peace and disarmament would move forward faster than before. But in the meantime a shift in the Soviet policy occurred in regard to matters directly affecting India including the Kashmir issue. In view of Gorbachev's desire to establish positive equations with USA and other western countries, the Soviet diplomats in important countries started conveying to their Indian counterparts that India should not expect the Soviet Union's categorical support as was the practice in the past. As a result of precipitate restructuring policies of Gorbachev, there was a slump in the economic and technological cooperation between India and the Soviet Union.

By the middle of 1989, the Indo-Soviet relations lost the warmth and confidence which had characterised their ties during the last four decades and more. Yeltsin replaced Gorbachev and in India Rajiv Gandhi also lost power. From 1990 onwards a new chapter in the Indo-Soviet relations became inevitable. During the terms of two successors to Rajiv Gandhi viz. V.P. Singh and Chandra Shekhar it became difficult to take firm control of relations between India and Russia. Owing to almost chaotic ideological and economic conditions in the Soviet Union, the V.P. Singh government found it difficult to take the grip over our relations with that country.

Gorbachev was going downhill in his control over the Central Asian Republics as well as over the East European nations.

A natural fallout of Gorbachev's Glosnost and Presteroika was globalisation. This and the New World Order reset the agenda for Indian-Russian bilateral relations. Globalisation received an impetus with the disintegration of the Soviet Union and the collapse of the East European bloc. Russia became dependent on the western technology, which resulted in countries like India, with structural ties to the former USSR, to look elsewhere. Defence links between Russia and India were disrupted after Soviet disintegration, because of the breakdown of overall commercial and financial arrangements. Moreover, the Yeltsin regime initially succumbed to US pressure which attempted to curb Russian sale of dual use technology to India. US pressurised Russia not to supply cryogenic engines for the Indian space programmes, though the supplying firm, Glavkosmos, which had become autonomous, had already delivered a substantial portion of the controversial technology. Since a bulk of the Indian frontline defence equipment, provided by the Soviet Union could not be upgraded or replaced by the western sources, the need for reestablishing supply lines from Russia was urgently felt.

Russia also felt that arms market was vital to its economy and India formed an integral part of the economic revival strategy of the Russian economy. Earlier, Yeltsin was persuaded by his Foreign Minister, Kozyrev to yield to the US pressure and halt the transfer of cryogenic rocket technology to India. His successor, Primakov had another angle. He strove hard to strengthen Moscow's ties with New Delhi and Beijing. Kozyrev had advocated Russia's exclusive dependence on the United States. Yeltsin began to realize the need for modifying the course of the Russian Federation. During his visit to India in December 1992, Yeltsin emphasized the conduct of Russia's relations with this country in a deideologized manner so as to prevent their being directed against a third party. President Yeltsin mentioned about an Asian tilt in Russian foreign policy. A new Treaty of Friendship and Cooperation with India was signed in place of the 1971 Treaty of Peace, Friendship and Cooperation. Yeltsin denied that the change in the name of the Treaty indicated any downscaling of the importance of the Indo-Russian strategic and defence cooperation. Yeltsin declared unequivocal Russian support for 'settlement of Kashmir' according to the Indian version. The rupee-rouble parity issue was also resolved satisfactorily between the two countries.

The visit of Prime Minister, P.V. Narasimha Rao to Moscow in June 1994 further underscored the strategic aspect of the Indo-Russian relations. A document called the Moscow Declaration was signed. That document brought out the travails of multiethnic states - both India and Russia - who had to cope with problems of terrorism on their borders. India's reference was naturally to Kashmir, whereas Russia was plagued with the situation on its southern borders in Georgia, Armenia, Azerbaijan etc. The declaration underlined the importance and the rights of multiethnic states in the changing world. The declaration was an indication of the growing realisation of both the countries to raise once again their relationship to a strategic long-term level. By September 1994, the first meeting of the joint commission, primarily to promote trade and economic cooperation had taken place. When the third meeting took place under the chairmanship of the then Minister for External Affairs, I.K.Gujral and Russian Deputy Prime Minister, Viktor Ilyushin, the Commission had grown into ten working groups: trade and economic cooperation, power and non-conventional sources of energy, petroléum, ferrous and non-ferrous metallurgy, science and technology, information technology, coal, culture, environment and natural resources and pharmaceuticals. Gujral told the meeting at Moscow that he was happy that both sides would take steps to imbue our close and multifaceted ties with even more meaningful content. An agreement on joint liner services was also signed to run ships along the Novorossisk-Mumbai/ Chennai route.

The Russian Prime Minister Viktor Chernomyrdin's visit to India in December 1995 marked a distinct move in the direction of restoring the strategic character of the Indo-Russian relations. He categorically stated that Russia was not supplying any military equipment to Pakistan and it had no intention of doing so in the future ended speculations about Moscow's plans to sell sophisticated military hardware to Pakistan. Among the several agreements signed between India and Russia in New Delhi, an agreement on military and technical cooperation till the year 2000 was of great significance. There was a rapture with the collapse of the Soviet Union in 1991, and the later years not only saw the revival of their ties, but their level went up much higher.

Yevgeny Primakov chose India for his first visit as Russia's Foreign Minister, which opened a new chapter in the Indo-Russian relations. He ardently advocated a Russia-India-China collaboration not only for the economic benefit of the three countries, but also in the international decision making. In India, however, there were certain reservations about a possible trilateral collaboration between Russia-India-China largely due to the Chinese policies with regard to India. In any case, some important members of the Russian Duma openly articulated the view that India was, is and should remain, Russia's first priority. President Yeltsin too spoke of Russia-China-India axis for building durable peace in Asia.

The United Front Government's Prime Minister, H.D. Deve Gowda visited Moscow in March 1997, against the backdrop of the largest-ever military hardware deal to be negotiated by India. India decided to buy $ 1.5 billion worth of fighter aircraft and other equipment. The new Russian state had come into being just five years earlier. Though there were differences on a few matters like modalities of repayment of the rupee debt, both countries agreed to cooperate even in sensitive areas. During Deve Gowda's visit, President Yeltsin gave a commitment to sell two light water nuclear power plants of 1000 MW each to be built at Kundankulam in Tamil Nadu. Though the deal was on the cards since 1988, when Mikhail Gorbachev had visited India, no progress was registered in its implementation as the Soviet Union had been embroiled in domestic difficulties leading to the dismemberment of the Union. The Russian Federation had joined the Nuclear Suppliers Group, which prohibited nuclear technology to all those countries who had not signed the Non-Proliferation Treaty. As soon as the Americans came to know of the Russian plan to act on the agreement signed in 1988, they were alarmed and debated the point with the Russians. But the Russian leaders argued that the deal with India had been reached much before their country had become a member of the NSG. Earlier in 1993 the USA had tried to stall the supply by Russia of cryogenic engines to India and now they were once again at the game without much regard to Indian sensitivities and needs. By denying the supply of power plants to India, the Russian leadership would have had to face the ignominy of playing a second fiddle to the Americans and would have also lost the confidence of India, besides inviting the disapproval of the Russian masses and intelligentsia on the issue.

Vladimir Putin, the successor to President Yeltsin, visited India in October 2000. Putin and the Indian Prime Minister Atal Behari Vajpayee transformed the vision of strategic partnership into a multipolar and multilateral world order as against a unipolar one. Soon thereafter, President Putin said that the project of creating a new architecture for international security, building a safer world has become particularly important after the two-polar world ceased to exist. We are in favour of improving the existing mechanism of the United Nations, mechanisms of improving international peace and security. On the issue of trilateral cooperation between India, China and Russia, which was for the first time mooted by Primakov, President Putin asserted: "We are convinced of the need for positive development of relations between Russia and India, Russia and China, and China and India. I think that all the three parties within this triangle are interested in this development. At the same time, I think we shouldn't go ahead of time, or move ahead without proper preparation."

While hosting a banquet in honour of President Putin, the President of India, K.R. Narayanan emphatically pointed out that the "multifaceted relationship between India and the Russian Federation is substantive in context and extensive in scope. As we consolidate our cooperation, the main challenge before us is economic development in order to meet the aspirations of our people." President Narayanan must also have been thinking of Indo-Russian bilateral economic cooperation, which had to some extent lost its ardour after the breakup of the Soviet Union. Whereas major global and bilateral issues like defence, space, technology and terrorism etc. have been adequately addressed, bilateral trade and economic relations had stagnated. Whereas the former Soviet Union was India's biggest trade partner, the bilateral trade had fallen to the level of a measly 1.5 billion dollars now. It was obvious, therefore, that there was need to impart a dynamic impulse to the mutual cooperation between the two countries.

The historic visit of Prime Minister Vajpayee to Russia in November 2003 became another landmark in the close and strategic relations between India and Russia. Vajpayee and Putin signed ten accords in the Kremlin after in-depth discussions. They proposed a consistent and uncompromising approach in tackling the menace of terrorism and called for giving up double standards in dealing with the problem. In a declaration inked by the two leaders, both countries proposed a concrete and time-bound action plan to be adopted for the earliest restoration of Iraq's sovereignty under the aegis of the United Nations. Among the accords signed by the two leaders, one related to cooperation in space research, which would include Russian assistance in an Indian lunar mission. Putin reiterated that cross border terrorism must end and the terrorist infrastructure in Pakistan must be dismantled as a prerequisite to peace in South Asia, which could follow a purposeful dialogue. There was complete agreement between the two leaders that international problems could be solved only through collective action on the part of the United Nations.

There was unanimity between Vajpayee and Putin that India-Russia defence cooperation had acquired great versatility and it encompassed a wide range of joint research, design, development and co-production. The two countries agreed to coordinate positions on key global issues, which were building blocks of the bilateral strategic partnerships. They called for effective implementation of the UN Security Council Resolution which was aimed against those who supported, funded or abetted terrorists or provided them shelter or asylum to engage in cross-border terrorism. Both India and Russia affirmed that "the future international order based on multipolarity should be determined by collective and multilateral processes rather than unilateral ones." Russia called for lifting of sanctions against India on the supply of nuclear technologies. "It is high time to review bans on nuclear cooperation with India imposed in 1992 by the Nuclear Suppliers Group," the Russian Atomic Energy Ministry said.

Addressing the Russian Academy of Sciences in Moscow, Vajpayee stressed the interest of both the countries in the evolution of a multipolar world based on a "cooperative security order." Vajpayee lauded the Russian support for India's permanent membership of the United Nations Security Council. "The Indo-Russian "strategic partnership" is a strong factor in promoting peace, security and stability both in Asia and the world. Talking of terrorism, Vajpayee said that it was threatening the unity, territorial integrity and sovereignty of both India and Russia. Putin minced no words in his address to the Indian Parliament three years earlier, when he had said that the same individuals, the same terrorist and extremist organisations were involved in terrorist acts from the Phillipines to Kosovo, including in Kashmir, Afghanistan and Chechnya."

Addressing the Russian Academy of Sciences on November 12, 2003, Vajpayee referred to the deep spiritual and cultural affinity between India and Russia, which manifested in the extraordinary resonance between the best minds of our two countries. This mutual resonance is also seen in the long tradition of intellectual interaction between our two countries in the various disciplines of the humanities and sciences that comprise the totality of human knowledge. In Vajpayee's words, it is a matter of immense satisfaction that Indo-Russian cooperation in science and technology has evolved continuously. Now it represents perhaps the most dynamic aspect of our overall relationship. The Integrated Long Term Programme of cooperation in science and technology is one of the most elaborate bilateral programmes in the world. Keeping with the challenges of modern times, our scientific cooperation now extends to the frontier areas of scientific research including biotechnology, informatics, nano technology, environmental protection, drugs and development of new materials. This is in addition to the traditional area of cooperation in space, atomic energy and defence technologies. Both India and Russia are multi-ethnic, pluralistic, democratic countries. Therefore, intellectuals, scientists and all public figures have an important role to play in the fight against the forces of intolerance and violence. There is a bright future for Indo-Russian relationship. But we should not rest on past laurels. We must follow a determined course towards continuous strengthening of political, economic, scientific and cultural ties.

In his keynote address at the joint meeting of Indian and Russian businesspersons in Moscow on November 13, 2003, Prime Minister Vajpayee described India and Russia as dynamic economies with tremendous potential for growth. India's economy is receiving more and more attention around the world. A quiet revolution has been going on in the integration of the Indian economy into the global mainstream. In many areas of the Indian success story, there is a strong Russian connection. The longstanding, robust and multifaceted bilateral engagement is the firm base on which a more modern economic edifice is sought to be built.

Energy cooperation is a key area of interest. Russia has emerged as one of the leading suppliers of energy and India is one of the largest and fastest growing markets for energy. Another sector of great potential in India-Russia collaboration is small and medium enterprises. The Russian Public Organization of Small and Medium Size Enterprises has concluded an MOU with the Federation of Indian Chambers of Commerce and Industry to explore synergies in this vital sector. Our cooperation can span a wide spectrum, such as training, exchange of experts, management, supply of machinery and equipment and even turnkey execution of projects.

India supported Russia's accession to the World Trade Organisation, not only in the spirit of our strategic partnership but also in the firm belief that Russia's membership would bring balance and strength to the WTO. India and Russia can play an important role, in concert with other major emerging markets, in encouraging the WTO to operate for the common benefit of all its member countries. India and Russia have developed strong bonds of friendship and cooperation over many decades. A dynamic and multifaceted economic partnership provides a secure underpinning to the other elements of this relationship.

The December 3-5, 2004 visit of Vladimir Putin was another milestone in the strategic partnership and time-tested friendship between the two countries. Apart from the multi-faceted cooperation and bilateral relations between India and Russia in the world arena, their determination to expand the area of their collaboration in the interest of their peoples and to enhance the cause of universal peace were the factors which could hardly be overlooked by Putin and Prime Minister, Manmohan Singh. After a little hiccup, his candid and articulate support for India's permanent membership of the Security Council had a salutary effect in most circles. Putin asserted vigorously that India's membership of the Security Council should be with full rights, including the right of veto.

In a joint Declaration released after the talks between Manmohan Singh and Putin, it was stated that India and Russia were guided by mutual trust and respect inherent in their bilateral relations. They were committed to promote global peace and progress and to counter challenges arising out of international terrorism. They confirmed their adherence to the common ideals of secularism, democracy, rule of law, cultural diversity and pluralism. They also reaffirmed their commitment to develop further and enhance the strategic partnership based on nation-wide consensus in both the countries.

Putin averred that Russia was interested in expanding trade in high-tech products with India and to improve forms and methods of cooperation in the investment sphere.High technologies -

computers, the internet, satellite communications and fibre optics-are the driving force of globalisation. Putin expressed his belief that the multipolar world of high technologies would help to balance the evolution of human civilisation. Russia and India both have an enormous potential to develop together advanced technologies, including alternative technologies. Defence Minister, Pranab Mukherji informed the Russians that India has decided to include the element of intellectual property rights in defence deals. He said this after co-chairing a meeting of the India-Russia inter-governmental Commission on Military-Technical Cooperation with his Russian counterpart Sergei Ivanov. Over 70 per cent of equipment available to the Indian military is of Russian origin.

Putin highlighted that India stood at the top of the Russian policy agenda. "Comprehensive strengthening of our cooperation has always been and remains a priority one of the top priorities of Russian foreign policy", he said and added, "India is a crucial factor in stability in the region and in the world as a whole. Russia would like to see India play a genuinely important role in international affairs."

The latest and the fourth official visit of Putin to India (January 2007) reflected a genuine consensus that is rare in foreign policy. The nine agreements signed and the statements made around them highlighted some important points. Both nations strongly believe in a multipolar world as against a unipolar world projecting hegemony. Putin agreed to collaborate with India in civilian nuclear energy, as Russia has undertaken to provide at least four nuclear power plants at Kundankulam in the Tamil Nadu state. She would also construct Russian designed nuclear power plants at new sites in India. Russia had started collaboration in this sphere when USA and others had imposed sanctions on India. Russia would not impose any conditionality as the US Hyde Act on transfer of nuclear technology to this country does. Russia has promised to give these plants perpetual supply of nuclear fuel and would not stop it even if differences with India arose. India would be free to conduct its indigenous research on nuclear technology without any conditions. The Russian commitments in the field of nuclear power would allow India complete independence in foreign and internal policies. Similarly Russia would give free access to India to navigation signals of the Russian Global Navigation Satellite System (GLONASS) for peaceful purposes. This, and further, cooperation with Russia will take India on the high road to greater confidence in the present day competitive world.

Cooperation in the field of defence between India and Russia has been a high water mark in their close overall relations. A bulk of India's defence needs has been met by Russia. But now they have reached a stage when they have to come face to face with diverse markets in the globalised world both in demand and supply. Russia inherited from the composite Soviet Union the lion's share of its Military Industrial Complex. About 2000 enterprises with over 900 research organisations have a complement of approximately 5 million workers and technicians.

Though Russia alongwith other permanent members of the Security Counci] condemned India for its nuclear tests in 1998, it did not impose sanctions on India. It went ahead, inspite of US pressure, to build two light water megawatt nuclear reactors at Kundankulam. During Premier Primakov's New Delhi visit in 1998, Russia and India extended long-term agreement on military technical cooperation upto the year 2010. As the country's Prime Minister, Vladimir Putin observed, only 20 per cent of Russian defence industry plants were working. After taking over the presidency, he revived and restructured the Military Industrial Complex through consolidation into viable conglomerates. As a result Russia became the second largest arms exporter after the United States.

During the first visit as President of Putin to New Delhi, arms deals worth $ 3 billion were clinched. The India-Russia intergovernmental Commission was upgraded from the secretary level to the Ministers' level. India has since purchased Su-30MKI multi-role fighter aircraft, II-78 tanker aircraft for use as platform for Airborne Warning and Control System (AWACS), Mi-17-IV military transport helicopters, R-77 air-to-air missiles, Kilo class/ type 877E submarines, frigates, Ka-31 Helix airborne early warning helicopters, aircraft carrier Admiral Gorshkov, MiG-29K, including MiG-29KUB version for use on aircraft carrier Admiral Gorshkov, Ka-27PL (Ka-28 version) and Ka-31 helicopters; T-90 tanks, fire control radar, air and sea surveillance radar, combat radar, aircraft radar, anti-tank and anti-ship missiles etc. Admiral Gorshkov has still to be delivered,after negotiations of cost escalation, to the Indian Navy.

The recent setting up of a consignment warehouse and a service centre in India called Rosoboron Service may go a long way in meeting India's requirements for uninterrupted supply of spare parts and repair and maintenance of equipment of Russian origin.

The payments for military hardware have shifted from the rupee payment regime to the hard currency. There have been certain delays in the delivery of weapon systems as also a number of items have lacked critical components. Russia has also promised to adhere to the delivery schedules by issuing a "comfort letter" instead of providing bank guarantees. There have been some complaints about the quality of certain systems as well. However, Indian pilots have found the performance of various Russian aircraft as highly satisfactory.

During Prime Minister, Manmohan Singh's Moscow visit in December, 2005, an Intellectual Property Rights (IPR) Agreement in respect of military equipment was signed. It was after Russia had put a lot of pressure on India and had warned that in the absence of an IPS Agreement, she would not be able to transfer technology to this country. It was agreed, however, that the IPR provisions would apply to future transactions only. Russia has offered to conduct "joint development and production" of weapon systems, which would entail designing and manufacturing of components. The major joint development and production projects include the supersonic cruise missile BrahMos with a range of 280 km, which are to be jointly marketed by the two countries and 5th Generation Fighter Aircraft and Medium Transport Aircraft. Cooperation in Space - the GLONASS has also been agreed to.

In October 2005, the Indian and Russian armies and navies held joint exercises in the desert of Rajasthan and off the coast of Vishakhapatnam, respectively.

After the removal of post-Pokhran sanctions on India by the United States in November 2001, Israel has emerged as the second biggest arms exporter to India after Russia. The Russian Defence Minister Sergei Ivanov conceded that India has tried to diversify arms acquisitions and Russia understands this country's desire to get the best available technology. Russia must compete with other countries in supplying advanced arms to India. In any case, the Indian Defence Minister stated in his keynote address to the General Staff Academy of the Russian Armed Forces that Russia "has been, and remains the largest source of our arms, weapon systems and technology imports." India would like to retain its strategic autonomy and take decisions on the basis of merit. It would safeguard its national interests.

Cooperation between India and Russia (after Soviet Union) has helped India build its defence potential. Continued cooperation would serve their strategic and geopolitical interests better and would be mutually beneficial. On March 16, 2006 the Russian Prime Minister Mikhail Fradkov said in New Delhi that the supply of uranium to Tarapur plant did not contradict or violate any international commitment since it fell within the four corners of the international framework. "We have informed the Nuclear Suppliers Group about the supply of fuel to the Tarapur Atomic Power Station. The sale of uranium is in the interest of both the countries." Russia heeded India's urgent request for 60 metric tonnes of uranium to TAPS to enable it to function with safety. Fradkov identified information technology, telecom, air space, nuclear cooperation, metals and construction among high priority areas for trade cooperation between India and Russia. Their trade turnover is expected to triple by 2010.

The Russian Foreign Minister Sergei Lavrov has written in an article on the 60th anniversary of diplomatic relations between India and Russia that the relations between the two countries have stood the test of time and have acquired a strategic dimension that will grow stronger in the twentyfirst century. "Strategic partnership embraced by our countries is based on a shared belief that there is no alternative to a multipolar world, on the responsibility of Russia and India for the future of the modern civilisation on a prudent, calibrated pursuit of their national interests" he wrote. The Minister emphasised that the relations between India and Russia have never been marred by any serious disagreement or contradiction. "On the contrary, they have always reflected mutual awareness that the two countries and peoples are close to each other, share long-term national interests and take similar stands on key international problems", Mr. Lavrov said. In a Kremlin foreign policy review approved by President Vladimir Putin, Russia reiterated its commitment to strategic relationship with India. Among other things, it said that "Development and deepening of strategic partnership with India in all directions - political, trade and economy, scientific-technological, cultural and defence - will remain one of the priorities of the Russian foreign policy." This document called for continuing "the development of dialogue and expansion of interaction in the trilateral India-Russia-China format, which the Russian leaders of late have been emphasizing. The twentyfirst century might open new vistas for India and other countries in cooperation for mutual interest.

References

1. India-Russia Partnership : Kashmir, Chechnya and Issues of Convergence by Debidatta Aurobinda Mahapatra - Published by New Century Publications.
2. India's Foreign Policy 1947-2003 by J.N. Dixit - Published by Picus Books.
3. Indo-Russian Relations : Prospects, Problems and Russia Today - Editor V.D. Chopra - Published by Kalpaz Publications.
4. New Trends in Indo-Russian Relations - Editor V.D. Chopra - Published by Kalpaz Publications.
5. Prime Minister Rajiv Gandhi visits USSR : Soviet Land Booklets-Published, by the Information Department of USSR Embassy in India.
6. Devendra Kaushik, India, USSR and East Europe, in India Quarterly - A Journal of International Affairs, January-March 1985 - Indian Council of World Affairs, New Delhi.
7. Global Significance of Indo-Russian, Strategic Partnership - Editor V.D. Chopra—Published by Kalpaz Publications.
8. Sumit Chakravarty, India and Russia, in World Focus 179-180.
9. Sumit Chakravarty, India-Russia: Strategic Partnership, in World Focus 238-239-240.
10. Anuradha Cheny, Cordial Relations with Russia, in World Focus 202-203-204.
11. Jyoti Malhotra, Indo-Russian Relations, in World Focus 209.
12. Joint Declaration by the Russian Federation and the Republic of India, http://www. india.mid.ru/summits/05d__02.html
13. Prime Minister's address at the Russian Academy of Sciences 12/11/2003, http://meaindia.nic. in/speech/2003/11/12ss01. htm.
14. India's Relations with Russia and China - Editors M. Rasgotra and V.D. Chopra—Published by Gyan Publishing House, New Delhi.
15. Keynote address by Prime Minister of India Shri Atal Bihari Vajpayee at the Joint Meeting of Indian and Russian Businesspersons, https//meaindia. nic.in/speech/2003/11/13ss0l.htm.
16. Joint Declaration by the Russian Federation and the Republic of India: Signed by President of Russian Federation Vladimir Putin and Prime Minister of the Republic of India, http//www.kremlin.ru/eng/text/docs/2004/12/80552.shtml.
17. India's Foreign Policy since Independence by V.P. Dutt—Published by National Book Trust, India.

18. The Hindu, March 17, 2006.
19. Anuradha M. Chenoy, Meaning of the Putin Visit in Mainstream February 10, 2007.
20. Jyotsna Bakshi, India-Russia Defence Cooperation, Strategic Analysis, Vol. 30, No. 2, Apr-Jun 2006.
21. R.R. Sharma, Indo-Russian Strategic Partnership, in World Focus 286, 287, 288.
22. The Hindu : International/India & World. India-Russia ties to grow stronger, says Lavrov, http://www.hindu.com/2007/04/08/stories/2007040801 220900.htm.
23. India's Foreign Policy in the 21st century—Edited by V.D. Chopra—Published by Kalpaz Publications.

6

State of US Relations with Russia and its Implications for India

B.K. Shrivastava

In the euphoria generated by end of the Cold War and the collapse of the Soviet Union, the United States nourished high hopes of the Russian Federation, if not speedily at least gradually, developing into a western style democracy in which there would be rule of law, the media would be completely free, there would be multi-party system, free and fair elections, an independent judiciary and free market where private enterprise would flourish. Although the American officials readily concede that, since the end of the cold war, in the last decade and a half, Russia had more freedom than it ever had in its entire history, yet they are disappointed that the developments in Russia have moved in the opposite direction. Democracy backtracked, media is restrained by government, private corporations have been chained and Russia is trying to dominate its neighbors; Georgia, Moldova, and Ukraine, former Republics of the Soviet Union. While Yeltsin was the President, economically weak Russia, after protesting vigorously said yes quickly and no at great length. Since Vladimir Putin's accession to the presidency of the Russian Federation, things began to change. What contributed to the hardening of the Russian resolve not to be pushed around was rapidly strengthening Russian economy due to soaring global oil and gas prices. According to The *Economist,* Russian GDP increased nearly three times since 2002 and has grown at 6 or 7 per cent each year since 2003. Inflation fell to under 10 per cent last year and its trade balance increased three-fold in four years. In 2006 the economy grew by 6.7 per cent[1]. But it is still smaller than the economies of other G-8 countries. For the last few years the United States relations with Russia have been passing through one of their worst phases. It appears to have touched its lowest point.

The relation between the two countries is complex. In a speech on May 31, 2007 before the Baltimore Council of Foreign Affairs, deputy assistant secretary for European and Eurasian affairs David Kramer observed that the developments in Russia in the last fifteen years could not be described in the absolutes of black and white. Certainly, Russia has become more free than anytime in its entire history. However, he argued that this appeared as great only because it started from a low threshold. And from the western perspective, it is much less than their expectations. As a more positive element he pointed to the rapid growth of economic relations between the two countries. In 2005, the US investment in Russia shot up almost by 50 per cent. Companies such as Alcoa., International Paper, Coca Cola, GM, Proctor and Gamble increased their stakes in the Russian Federation. Proctor and Gamble employed more than 20,000 Russians and Boeing employed 1300. Last year Boeing signed an $18 billion agreement to buy titanium from Russia. It initiated a contract valued at $2.4 billion with the second largest Russian airline S7 for the purchase of 15 long range jets. Kramer went on to describe the Russian market as "an incredible one in recent years". As Russian economy gained in its strength, it offered greater opportunities to American corporations for trade and investment. More American corporations are interested in investing in the Russian Federation. The US hopes that after Russia joins the WTO, the opportunities for American business would expand further.

There are areas where interests of the two countries overlap. The US feels happy with the cooperation it receives in combating international terrorism, stopping nuclear proliferation, checking drug-trafficking and efforts to secure peace and stability in the Middle East. Even on Iran the US plays down the differences and argues that differences with Russia on preventing Iran from acquiring nuclear weapons are only "tactical." After all, not withstanding its high stakes in Iran, Russia voted with the United States on the UN Security Council Resolutions 1737 and 1747which imposed economic sanctions on Iran until it suspended its nuclear enrichment program and came into compliance with its obligations under NPT. It also voted in favor of Resolution no 1718 on denuclearization of the Korean peninsula and imposing Chapter VII sanctions on North Korea.

There are three primary issues where the interests of the two countries are opposed; backsliding of democracy, simmering regional conflict among former Soviet Republics and Russia's increased cooperation with Iran and Syria. In the middle, between cooperation and conflict is the area of cooperation and competition in the field of energy, more specifically in oil. The US is constructing Baku, Azerbaijan, Ceyhan oil pipeline (in Turkey) to bypass both Russia and Iran. It accuses Russia of using oil and gas as a political weapon to pressurize Western Europe and its neighbors who are dependent on it for their energy. And as the ice is melting in North Pole a new struggle for oil has begun among the United States, Russia, Canada, Norway, and Finland who are claiming the right to own North Pole oil. Kramer summed up the US policy towards Russia in the following words: *"cooperate wherever we can, push back whenever we have to." ... "preferred approach is cooperation where our interests overlap. We push back when we must. We do so privately when possible, publicly when necessary in the interest of our values, national interests and friends." (Emphasis added)* Pushing has gone a little too far. As a result differences have been exacerbating. Russia has come to believe that in the last two three years the United States has been pushing policies that threaten the Russian security and NATO is expanding eastward closer to the Russia border. The Russian leadership is not only irritated but is really angry with the US proposal to construct a missile defense site in Poland and a radar site in the Czech Republic so close to Russia's borders. It is now firing warning shots to indicate that it is losing patience and unless such policies are given up, it would be forced to initiate measures that would endanger cooperation with the West and may threaten European states.

It was Lt. General Ronald Kadish, director of the missiles defense agency (MDA) who in his testimony to the Congress in early 2004 first disclosed the plan: "In Block 2006 we are preparing to move forward when appropriate a third (ground based interceptor) site at a location outside the United States." (Block referred to two year period from 1 January 2006 to 31 December 2007). It was reported that the United States was holding discussions with the Czech Republic, Hungary and Poland about building the site on the territory of one of them. No final decision had been reached. Secret discussions with Poland were still in a preliminary stage. By mid 2006 the secret negotiations were moving towards finalization. The director of MDA, General Henry Obering, declared in August 2006 that within months he would recommend where the radar and interceptor missile sites would be located in Europe to counter the missile threat from Iran. The General said "we are facing a real threat...one that is growing. It is one that I consider to be one of the preeminent threats that we will be facing in the 21st century." Iran has tested Shahab-3 missile with the reported range of 1300 kms.(about 800 miles). The Iranian missiles could reach European States but not the United States. But according to the General, Iran was trying to increase the capacity of its missiles and therefore there was a potential threat to the security of the United States. The US plan called for the stationing of ten interceptor missiles in eastern Europe by 2011.[2]

Analysts described the project as "the most controversial" since the end of the Cold War. Russia views it as an unacceptable challenge to its own sphere of influence. It considers the proposal to construct interceptor missile site near its own border not as an isolated threat but as a part of a design to strategically and economically integrate erstwhile Soviet Republics in European Union leaving Russia isolated. Russia knew all along what was going on. The United States tried to take Moscow on board. A high ranking Pentagon official met Russian officials on March 17, 2006 to discuss the issue. On April 3, a full delegation went to Moscow to apprise status of the missiles program. Former Secretary of Defense Donald Rumsfeld spoke to his counterpart Sergei Ivanov twice. The subject was placed on the agenda of the meeting of the NATO- Russian Council in 2006. But all these attempts failed to convince Russia that the missile project was not directed against it. The question also remained what the Russians were told in these discussions. Probably, the information given was "vague" and "sparse." Any way, the Russians had not been taken in as a partner when the plan began and developed but only when it had reached the decisive stage, the US tried to convince Moscow that it was in the larger interest of Europe's security against threat arising from the Middle East which was shared by Russia too. Obviously Moscow did not find the argument convincing.[3]

Russians were becoming angry became evident by the speech Vladimir V. Putin gave at the 43rd meeting on Security policy in Munich on February 10, 2007. He launched a blistering attack on the United States charging it with pursuing the goal of a unipolar world, imposing its economic, political, cultural and educational policies on other nations. This inevitably encouraged, he said, a number of countries to acquire weapons of mass destruction and because of it terrorism took on a global character. He contended that unipolar world was not only unacceptable but impossible. The new centers of global economic growth like China and India, would inevitably convert in to influence and that would strengthen multipolarity. Speaking pointedly on the issue of construction of anti-missile defense system in East Europe, he said: "Plans to expand certain elements of the anti-missile defense system to Europe cannot but disturb us" and warned that "this would lead to an arms race that no one wanted". He pointed out that missile systems with a range of about five to eight thousand kilometers that would really pose a threat to Europe do not presently exist in any of the "so called problem countries" nor is there a possibility that this would happen in the foreseeable future. Then where was the need for constructing a site for an interceptor missile defense.[4] Subsequently, he warned that if the proposal was implemented despite Russia's objections, then Russia would aim its missiles on sites in Europe. This warning unsettled Europe.

Putin's personal envoy Sergei Yastzhenbesky told Rossiiskya Gazete that Putin's speech, was based on information that western countries were prepared to discuss only behind the closed doors. The envoy did not strike a belligerent pose. The speech, he suggested, had the effect of the "cold shower and not a Cold War". There was no question of going back to the confrontational era of the Cold war. Russia only wanted to let it be known how it looked at the proposal.. "We are no longer in ideological conflict with the West," he said, "Russia is a totally different country."[5]

The United States continued its efforts to assure Russia that the construction of the anti-missile site would not pose a threat to it. In the first week of March 2007, General Obering, director of MDA, addressed ambassadors from twenty-six NATO countries and answered questions from the edgy ambassadors. He claimed that anti-missiles defense system was entirely defensive in nature and provided protection against threat from Iran.[6]

After blowing hot, time was ripe for blowing cold. Nearly four months after his Munich speech, on June 7, after a private meeting lasting two hours between himself and President George Bush on the sidelines of the annual gathering of G-8 in Germany, Putin surprised the Americans by proposing to jointly build a missile defense system in Azerbaijan. But said nothing on interceptor missile site in Poland. In his February speech he had questioned the necessity of the missile defense system because neither the threat existed nor was it likely to develop in the near future. Now he was willing to consider the possibility of a threat of a missile attack and offering to jointly build the system. Putin gave the appearance of his readiness to compromise and calm the fears which his threat to again aim missile at Europe had raised. He said "this would make it impossible - unnecessary for us to place our offensive complexes along with borders with Europe." Bush did not immediately reject the proposal. He told the press that the Russian President had put some interesting suggestions. The two leaders announced the formation of a group of military and diplomatic officials from both the countries to study the feasibility of the Russian proposal. Bush said the group would examine how the two countries could cooperate in building the missile defense system. "There will be serious strategic discussion and we want to make sure that we all understand each other's position clearly."[7] From this exchange *the New York Times* concluded that this "indicated a desire on both sides to cool hostile exchanges" that had driven the US Russian relations to a low point. Secretary of Defense Robert Gate's comment was that the Russian proposal was not a substitute but only complementary to the American plan, a position that Russia would have rejected without giving it a second thought. There were other American officials who argued that there were technical problems in the acceptance of the Russian offer. Russia did not own the facilities in Azerbaijan but only had the lease of the property. Another problem was that the Russian facility was only a tracking station and not the X band radar that is used to guide anti-missile interceptors. But these objections were baseless and frivolous. If Azerbaijan was willing to cooperate, as Putin said that it was, it did not matter whether the facilities were owned by Russia or on lease to it. If the radar in Azerbaijan was not up to the requirement, it was non-existent in the Czech Republic and was going to be constructed. What Putin had proposed was joint development of the missile defense system and not sharing of the existing facilities only.[7]

Russia warned the United States against rejecting its proposal. General Yuri Baluvesky, the Chief of General Staff of Russian armed force, said that as Iran posed no immediate threat, the aim of the planned US site in Poland and the Czech Republic must be clearly against Russian nuclear arsenal. And if Washington rejected Putin's proposal, it would clearly show United States' real intention.[8]

Europe's response to US proposal is divided. If the "Old Europe" is lukewarm because it does not want to disrupt its relations with Russia which is a major supplier of its energy needs, the "new Europe" sees it as an opportunity to further strengthen its ties with the United States. One should recall that Ukraine, Poland and Azerbaijan contributed troops to the US led Iraq war and did not toe the Russian policy. Europe wanted to cool the exchanges that were becoming sharper by the day. NATO' Secretary-General Japp-de Hoop Scheffer, who visited Moscow in early June told reporters during his visit : " there is no reason to speak with megaphones. It is advisable to lower the comments on both the sides." Commenting on the Russian warning that it could hit the anti-missile defense site, the Secretary-General said: "The NATO-Russian relationship is one of partnership, and in the framework of partnership, these remarks about targeting missiles do not fit and they do not have a place in the discussions."[9]

At the meeting in Germany Putin offered to stop in the United States on his way to attend the meeting of the Olympic committee in Guatemala to lobby Russia's case for hosting winter Olympic in 2014. George Bush instead of fixing the meeting in Washington decided to invite him to their family resort in Kennebunkport, Maine. There was skepticism in Moscow as well as in Washington that the two countries would be anywhere near an agreement on this thorny issue. President of a Russian think tank "Policy Foundation," Vyacheslav Nikonov said: "I do not expect any break-through. Bush and Putin would communicate to cool down the friction between the two countries which has surpassed all reasonable limits now."[10]

In the meeting on 1-2 July, Putin went farther than his proposal in Germany. He offered to build a regional European missile shield that could include a new radar facility in south of Russia. Responding to some of the problems raised earlier, Putin said, if the radar in Azerbaijan was not adequate, Russia would modernize it. And if that was not feasible Russia would build a modern Russian facility in southern Russia. He proposed that the system be put under the auspices of NATO-Russian Council to make it a European missile shield. He also advocated setting up of advance early warning system in Brussels and Moscow. Bush welcomed the proposal. And his advisers were convinced that Putin was serious in working together. However, it was not clear whether Bush would still go ahead and deploy the interceptor missiles in Poland despite

Russian opposition. The media pointed out that in the past the two countries, effort to devise a system that would guard against accidental rogue missile launches had failed to take off because of politics and bureaucratic hassles. Russia had made its offer and was waiting for the American response. By his offer he wanted to obviate the prospect of a missiles system close to its own border. One forceful argument advanced was that if the interceptor missile was situated in Poland, collision of the missiles - the one coming from the Middle East and the interceptor missile, would take place over the Russian territory and the falling debris would damage the Russian property and kill people. Putin added that if his proposal was accepted there would be no need to place any more missile in Europe and the relations between the two countries would rise to a new level. *Gradually it would be like "a strategic partnership".*

Bush called Putin's proposal "very constructive" and "bold" and said he was in "strong agreement with it" He told Putin that he wanted Poland and Azerbaijan to be integral part of the system. The National Security Advisor Stephen J. Hadley called Putin's proposal "a very interesting shift" and some real progress on the issue. But there was no indication given either by Bush or his National Security Advisor what the US was conceding. On the other hand Russia that had earlier denied that there was a threat of a missile attack on Europe or likely to develop had shifted its position and was offering its cooperation in devising a system to meet the potential threat. But it wanted it to be an European shield that would not be a threat to its own security. One way to achieve this objective was to be part of the system. But by accepting the proposal the US would send a message to the "new Europe" that it was not interested in standing by them against Russian domination and accepted that the East Europe was within the Russian sphere of influence. By insisting that the Poland and Azerbaijan be integral part of the system it was conveying the message that the US was not withdrawing from the region.[11]

While greeting US on its independence day on 4th July, Putin's message was conciliatory. He observed that despite disagreement relations with the United States would only grow. Disagreements were unavoidable in an open and honest dialogue. He significantly added: "the deck has been dealt and we are here to play. And I would very much hope that we are playing one and the same game." The first deputy prime minister and former defense minister Sergei Ivanov ominously added from Central Asia where he had gone on a visit that Russia has found a symmetrical and effective response to the US plan. He did not, however, spell out this Russian plan.[12]

In the exchanges that took place in Germany between the two leaders two other issues came up for discussion. On Iran the United States has pursued Janus like policy that looked in two opposite directions. The United States has been accusing Iran of supporting terrorist groups in the Middle East, Hizbullah in Lebanon, militant Shiite organizations in Iraq and Hamas in the Palestine. Iran provided these organizations with weapons, training and finances. Thus US views Iran as a destabilizing force. On the other hand the US also knows that for peace and stability in the region it is under compulsion to take Iran and Syria on board. Therefore, on the one hand it is negotiating with Iran for peace in Iraq and on the other it wants to impose strong sanctions on Iran to deter it from acquiring nuclear weapons. Russia on the other hand is assisting Iran in building nuclear reactors in Busehar. At the same time, it shares with the United States the goal of nuclear nonproliferation and is opposed to Iran's acquisition of nuclear weapons capability. It therefore went along with the United States in imposing sanctions on Iran. These sanctions did produce some result as was evidenced by the imposition of rationing of oil in Iran, the second largest producer of oil, second only to Saudi Arabia. Most of its oil is refined outside the country. And the refusal of countries refining Iranian oil has led to this crisis. The United States is interested in further tightening of economic sanctions. It wants provisions that would permit the searching of ships suspected of carrying nuclear material to Iran to further constrain Iran's capability. It needs Russia's cooperation in the UN Security Council for this. Russia can easily tie up the question of cooperation on Iran with the issue of US missile defense plan.[13]

Another important issue on which the two sides differ is the future status of Kosovo;[14] whether it would remain part of Serbia or would become independent. Albanian Muslims constitute nearly 90 per cent of Kosovo's population which is keen on independence. A very large number of- Serbs in Kosovo immigrated fearing reprisal from the Albanian majority. The Serbs in Kosovo as well as in Serbia consider it to be part of Serbia on historic and cultural grounds. In 1999 NATO carried out military operations against the Serb forces that were trying to crush the Albanian-Kosovars movement for independence. After the military operations were over the UN Security Council sent a UN Mission (UNMIK) to administer Kosovo the autonomous province of Serbia - Montenegro. Its future was to be decided later. Kosovo has been under the Mission since 1999 and its internal administration is carried on by local institutions. The international community recognizes nominal sovereignty of Serbia over it. In 2006, the UN Security Council appointed a committee headed by Martti Ahitisaari of Finland to discuss the issue with the Kosovo-Albanians and the leaders of the minority Serb population. The Committee worked for nearly thirteen months and submitted its report even though discussions were deadlocked as the Serb minority in Kosovo, encouraged by Belgrade, refused to participate in the negotiations. The Ahtisaari Committee recommended independence managed by European Union with cultural autonomy for the Serbs that still remained in Kosovo. The committee also assured the presence of the Orthodox Church in Kosovo. Serbia hoped for the Russian support. Vitaly Churkin, the Russian Ambassador, declared in June that any plan recommending independence was unacceptable to Russia and it would veto the resolution moved by the United States, the UK, and France. The draft proposal before the Security Council was changed three times to accommodate the Russian objections. Under the last modification it was provided that the plan would go into effect one hundred twenty days after the passage of the resolution. This would give some more time to evolve a consensus. The UN Secretary General Ban Ki-moon said on 5th July that unless swift action was taken, progress in stabilizing Kosovo would be reversed. The subject was scheduled for discussion in the Security Council on 9th July. Putin argues that his opposition to the independence is not on the ground of Russian affinity with the Serbs or on the basis of ethnicity (both being Slavs) but on the ground of stability of the region. If Kosovo is granted independence then similar other area like Abkazia and South Ossetia in Georgia would demand independence. In both these regions Russian population is nearly 80 per cent and they hold Russian passports and are Russian citizens. If the resolution fails because of the exercise of veto by Russia, the restless Kosovo-Albanians can still go ahead and unilaterally declare independence. Some other countries then can go ahead and recognize Kosovo's independent status and Russia could retaliate by recognizing the two separatist movements. Unless some compromise is reached, the situation is fraught with great risk of instability and enhanced tension in relations between the West and Russia. It was presumed that the meeting in Kennebunkport between Bush and Putin would discuss Kosovo but the meeting focused only on missile defense plan. Security Council meeting on 16th July again ended in a deadlock over Russian objections. Churkin said that the chances of the passage of the resolution were zero.[15]

The United States has been accusing Russia of trying to keep Georgia and Moldova in turmoil by supporting the secessionist movements in the former Soviet Republics. Richard Haass, in the Cato report that was submitted to the Congress in June 2004, suggested that the US tread carefully on the issue. He argued that Georgia is going to be the neighbor of Russia forever where as United States is faraway. He implied that the problem between Russia and Georgia should be resolved through negotiations between the two countries. And the United States should not make promises to countries in Eastern Europe which it would not be able to deliver.[16]

Thr Cato report's suggestion made no impact on the US policy in this regard. At the OSCE summit in Brussels in the first week of December 2006 Nicholas Burns said: "some countries were imposing economic and financial pressures on Georgia and Moldova." And as long as these countries remain torn apart from within and as long as open support for separatist regimes continues from without these two countries they would find it difficult to realize their potential." The Russian representative Lavrov counter-charged that the OSCE was exacerbating the conflict in the region. The OSCE was trying to force one side solution to long lasting disputes. . .such action leads to exacerbation of the tension and mistrust and puts back the clock of any possible solution."[17] The overwhelming majority in Abkkazia and South Ossetia in Georgia want to be part of the Russian Federation rather than remain with Georgia. This is a long standing dispute and can only be resolved by an outcome satisfactory to both the sides.

Putin in a statement to the Russian Parliament on 26th April had warned that Russia would abrogate the CEF treaty in response to the abrogation of the ABM treaty. The statement also noted that the NATO governments have not ratified the 1999 amendment to the treaty which Russia did in 2004. Western Governments had stated that they would not ratify the treaty till Russia withdrew its forces from Georgia and Moldova. Putin stated that Russia has withdrawn its forces from Georgia and has explained to Moldova that it would withdraw its forces after stability has been restored.[18]

The meeting between Bush and Putin in Kennebunkport, Maine did not ease the escalating tension. On July 14th Russia gave notice to NATO governments that it would suspend its obligation under Conventional Force in Europe Treaty (CFE). As the treaty stipulates, the decision would be implemented within 150 days. This delay leaves some possibility of renegotiation of this important limitation of armament treaty signed in 1990. Some analysts viewed it as a gesture to the growing anti Americanism feeling in Russia in view of the forthcoming presidential election in March. The treaty has no provision for suspension, it has only provision for withdrawal. The Russian statement explained that the decision had been taken due to "extraordinary circumstances that affect the security of the Russian Federation and require immediate measures." Russia gave six reasons for the decision. One of these was that NATO's expansion into Eastern Europe had soared up the military capability of the Alliance. Latvia, Lithuania, and Estonia are not the members of the Treaty yet NATO weapons are deployed on their territories. Russia maintains that in 1999 NATO committed that it would not have bases in new member countries though now it is building facilities in Bulgaria and Romania. NATO, of course, denies the charges claiming that it has not established any bases and these are only training sites. Another important reason that has angered Russia is American decision to abrogate the ABM treaty so that it would be free to develop a global anti-missile shield. Russia may not be facing threat to its security now but it strongly believes that such a global missile shield would completely undermine its own and China's offensive missile capability.[18] The US expressed its disappointment at the announcement and stated that it would continue to meet Russian officials to resolve the differences over the treaty. A Russian political analyst, Gleb O. Pavlovesky said that Russia is conveying a message to the West by suspending its obligations under the treaty and if the message is ignored then the Intermediate Nuclear Force Treaty would be the next[19].

The Council on Foreign Relations, an American Liberal think tank appointed a bipartisan committee that was headed by former Senator John Edwards and Jack Kemp, former Congressman and Secretary of the Department of Housing and Urban Development. The Committee submitted its report: "Russia's Wrong Direction, What the United States Can and Should Do" in March 2006 that coincided with the G-8 meeting in Russia. It found that "US Russian relations are clearly headed in the wrong direction," and concluded that the very idea of "strategic partnership" no longer seem realistic." At the meeting releasing the report Kemp conceded that " Russia's Cooperation is central to achieving American interests". He went on to enumerate some of them: Iran, energy, Hiv/Aids, preventing terrorists from acquiring weapons of mass destruction. It is "vital to have Russia on our side," he said. Edwards added that the report was a "wake up call to get US-Russia relations back on track." But among the recommendations was the suggestion that "the US should cede no veto or undue deference to Russia over American relation with the states on the Russian periphery. It recommended greater support to these states. Partnership was the right long term approach but "not a realistic prospect over the next several years". Therefore it recommended "selective cooperation and selective opposition." In 2007 David Kramer was recommending the same approach.[20]

BBC correspondent Paul Reynolds wrote on 28 June 2007 that West will have to live with Russia for the foreseeable future. Russia is not an enemy but is not a close friend either. It is a competitor playing by some international rules and some it has made itself. There are more voices in the West now that are calling for an understanding and accommodation with Russia. Sir Rodric Braithwaite, the British ambassador in Moscow from 1988 to 1992, wrote in his recently published book: "Russia has now to be taken in to account. It has lot of levers after years of weakness. It has come back quickly from the depth of humiliation and this makes Russians feel better. The most sensible way to look at Russia is not as an appendage of the West but as a substantial non-aligned country like China or India. We do not worry when these countries define their interest differently from ours. The Russian leadership is not seeking confrontation with the West but is seeking a basis for remaking the relationship."[21]

The United States establishment does not appear to be greatly perturbed by sharp deterioration in relations with Russia. It believes that if there are differences between the two countries, there is also area of extensive cooperation underlining shared interest. Together they have addressed the problem of nuclear programs of North Korea and Iran. On the negative side, however, they concede that the United States is concerned about the growing authoritarianism in the Russian society, its opposition to independence of Kosovo and its vehement opposition to the extension of NATO to the very borders of Russia and setting of missiles defense system in eastern Europe. As Daniel Fried, assistant secretary of state for European and Eurasian affairs told the members of the Senate: "We defend and advance our interest while building on areas of common concern, find right balance between realism about Russia and higher realism of commitment to defend and advance our values." He argued that there was a new order in which NATO's role was expanding in the former eastern bloc and the western orientation of the former Soviet republics. Russians saw this as a period of decline and chaos.[22] Fyodor Lukyanov, editor of foreign affairs journal "Russia in Global Affairs," in an interview to BBC made an apt comment on the reasons for the Russian anger. He said in Putin's eyes Russia has done a great deal for the United States, he removed military bases from Vietnam, shut down the radar station in Cuba, he did not stand in the way of the US setting bases in Central Asia. The US believes that Russia had no choice and what it did was in Russian interest any way. If it permitted the United States to establish bases in the Central Asian republics before the war led by the United States in Afghanistan began, it served Russian interest as well. After all, it had been supporting the Northern Alliance which had been pushed by the Taliban to a tiny corner. But Russia believes that all it got for its efforts was the Orange revolution in Ukraine, disputes in Georgia, NATO expansion and now these missiles sites. Had it been only a matter of a radar site in Azerbaijan and a missile interceptor site in Poland, Russia would have nothing to fear but if the idea of a global missile defense becomes a reality, it would undermine the Russian and the Chinese missile capability. There has to be a balance between the sword and the shield. The ABM treaty had established that balance. By abrogating the ABM treaty the United States signaled that it is no longer committed to that balance. Reasons enough for the Russian frustration and anger. Lukyanov added "We must be wrestling with the US or EU but there would be enormous countries on the sidelines, enjoying the spectacles. I mean China, India, and others. Of course, Russia wants to be a great power but not a super power. It wants to be a member of the elite club which sets the rules and review the rules which were drawn up when it was weak."[23]

Russia is not a super power any more but it has a vast land mass with very large resources. It may not have a global reach but it certainly has great influence along its periphery. It is a nuclear power and above all it has veto in the Security Council. Therefore, if the United States in its own interest wants to take any collective action through the United Nations it has either to take Russia along or act unilaterally or in cooperation only with its close allies. None of the later alternatives would have the legitimacy in the eyes of the international community. It has been demonstrated again and again that unilateral economic sanctions are not effective. That is why the resolution before the UN Security Council on the independence of Kosovo has been revised several times to meet Russian objections. Kosovo has declared that it would unilaterally declare its independence soon because the UN Security Council has been unable to resolve the issue. That would be the beginning of another crisis in US-Russian relations.

There were many in the United States who felt that the Soviet Union ended the Cold War because of the pressure the United States exerted on it. But that is not the way the Russians see it. They believe that they ended the Cold War not because they were militarily defeated but because they realized that their political and economic system was flawed. They abolished the Warsaw Pact, withdrew their forces within their own territory. They cooperated with the United States on issues of concern for the international community. They expected that their action would result in their acceptance as a partner by the West and more particularly by the United States. Russians are enraged that they are not being accepted as an equal partner. The present tenor of Putin's statements reflect this rising anger. Viktor Chernomyrdin, former Russian Prime Minister articulated this frustration: "Nobody awaits either Russia or Ukraine in the West. They will try to be friends with us, they will promise a lot to us but they will never declare us as their natural partners."[24]

The Russian feeling of disenchantment with the West has been growing. Even minor issues result in Russian warnings that it would review its relations. For instance, the issue of Kaliningrad. With the collapse of the Soviet Union, Kaliningrad became separated from the Russian territory. If the Baltic states join EU then Kaliningrad would be cut off from Russia. There were statements by the Baltic state that visa requirement would be introduced. . Responding to this Putin said in 2006 "What we hear today is worse than the Cold War, because it divides the sovereignty of Russia.... We will never agree to the division of Russian sovereignty." Russian Defence Minister Sergei Ivanov told a Finnish newspaper that if Baltic states joined NATO, "Russia would then be forced to review not only its own military positions but also the entire spectrum of international relations with the alliance as a whole and the mentioned Baltic state."[25] When Britain announced that it would expel four Russian diplomats because of the Russian refusal to extradite Andrei K. Lugovoi, suspected murderer of Alexander V. Litvineko, a Russian fugitive who had become British citizen, for trial in the UK, Russia warned that it would have "serious consequences". If nothing more it could end the Russian cooperation in counter terrorism. These two instances show how even something of a minor nature is turning out into major controversies.

In the last five years US-Russian relations have worsened, and in the next five years it is more likely that they would worsen even more. Russia may feel howsoever frustrated and angry with the ways the West is pushing it, yet it is unlikely that it would return to confrontation. Russia is no Soviet Union. It has no ideological confrontation with the United States. It would however strongly defend its own vital interest. In the post cold war era interests of countries are inextricably tied up. They join a number of groups instead of being part of one grand alliance. These groups are based on specific common interest. Russia still wants a relationship with the United States that would ultimately be like strategic partnership. But before that long term goal is realized it would like the United States to be more sensitive to its national interest more particularly in Eastern Europe and Central Asia.. The harsh reality is that these states having lived for decades under Soviet control want to be free of Russian dominance and are leaning towards the United States and the EU. Integration with EU or the presence of the United States in the region appears to them as an insurance of their freedom. There is thus a basic contradiction between what Russia wants from its relation with the United States and what the United States is willing to concede. The United States would prefer to see Russia as an European country like Germany or England that may occasionally define its interest differently but not claim a sphere of influence beyond its own borders. Differences can be negotiated and a compromise can be reached but accepting a sphere of influence means exclusion from an area. The US would not willingly concede an exclusive sphere of influence to Russia or even concede primacy to it in the region. It would like to be free to develop its relations with the country concerned. This contradiction is not easy to resolve especially as the Russian economy is growing at a rapid pace and it is no longer dependent on either the US or the EU. It is looking for a greater role for itself in the world. It wants to be a member of the group that formulates the rules. Nothing less than equal partnership in the management of the world affairs will satisfy Russia. The fact is that Putin's policy is approved by a very large per cent of the Russian population. And therefore it is unlikely to change even after President Putin demits office in 2008.

In the foreseeable future Russia's relations with the United States would remain in the gray area: neither, black nor white. Russia does not threaten the security of the United States and it does not want to confront it. If the United States continues to push it hard, it may not extend cooperation any longer on issues of vital interest to the West. It may signal this by gradually withdrawing from the agreements it has already entered into. It has already served notice that it is suspending its obligations under CFE treaty. It has announced its intention to have a base in the Mediterranean sea without indicating where it would have that base. The US offers assurances that the measures it has adopted are defensive and not aggressive. It wants Russia's cooperation but is unwilling to offer anything as quid pro quo.

Russia welcomes the rise of China and India and hopes that their economic prowess would lead to a multipolar world. It would like to quicken this process by deepening its relations with both these countries. After the collapse of the Soviet Union, Russia became keenly interested in being part of the European home. But after a decade and a half it is disillusioned. It now realizes that perhaps it would never be accepted as a friend or an ally of the United States and as an integral part of the West because of a lack of trust. China and India share the Russian objective of a multipolar world. Russia has patched up its differences and has forged new ties with China by selling it sophisticated weapon systems. China's relations with the United States are complex. It has areas of cooperation as well as conflict. The status of Taiwan is a constant source of tension. But their economies are more in sync. The US is the largest trading partner of China. Russia is tenth. Last year China's world trade was valued at $969.1 billion. Its bilateral trade with the US was worth $343 billion and it had trade surplus of $232.5 billion. The US cumulative investment in China was estimated at $54 billion through the end of 2005. In contrast, Russia's bilateral trade was only $30 billion. Its exports to China were worth $15.89 billion and imports $13,21 billion. Energy and commodities dominated its exports while China sold more high tech products. In 2007, Russia trade is estimated to be nearly $40 billion. Both the countries hope that in the next five years it would touch $60 to 80 billion. China uses its trade surplus on purchase of US government bonds. Dollars spent thus return to the US to finance more purchases. The spiral thus rises higher each year. Since 1995 there has not been a single year in which the trade deficit of the US with China has not increased. While China is willing to enter into bilateral agreements with Russia for the acquisition of sophisticated weapons and expanding its economic ties, it has no interest in becoming part of an anti American alliance, or take a position against it if its interests are not directly involved. It did not break rank and voted along with the United States in imposing sanctions on Iran.[26]

Russia has been paying close attention to its relations with India. In 2002 during Putin's visit the two countries set up a joint working group on terrorism. The group has already met several times. The bilateral trade has been very modest. In January-December 2002 it was just $2.1 billion. In 2003 it increased to $3.3 billion. During Putin's visit a road map was prepared to take it to $8 to 10 billion by 2010. But compared with the United State $ 18 billion and China's $6.6 billion in the same period it is still very modest. But the important point is there has been no point of contention between the two countries. There is great scope for cooperation in the area of energy. Russia is helping India in building Kundankulam nuclear power plants and is associated with the construction of Tehri hydropower plant. And if Nuclear Suppliers Group accords its approval to US-India nuclear civilian cooperation agreement, India can expect Russian entry into the Indian nuclear market in a big way. Though its investment in India may not be large, it has permitted India to invest in Sakhlin I. The Indian investment of more than $2 billion in oil industry is the largest. If Russia would move closer to India, it would find the environment much more congenial than it would in China even though India has moved closer to the United States.

As in the case of China what primarily drives India's relations with the United States is their mutual economic interest and shared interest in combating international terrorism. The United States is India's largest trading partner. Bilateral trade in 2005 was $26.8 billion. It is also India's largest investment partner with a share of 13 per cent. FDI from the US in 2005-6 was more than $5 billion. The United States is an important source of investment and technology. IT industry is forging new ties. Software exports crossed $22 billion in the same year. In 2006-07, It and BPO exports are projected to grow nearly 27-30 per cent.[27] Apart from official relations between the two countries, people to people relations consolidate the Indo-US relations. More than two million Americans of Indian origin in the US and nearly 76 thousand Indian students, largest number than from any other country, in American educational institutions serve as an underpinning of relations with the United States. During the decades of Cold War, Indian elites believed that the US opposed the emergence of India as an important player in international arena. That impression has considerably eroded. Indians are aware that the US-led war in Afghanistan and Pakistan against the militants serves India's interests. The militant groups have declared India, Israel and the United States as their primary targets.

It would be wrong to assume that a complete break up of relations between Russia and the United States is going to occur in the foreseeable future. The Bush Administration has just a few months more in office. Its approval rating is at the lowest point. But the low approval rating is because of the failure of US policy in Iraq and the Middle East and not due to policy towards Russia. Indeed, the Bush Administration policy on Russia reflects the views of American people. Therefore, the present tension in US-Russian relations may ease under the new dispensation but is unlikely to totally disappear. It would have to be taken as a fact.

India would have no interest in a wrestling match between the two, certainly not in watching it from the sidelines waiting for the outcome. It would be a matter of serious concern. India needs peace and stability in the international system so that its own development can proceed at a much faster pace. India's interest lies in maximizing its national interest, in developing closer economic, political and strategic relations with both the big powers. India has a history of closer relations with Russia. India, Russia and Iran supported the Northern Alliance against the Taliban. There is convergence of Indian and Russian interests in Central Asia. India, China and Russia are members of Shanghai Cooperation organization. Such relations would further increase if Russia turns its attention from Europe to Asia. It is the recognition of India's growing importance that every major country wants to develop closer relations with it. The US officials never tire in asserting that US relations are now better than ever before. The US is willing to walk an extra mile to accommodate India's interest as is shown in the conclusion of civilian nuclear agreement. Russia has assured of its cooperation when the agreement is placed for the approval of the 35 members Suppliers Group. India expects the United States to persuade China and Pakistan not to oppose it. Russia is equally interested in the opening of civilian nuclear market in India. What is needed is a dynamic balance in India's relations with both the countries, United States and Russia.

Notes

1. These figures have been cited by Paul Reynolds in his article in BBC on June 28, 2007.
2. .htlp://arms control.org/oct2004_07c); http;//www.spacewar.com/report/ger
3. "Europe Divided Over US Missile Defense" Spiegel On Line. March 7, 2007.
4. Full text of Putin's speech is available on http://www.mindfully.qrg/Reform 2007, Putin-43Munich.l0feb07.html.
5. (http://www.edi org./russia/johnson/2007-44-8
6. Spiegel On line, March 5, 2007.
7. The New York Times, on line June 7, 2007.
8. http://iht.articles./ap/2007/06/21/Europe/Eu-Gen-Rus.
9. http://news.bbc..co.uk/2/hi/europe/6242512.stm.
10. Indian Express, June 1, 2007.
11. Washington Post, July 3, 2007.
12. Indian Express, July 5, 2007.
13. Guardian Unlimited, 3 July 2007.
14. Kosovo has 10,887 square kilometer of territory according to the last census carried out in 1981. Its population then was 1,585,000 of which 77 per cent were Kosovo-Albanians and 13 per cent were Serbs. In 1991 Kosovo-Albanians boycotted the census. The percentage of Serb population had gone down because Serbs migrated in search of employment in a Serb dominated Yugoslavia, but Kosovo-Albanians have no place to go. Their share of the Serbs in the population was reduced to 5 from 10 per cent. After 1999 Serbs fearing reprisals from the Kosovo-Albanian majority, migrated again in search of safety. Their population fell further.

While Kosovo-Albanians are Muslims and want independence, Serbs regard Kosovo to be an integral part of Serbia as it was the seat of Serb power in the medieval period and has the sacred site of the battle where the Serbs had fought the Turks in 1387.

15. The New York Times, July 6, 2007.
16. Cato's Handbook For Congress: Policy Recommendations For the 108th Congress. Chapter on "US— Russian Relations in the Post Cold War World," www.cato.org/pubs/handbook/hb 108/hb 108-59.
17. (http://news.bbc/2/hi/ europe/62).
18. The New York Times, July 14, 2007.
19. *Ibid.*
20. News Release CFR http://www.cfr.org.publication/10020.
21. Quoted in Paul Reynolds article in BB on 28 June 2007.
22. eov/xarchieves/display.htmlpp=washfile.eng&y=20078m= Junex=20070621175427idybe ek cm o.6718495.
23. Interview on 7 June 2007 (http://news.bbc.co.uk/2/hi/europe67)
24. Cato's handbook, p. 594.
25. *Ibid.*
26. The US-China trade statistics have been compiled by the US-China Business Council.
27. US Department of State, Bureau of South and Central Asia. Background Note: India.

7

Indo-Russian Relations

Brig Chandra B. Khanduri

The Indo-Russian relations span back to the period 1947 when India gained its independence and the World began to mark it on the atlas. The non-aligned policy India adopted in a world with growing schism of the so-called 'Cold War' had little or no importance to Stalin's Russia or the Soviet Union. Although some understanding developed between the two countries, it was only in the post-Stalin era that Russia acknowledged the importance of a 'Third-World Country India' and began to develop a 'rouble-rupee' trade, assist India in infrastructural developments such as steel and coal industry, besides hydro-electric projects.

On the political side, Russian leadership salvaged the Indian position and stand on the Kashmir issue by exercise of its veto in UN Security Council more than once, to which India remained grateful. However, it was wrongly dubbed as a Russian ally, for India zealously guarded its position as a neutral nation, a leading member of the Non-aligned nations of the Afro-Asian solidarity. To NAM, India's contribution has remained steadfast and substantial. Nonetheless, it created a warm and mutually supporting 'New Delhi-Moscow Axis' as Dr. Nick Evsenkin called it.[1]

In the absence of its own indigenous industry and growing threats from Pakistan and China, the post-1962 expansion of its armed forces, India began to lean upon the Soviet Union for supply of arms and technology connected with it. The Russians obliged this country by accepting the rupee-rouble trade and loan at easy repayment terms.

Consequently, a very healthy collaboration and understanding developed between the USSR and India, which blossomed to fulsome in 1970s and lead to the signing of the Peace, Friendship and Cooperation Treaty in 1971. Largely, the success of the lightning campaign fought by the Indian armed forces stemmed from the moral and material help received from the Soviets. Besides the supply of much needed military equipment, India received from the Soviets key diplomatic support in the international fora, including the UNO. And it mattered substantially.

Moving into the fateful 1990s, the world saw the 'crumbling down' of the mighty Soviet Union, a fragmented Russia—that had shrunk its borders, that abandoned the 'Soviets' and a Russia decisively defeated by the capitalist world.[2]

It was a demoralised Russia, desperately trying to cling to the countries on its rim that comprised the Baltic, the Central Asian countries but facing a secessionist Chechnya in its heartland. Fortunately, for Russia, strong leaders like Yeltsin, Gorbachev and now Vladimir Putin have held the Russian flag flying.

India felt the impact of disintegration of the USSR, greatly. For, 70 percent of the defence inventory of arms and equipment of the Indian Armed Forces had, willy-nilly, become of the Russian-Soviet origin. The sudden drying up of this vital source threatened to turn the Indian equipment obsolescent and unserviceable. It warranted immediate search for alternative sources. Some were found but the country had to pay through its nose and yet there was no guarantee that when more was required, the hard earned foreign reserve resources would not be dried up. It was also realised, how the indigenous Research and Development had failed the country.

With crises at hand, India signed yet another treaty with Russia—the 20-year Treaty of Friendship and Cooperation in January 1993. President Boris Yeltsin and Prime Minister P.V. Narsimha Rao were the signatories. This then not only revised the flagging situation on the armament front, but also re-anchored the Indo-Russian relations afresh. The signing of a bilateral Military Technology Cooperation, a year later valid until 2010, followed.

The Appendix ('A') showing the state of India, dependence on Russia would be clear as readers peruse the major Russian equipment still held by the Indian Artillery and the Navy. The bulk of the IAF fighter and transport fleet continue to remain Russian and most of the armoured vehicles are still of the Russian origin.

In the continuing mutual friendship or patron-client arms supply relationship, a 10-bn dollar deal was signed for purchase cum joint development of SU-30 Mk I, in India. The deal will also include the licensed manufacture of T-90s tanks, the negotiations for the refitting of the Russian Aircraft Carrier GORSHKOV along with the aircraft, helicopters etc. There is a long list of major weapon platforms.

New Russian Paradigms

By 1993, when Russia woke up to new realities, the burgeoning dangers of the US 'Sole Super Power' bogey and the globalization challenges, it evolved its new strategy based on its perception of globalization and hard-nosed business proclivities:[3]

- Strengthening Russia's military-political positions in different regions of the world.
- Raising hard currency for state needs, defence conversion projects, defence production, destruction and disposal of weapons and restructuring of defence industries.
- Maintaining the required level of exports of conventional weapons and military hardware.
- Developing a scientific and experimental basis for the defence industries and their scientific research and design institutions and organisations.
- Providing social support for the personnel of industrial plants, institutions and organisations that develop and produce weapons, military and special hardware and other items.

With India, however, there was a departure from the above listed paradigms as Russia agreed to 'joint development and joint production of weapons' . It was intended to not only jointly explore the technological wherewithal but also help develop the Indian exports.

Before proceeding any further, a look at the geostrategic developments shaping the world of the 21st century may be necessary.

First and the foremost, the world is hardly 'peaceable' . There are civil wars going on in Anglo-American occupied Iraq and Afghanistan and what were expected to be 'democratically transformed countries' are dangerously heading for fragmentation.

Second, the nuclear proliferation continues with Indian and Pakistani nuclear tests, the clamour of North Korea and Iran to acquire nuclear weapons capability keeps troubling the nuclear haves.

Third, Terrorism (with capital 'T') has shown its new face since 1990s. Pak-promoted proxy war in Kashmir, militancy in Chechnya, the Islamic fundamentalism perpetrated by fundamentalist groups such as Taliban, al Qaida, and an host of such organisations have caused traumatic experiences such as '9.11', '7.7', '6.12' and so on.

On the positive side, a few more developments are reshaping the world.

- As a sequel to US domination, the concept of 'US, the Sole Super Power', the 'unipolar world', the unilateral actions by USA not only in invading Afghanistan and Iraq but extending NATO (and EU memberships) to countries on the Baltic, besides deploying anti-missile shields in Eastern Europe, Russia is adopting suitable counterpoise for a Polycentric world.
- Buoyed by its economic growth, export of gas and oil, armament industry, modernization of the Russian armed forces including strategic weapons, it is redeploying its forces in its power projections for containment of the American expansion.
- It has also developed its strategic partnership with China, thus achieving a coalition of forces for a joint stand against the Americans. The world is gradually getting into blocks - of the yesteryears of the 'Cold War' period.
- The rise of the Chinese in Asia is another factor that has distinctive features. While Russia-China are combining their stand against what they call, 'unilateralism', 'exploitation' and 'terrorism', a new forum is emerging in Asia: the strategic forum comprising Australia, Japan, India and the US. In what shape this strategic grouping blooms is yet to be seen. However, as perceived it would act as a bulwark (?) against the Chinese expansion into the Indian Ocean.[4]

Therefore, a constant coalitional activity would carry on throughout the century.

Geo-strategic Commonalities

It is imperative to appreciate the geo-strategic including the geo-political commonalities that turn our relationship on a stronger 'keel'. It is more deep-rooted than the contemplated Indo-American strategic relationship.[5] These commonalities are :

- Russia supports the Indian stand on Kashmir, terrorism, a polycentric world besides its entry as a member of UN Security Council.
- India opposes the NATO expansion to the borders of the country; it opposes NATO's deployment of BMD (Ballistic Missile Defences) in Europe.
- Both Russia and India opposed US led unilateral military actions in Iraq, Yugoslavia.
- This commonality expands to weapons, as averred. For the IAF, the range of MIG fighters and bombers and now SU-30s, the multi-role fighters, besides what appears tempting, the MIG-35s. For the Army 1,000 BrahMos have been added to its artillery, besides the MBT T-72 and T-90s.

The Continuing Link

The SU-30s supply line is based on contracts signed in 1996 and 2000. The first one was for 40 aircraft with an additional 20. In December 2000, a $3.3 billion deal was signed for the supply of 140 Su-30 MKIs to India in the next 14 years. HAL was to build the aircraft with IAPO.

In late 2000, the IAF took deliveries of the first two MiG-21Bis fighters upgraded to the MiG-21-93 configuration at Sokol. The contract worth $343 million envisaged modernization of 125 MiG 21 Bis around 2004-05.

Kazan helicopters delivered 40 Mi-17 transport helicopters to India between October 2000 and June 2001, while Kamov had signed contracts worth $108 million for supply of nine Ka-31 AEW helicopters to the Indian Navy.

For the navy, Russia delivered a number of missiles for fitting onto ships. As of the beginning of 2001, around 100 Kh-35 missiles had been delivered. Since 1998, the Uran system deliveries have commenced also for the three Brahmaputra (Project 16A) frigates. In July, Russia handed over S64 Sindhushastra, an 877EKM diesel-electric submarine with Klub-S ASMC. Concurrently, four Indian projects, 877 EKM, had been overhauled and retrofitted with the Klub-S.

Work had also been carried out on INS Talwar and INS Trishul.

Tula based KBP signed with India in 1999—a $34.5 million contract to supply 1,000 Krasnopol-M 155 mm artillery guided projectiles. The Design Bureau of Engineering or KBM of Kolomna has delivered several hundred man-portable Igla SAM systems. The biggest deal is for the supply of over 300 T-90S MBTs. Contract provided for the delivery of 124 T-90S tanks in several batches and the licensed assembly in India of 186 using Russia-provided components.

The IAF had also decided to buy the A-50EI AEW&C aircraft created round the Russian II-76MD but with installed Israeli-Phalcon-phased-array radar. (One is not sure how far this project has progressed.)

Perhaps the most significant development is the idea of leasing from Russia four Tu-22M bombers for the Indian Navy to offset refurbishment of its fleet of II-38s and Yu-142s. The Tu-22M is a strategic platform with the capability of carrying nuclear weapons. If eventually supplied, the Indian Navy will significantly increase the surveillance capabilities of the Indian Navy in the Indian Ocean region.

The other area of interest is air defence.

BrahMos Missiles

The export version is basically of the anti-ship variant of the 290-km range BrahMos, already inducted into Indian Navy. Incidentally, the land-attack, air and submarine launched versions of BrahMos are also in the pipeline for the Indian armed forces now. India is already augmenting facilities at Hyderabad to take the production of BrahMos missiles from the existing dozen or so to at least 50 per year.

This will also hope in its faster induction into the Indian forces, which have placed orders worth Rs. 3,500 crore for the missiles until now. What is interesting is that BrahMos Aerospace is even ready with the submarine-launched missile variant, which can be fired from an underwater depth of almost 60 meters. The work has centred on the Russian Amur-1650 Submarines, a frontrunner for India's second line of submarines after the French Scorpenes.

Meanwhile, with the frontline warships like Rajput-class destroyers having already been equipped with BrahMos vertical launch systems, the Army is now gearing up to induct the "precision-strike" land-attack version by converting three of its light artillery regiments into BrahMos missile regiments. Each regiment will have four mobile autonomous launchers on 12x12 Tatra vehicles and mobile command posts.

Stakes for MIG-35

In comparison with predecessors, in particular the MiG-29M2, the MiG-35 has more enhanced capabilities due to the new optical devices installed on the top and bottom of the airframe as well as on the wings' trailing edges. According to the team of MiG experts, these are part of the aircraft's self-defence system enabling it to trace hostile missiles and laser beams. Aside from the super-manoeuverability (i.e. at the high angles of attack and minimum speed), the MiG-35 also offers better three-dimensional stabilisation, which will reduce the aircraft's trimming requirements and, consequently, its fuel consumption.

These enhancements allow the aircraft's suite of guided weapons to be expanded with the addition of the Kh-31A anti-ship missiles with active radar seekers, the Kh-31 anti-radar missiles, Kh-29TE missiles and KAB-500Kr TV-guided bombs. When equipped with an external optical/laser targeting pod, the fighter can use the Kh-29L air-to-surface missiles and KAB-500 laser-guided bombs. These additions will allow the aircraft to engage aerial and land targets. Improvements have also been made to allow the MiG-35 for higher internal fuel capacity of 950 litres, through an addition of a strap-on tank behind the cockpit. The capacity of the external fuel tank suspended under fuselage has increased up to 2,000 lires. Ferry range with three external fuel tanks and two R-73 air-to-air missiles (for self-defence) has increased up to 3,100 km. with one in-flight refueling, the range will be 5,400 km. The fuel management system has also been digitized, and includes a new digital fuel metering system.

Progress on Admiral Gorshkov (INS Vikramaditya)

The 44,570 tonne Russian Carrier was paid Rs. 6,900 Crore-package deal signed in January 2004. Expected by August 2008. Getting further delayed.

Proposal to Acquire 126 Multi Role Combat Aircraft for the IAF

Decision whether to buy Su30s, F-16/F-18 or the Swedish Gripen, Russian MiG-35, the Euro-fighter or the French Rafale is under consideration. There is no doubt that the Russians would pitch in.

Future Scenario

Three factors help visualise the future Indo-Russian Defence relationship: the state of the Indian Defence Research and Development (R&D), the Russian strategy, and the Extraneous influences.

The State of Indian Defence Research and Industry

The DRDO that is responsible for R&D and the supplies has had a chequered history of miscarriages, if not total failures. Working under the MOD since its inception in 1962, it has been under the control of civilians generally bereft of understanding of the needs of the services besides their lack of sympathy and accountancy. Little wonder then, though mandated to 'enhance self-reliance in defence system through design and development of the state of-the-art weapon systems', it has not been able to meet most of its projects: Main Battle Tank (MBT), Light Combat Aircraft (LCA), the Advanced Jet Trainer (AJT) and now the Indigenous Aircraft Carrier (IAC) (due to be rolled out of the Cochin Shipyard in 2015) to name only a few yet vital projects. They have failed and floundered. Self-reliance, despite far-sighted planning is nowhere in sight. It has happened due to clear lack of political will, absence of bureaucratic and departmental accountancy, inability to adapt to the Revolution in Military Affairs, (RMA), suitable adoption of Information and Technology (IT).

It's regrettable failure was so evident even in 1999, during the Kargil War - some 37 years after the establishment of DRDO and its modernization in 1984. The country has suffered owing to the overall failure of the MOD and its bureaucracy, which lack a clear strategy.

It is inconceivable, otherwise, to think that while the civilian private industries, the IT, and availability of a pool of talented and trained personnel, nothing worthwhile has been obtained except an armed helicopter *Dhruv,* or an AJT prototype, which are yet to be accepted.

This is not decrying the progress we made elsewhere, especially in missilery. To quote the MILITARY BALANCE-2006:

"In August 2004, India carried out the third flight test of the Agni II medium-range (2,000 km) ballistic missile. It was reported that the first test of the longer-range Agni-III missile (estimated at 3,000 km) could take place in late 2005/early 2006, although this has already been postponed twice in the past two years. India reportedly started inducting its Agni I and Agni II missiles into the recently established Strategic Forces Command. Two tests of the Prithvi III short-range ballistic missile took place in October and November 2004. This test was followed by the test of a surface-to-surface version of the Prithvi II missile in May 2005. In addition, India carried out three tests of the joint Indo-Russian supersonic cruise missile, BrahMos...In mid-2005, the first Indian naval ship was fitted with the 290-km BrahMos missile; production had begun in late 2004. The BrahMos is currently being fitted alongside Russian-origin Klub antiship missile (220-300 km) on major surface warships. The air force version of the BrahMos was to begin testing in 2006, with plans for deployment on the Su-30 MKI.

"In December 2004, India and Russia agreed to protocols relating to intellectual property rights on jointly developed weapon systems (including a fifth-generation combat aircraft and a heavy multi-role transport aircraft), as well as the provision of spares and upgrades for Russian arms and equipment and technology transfers for the licensed production of the T-90 main battle tank in India. Russian investment in the joint venture BrahMos project was increased to 60% with both countries agreeing to market the missile together in third countries."

Let us hope the ad-hoc integrated headquarters and the MOD would impel the DRDO to fulfill its obligations obviating thus our leaning on foreign sources.

The New Russian Strategy cum Policy

Writing in *The Hindu* on January, 24, 2007, the Russian Foreign Minister, Sergey Lavrov, clarified the essential components of 'Russia's Foreign Policy Imperatives':

> "..Russia's consolidation has become a catalyst for positive changes... Russia made the right choice in 2000... in giving up ideology for common sense... Russia has equitable cooperation with all states. With many countries including our CIS neighbours, China, India, Egypt, Brazil, and G-8 we have established strategic partnership..."

He then goes on to say how the NATO and EU expansion had begun to 'lose flexibility and ability to achieve their fundamental goals' by trying to encircle Russia.

Of interest is the effect of the multi-vectored foreign policy that India has rightly begun to follow. Various Russian ministers who visited India during President Putin's visit to Delhi in January 2007 enumerated the effect of this policy and Russian flexibility.

The Russian ambassador at Delhi, commenting on the on-going talks on the Indo-US Strategic Partnership had said that 'while Russia would wait for negotiations between India and USA to conclude, Russia would continue to support India in the nuclear energy. Russia, he said, would construct four more nuclear power stations besides, Kudankulam (TN)'; Russia would supply 347, T-90 tanks, besides promoting the joining by the ONGC in the 'Sakhalin oil project'.

The Russian Deputy PM Serei Borisovich Ivanov said that Russia had supplied 35-bn dollar worth of defence equipment since 1962 and would remain the 'top arms supplier' to India in future. He outlined the Russian strategy of collaboration with India as he remarked,

"Now we are bringing our cooperation to a new level by moving from seller-buyer relationship to partnership in developing technologies and upgrading weapons, joint R&D, and manufacture of hardware... and take care of currency fluctuations through a joint mechanism."

Quoting him further the *Times of India* of 22 January 2007, added scientifically "India desire to pursue multi-vector foreign policy and develop mutually beneficial relations with all leading world powers, not only with the US, meets the realities of globalization era." He also welcomed India's observer status, to the Shanghai Cooperation Organisation (SCO).

Extraneous or Multi-Vectored Influences

By virtue of geography and history, the destinies of both India and Russia are rooted in diversity of culture and civilizations. It is these aspects of our existence, which encourage the seeping of multi-vectored influences, to and from, India as well as Russia. Our political system adds to this proclivity. Globalization has made further diversification possible. India's purchase of arms from Israel is outcome of these. So is the India-US Defence cooperation.

According to the Military Balance, 2006:

"In a significant development in June 2005, India and the US signed a 10-year defence cooperation framework agreement. While increasing military-to-military cooperation, including training, joint exercises and disaster response, it encourages joint weapons collaboration, co-production and R&D cooperation. For the first time, Delhi agreed to multinational military operations with the US without a UN mandate. This significant policy shift - a marked change from India's rationale in refusing to send troops to Iraq in mid-2004-appears to be the prelude to Indian participation in US-led counter-proliferation and counter-terrorism initiatives. The Indian-US nuclear deal three weeks later - whereby the two countries agreed to develop 'full civil nuclear energy cooperation' - also created better conditions for improving strategic ties. However, Pakistan has expressed concern over the transfer of missile defence technology to India.

"India actively continued its programme of naval and air exercises. In June 2005, the Indian Air Force carried out a fortnight-long joint exercise with the French Air Force (Garuda II) at the Istres base in France. In November 2005, the Indian Navy carried out its first exercises with nuclear-powered aircraft carriers - in the US Malabar-series of exercises in the Arabian Sea and the Varuna IV exercises with the French in the Gulf of Aden. For the second year running, the Indian Navy conducted exercises with a Russian naval flotilla in the Bay of Bengal (Indra exercises). The IAF carried out an exercise with the US Air Force in November. The Indian and Chinese armies were planning to hold joint counter-terrorism and peacekeeping training programmes for the first time along with a second round of bilateral naval exercises."

With these 'opening outs', India is turning into a global player and is determined to play its role actively. Russia realizes it and is therefore, following a policy that complements strategic initiatives rather than obstructs them. Like any other power it would, of course, protect its own interests and continue to promote them by remaining friendly with India. Once again, history, geography and our common interests would augment the endeavour.

FURTURE PROSPECTS OF INDO-RUSSIAN MILITARY COOPERATION-CUM-COLLABORATIONS

On January 25, 2007, India and Russia signed nine bilateral documents and adopted two more after summit talks between the visiting President, Vladimir Putin and Prime Minister, Manmohan Singh. Among the issues discussed were :

1. Joint Statement on the outcome of the official visit of Mr. Putin, signed by Dr. Manmohan Singh and Mr. Putin.

2. Programme of Cultural Exchanges between the Governments of India and Russia for the years 2007-09.
3. Protocol between the Indian and Russian Governments on holding "Years of Russia in India" in the Year 2008 and "Year of India in Russia" in the Year 2009.
4. Memorandum of Intent between the Department of Atomic Energy (India) and Federal Atomic Energy Agency (Russia) on development of cooperation in the construction of additional nuclear power plant units at Kudankulam (Tamil Nadu) site as well as in the construction of Russian design nuclear power plants at new sites in India.
5. Agreement between the governments of India and Russia on the access of the Indian Party to navigation signals of the Russian Global Navigation Satellite System GLONASS for peaceful purposes.
6. Agreement between the governments of India and Russia on access of the Indian Party to a part of the Russian Global Navigation Satellite System GLONASS Radio Frequency Spectrum.
7. Agreement between the Indian Space Research Organisation and the Federal Space Agency on cooperation in the joint satellite project 'YOUTHSAT'.
8. Protocol between the Central Board of Excise and Customs (India) and the Federal Customs Service (Russia) on exchange of information on the movement of goods and conveyances between India and Russia.
9. Cooperation Agreement between Saraf Agency Private Limited Vneshekonom Bank of Russia and Joint Stock Company Technochim Holding.

Besides, the two sides adopted two more bilateral documents - a joint statement on cooperation in the energy sector and on celebrating 60th anniversary of establishment of diplomatic relations between India and Russia, starting from April 17, 2007.

Reflections

Both the countries have remained truthful to their commitments, though shortfalls in delivery of *INS Vikramaditya* and such other defence items seem vexatious. Russia, that now possesses 25 percent of World's gas reserves, claims most of the Arctic Ocean for its mineral wealth and is deploying the Russian

Armed Forces to counter the expansion of NATO and its missile system, is a powerful country once again.

India is also well on its path of growth and increased prosperity with its GDP showing continuous remarkable growth. Its R&D too is expected to pick up and head for self-reliance, though the march is long and tedious.

Both the countries are expected to develop their relations to new high.

Notes and References

1. In *India & Russia: Rediscovering the Strategic Paradigm* (IDR 88).
2. The Russians sold some of their armory including the aircraft carriers *Kiev, Minsk* and now the *Gorshkov.*
3. The Japanese Prime Minister, Shinzo Abe, called it *"Arc of Freedom and Prosperity"* during his visit to India in August 2007.
4. *Military Technical cooperation between the CIS, Member States,* by Alexander A. Sergounin (in Russia and Arms Trade, Sipri 1998). Also Russian Military Cooperation: Structure & Processes, Strategic Analysis June 2001.
5. *The Indo-US Strategic Partnership,* also called Indo-US 123 Agreement, is intended to solve the enriched Uranium shortage that has constrained India's nuclear power programme for decades, pushing India's production to 27th position among the 30 countries using nuclear power. The political opposition to it is threatening its adoption.
6. Several references to other documents have been quoted in the text itself.

A Summary of Important Russian Equipment in the Indian Armed Forces

From Military Balance 2006

ARTY up to 12,675+

TOWED up to 5,625+

75mm 1,115: 900 75/24 mtn; 215 M-48 Tito Gun

105mm up to 1,350+

IFG 600+: 600+ Mk1/Mk2/Mk3 (being replaced)

LFG up to 700 M-56 50

122mm 550: 550 D-30

130mm 2,200: 1,200 M-46; 500 (in process of upgrading to 155mm); 500 in reserve in store

155mm • **FH-77** 410: 410 FH-77B

SP 150+

105mm 80: 80 *Abbot* in store

130mm 70: ε70 M-46 *Catapult* in store

152mm: some 2S19 *Farm*

MRL 180

122mm 150: ε150 BM-21/LRAR

214mm 30:30 *Pinaka*

MOR 6720+

81mm 5000+: 5,000+ E1

120mm 1500+: some (SP) **AM-50/E1** ε1,500 (some E1 are SP)

160mm 220: 20 M-58 Tampella; 200 in store

At (Anti-tank)

MSL: some AT-3 *Sagger* (being phased out); some AT-4 *Spigot* (some SP); some AT-5 *Spandrel* (some SP); some *Milan*

RCL • 106mm • M-40 3,000+:3,000+ M-40A1 (10 per inf bn)

84mm: some *Carl Gustav* (one per inf section)

HELICOPTERS

ASLT 12: 12 *Lancer*

UTL 150

SA-315 50: 50 HAL *Cheetah* (SA-315B) *Lama*

SA-316 100: 100 HAL *Chetak* (SA-316B) *Alouette III*

UAV: some *Nishant*

RECCE • TAC: some *Searcher*

AD

SAM 3,500+

SP 800+: 250 SA-13 *Gopher;* 180 SA-6 *Gainful*

SA-8 50+: 50+ SA-8B

SA-9 ***Gaskin*** 400

MANPAD 2,620+: 2,000+ SA-16 *Gimlet;* 620 SA-7 *Grail* (being phased out)

GUNS 2,339+

20mm • TOWED: some Oerlikon (reported)

23mm 395

SP 75: 75 ZSU-23-4

TOWED 320: 320 ZU-23-2 (some SP)

30mm • SP 24: 24 2S6 (60+ more on order)

40mm • TOWED 1,920: 1,920 L40/70

RADAR • LAND 12+: 12AN/TPQ-37 *Firefinder;* some BSR Mk.2; some *Cymbeline;* some EL/M-2140; some M-113 A1GE *Green Archer* (mor); some MUFAR; some *Stentor.*

AMPHIBIOUS • CRAFT 2:2LCVP

Navy 55,000 (incl 7,000 Naval Avn and 1,200 Marines)

Forces by Role

Navy 1 Fleet located at Mumbai (Bombay); 1 Fleet located at Vishakhapatnam.

Equipment By Type

SUBMARINES • TACTICAL • SSK 19:

2 *Kursurat* (FSU *Foxtrot*) each with 10 single 533mm TT (6 forward, 4 aft).

3 *Kursurat* in reserve (FSU *Foxtrot*) each with 10 single 533mm TT (6 forward 4 aft).

4 *Shishumar* (Ge T-209/1500) each with 1 single 533mm TT (+ 2 Types 1500 ordered locally).

9 *Sindhughosh* (FSU *Kilo*) each with 6 single 533mm TT (all *Kilos* to be fitted with SS-N-27).

1 *Sindhughosh* (FSU Type 636 *Kilo*) with 6 single 533mm TT each with SS-NX-27 *Club-S* tactical SSM.

PRINCIPAL SURFACE COMBATANTS 54

Aircraft Carriers • CV 1:

1 *Viraat* (UK *Hermes*) (capacity 30 *Sea Harrier* FRS MK51 (*Sea Harrier* FRS MKI) FGA ac each with *Sea Eagle* tactical ASM; 7 Ka-27 *Helix ASW hel / Sea King* MK42B ASW hel).

DESTROYERS • DDG 8:

3 *Delhi* (capacity either 2 *Sea King* MK42A ASW hel or 2 ALH utl hel) each with 5 × 1 533mm ASTT, 4 quad (16 eff.) each with 4 SS-N-25 *Switchblade* tactical SSM, 2 single with 24 SA-N-7 SAM, 1 100mm gun.

5 *Rajput* (FSU ***Kashin***) each with 1 Ka-25 *Hormone*/KA-28, 5 × 1 533mm ASTT, 2 Twin (4 eff.) each with 1 SS-N-2C *Styx tactical SSM*, 2 (4 eff.) each with 16 SA-N-1 *Goa* SAM, 2 RBU 6000 *Smerch* 2 (24 eff.), 276mm gun.

FRIGATES 17

FFG 9:

3 *Brahmaputra* (capacity either 2 HAL *Chetak* (SA-316B) *Alouette III* SA-316 Utl/*Sea King* MK42 ASW hel or 2 *Sea King* MK42 ASW hel) (2 awaiting full weapons fit) each with 20 SA-N-4 *Gecko* SAM, 2 triple 324mm ASTT (6 eff.), 4 quad (16 eff.) each with 4 SS-N-25 *Switchblade* tactical SSM, 176mm gun.

3 *Godavari* (capacity either 2 *Sea King* MK42 ASW hel or 2 HAL *Chetak* (SA-316B) *Alouette III* SA-316 Utl/*Sea King* MK42 ASW hel) each with 2 triple 324mm ASTT (6 eff.), 4 single each with 1 SS-N-2D *Styx* tactical SSM, 1 twin (2 eff.) with 20 SA-N-4 *Gecko* SAM.

3 *Talwar* (capacity either 1 KA-31 *Helix B* FW hel/KA-28 ASW hel or 1 ALH utl hel) (undergoing sea trials) each with SS-N-27 *Club* tactical SSM.

FF 8:

1 *Arnala* (FSU ***Petya***) with 3 × 1 533 mm ASTT, 4 RBU 2500 *Smerch* 1 (64 eff.), 476mm gun.

1 *Krishna* in reserve (UK *Leander*; trg role).

4 *Nilgiri* (UK *Leander*) each with 1 *Limbo* ASW Mor (triple), 1 HAL *Chetak* (SA-316B) *Alouette III* SA-316 Utl, 2 triple 533mm ASTT (6 eff.), 2114 mm gun.

2 *Nilgiri* in reserve (UK *Leander*) each with 1 *Limbo* ASW mor (triple), 1 HAL *Chetak* (SA-316B) *Alouette III* SA-316 utl, 2 triple 533mm ASTT (6 eff.), 2114mm gun.

CORVETTES 28

FSG 24:

4 *Khukri* each with 176mm gun, 2 twin (4 eff.) each with 2 SS-N-2C *Styx* tactical SSM, 1 hel landing platform (For ALH/*Chetak*).

4 *Kora* each with 1 quad (4 eff.) with SA-N-5 *Grail* SAM, 4 (16 eff.) each with 4 SS-N-25 *Switchblade* tactical SSM, 176mm gun, 1 hel landing platform (For ALH/*Chetak*).

6 *Veer* (FSU *Tarantul*) each with 2 quad (8 eff.) (quad manual aiming) each with SA-N-5 *Grail* SAM, 4 single each with 1 SS-N-2D *Styx* tactical SSM, 1 76mm gun.

8

Indo-Russia Defence Cooperation

Dr. Rajan Kumar

Indo-Russian defence cooperation is the mainstay of Indo-Russian relations today. The importance of defence relationship with Russia can be gauged from the fact that the expenditure on defence imports, since the late 1990s, has exceeded the spending on rest of the imports from Russia. This is largely because while India's commerce has diversified drastically, the military sector is still dependent on Russia. The dependence of the three branches of Indian military on Russian imports is so high that, despite the increasing efforts of the Ministry of Defence to diversify its defence imports, more than 2/3rd of the total military hardware is still imported from Russia. It is expected that, in the short term, India will remain dependent on Russian military exports. However, as the competition intensifies, states like Israel, France, UK and the USA are likely to apportion a large chunk of this arms trade. The growing bonhomie of India and the USA poses a serious challenge to the Russian arms exports to India. The ongoing strategic shift of India's foreign policy is likely to impinge on arms trade too.

The arms imported from Russia and other states were basically aimed to develop a minimal deterrent and protect India from Pakistan and China. This, however, also generated a perpetual arms race in the region. This paper, while focusing on defence cooperation between India and Russia, also touches upon some of these issues which remain unaddressed till today. First, it discusses the way defence cooperation, as it stands today, has been divested of any security framework. Second, it describes the defence trade between India and Russia in detail. And finally, it contends that the Indo-Soviet/Russian arms trade, though being a bulwark of the Indian defence build-up, also contributed to the arms race in the region.

Insularity of Defence Cooperation

Historically, India's 'defence cooperation' with the Soviet period was a part of the larger security and strategic cooperation framework between the two states. The Soviet Union provided unflinching support to India on its strategic issues and backed it unconditionally in international forums. Both countries were tied by an informal collective security agreement according to which Soviet Union would come automatically to India's rescue in case of crisis[1]. Further, the relations between the two countries were not just about military exchanges. The Soviet Union was the main force behind India's initial industrialization process and it also used to be the most important trading partner.

Compared to the Soviet period, the present relationship between India and Russia lacks the warmth and multiplicity of exchanges and appears lopsided. First, military imports from Russia have become the core item of trade while the total amount of non-military bilateral trade has plummeted to just about $ 3 billion dollars. Moreover, India remains the second largest importer of military hardware from Russia, even after 50 years of cooperation. There are little military exports from here to Russia or any other country for that matter. The joint development of weapons and transfer of technology has failed to make India self-reliant.

Second, the defence cooperation no longer carries the wider Soviet meaning and significance. The term 'defence cooperation' had an appropriate meaning in the Cold War period when most of the other western states were unwilling to provide crucial technologies and weapons to India. The Soviet Union 'cooperated' by providing cutting edge weapons and technologies to India when others refused. Today, the situation is different. India, unlike China, has the option of buying military goods from USA, France, Britain and other countries and this is likely to intensify further with the recent civil nuclear cooperation, the so-called 123 deal, between India and the USA. These states are willing to sell sophisticated weapons to India recognizing the potential market it offers on account of its insatiable appetite for military stockpile to fulfill its ambition of becoming the regional/global super-power and settle conflicts within and on the borders.

The defence cooperation between India and Russia today has been stripped of its strategic umbrella and it is surviving because of India's compulsion and Russia's shrinking choices elsewhere. Abhijit Bhattacharya argues that the present Russo-Indian defence mechanism is a "revival of the traditional marriages of convenience and realpolitik of Kremlin and South Bloc. Russia needs a steady market in the unsteady world of shrinking consumer base. For India it is a compulsion borne out of limited choice coupled with the fact that a major percentage of the equipment is of Russian origin."[2]

Russia's supply of weapons to India is determined not by geopolitics but by market conditions. The strategic advantages that accrued to India during the Soviet period, such as cheap prices, rupee-rouble barter and so on, no longer exist. The value of arms and weapons are determined by market conditions and 'geopolitical concessions' have become the things of past. The defence cooperation between India and Russia has been divested of any security framework.

In the recent years, however, some attempts have been made to revive the traditional cooperation, especially under the Putin administration. One positive outcome of this on defence is that several joint developments of defence projects have been initiated.

Preeminence of Defence Trade

It would not be an exaggeration if we say that the defence trade forms the backbone of Indo-Russian relations. This significance of defence trade can be better understood if we compare that with non-defence bilateral trade and see how the defence trade takes precedence over other trade.

Bilateral Trade: A Drop in the Ocean

The non-military cooperation of India and Russia today presents a very dismal picture. The total amount of trade between India and Russia in 2006 was just about 3 billion dollars. This can be seen in a better perspective if we compare this figure with the Sino-Indian trade. The trade with China, which was not even a billion dollar a few years back, is approximately 25 billion dollars today and is estimated to get doubled in the next 3 years. The trade of India with the USA was approximately 32 billion dollar.[3]

Bilateral Trade in US $ Billion

Year	*Indian Exports*	*Indian Imports*	*Turnover*
1990-91	3.5	1.7	5.20
2002-03	.69	.58	1.28
2003-04	.70	.95	1.67
2004-05	.59	1.2	1.8
2005-06	.74	2.02	2.76

Source: DGCI & S (Russian State Statistics).

Russian and Indian plan is to increase trade to $ 10 billion by 2010. ONGC Videsh Limited (OVL) has invested $ 2 billion in the Sakhalin-I oil block. India should raise the demands for stakes in Sakhalin-Ill, IV, V and VI fields when they are opened up[4]. The head of Centre for Indian Studies of the Russian Academy, Oriental Studies Institute, Tatiana Shaumian rightly remarked, "I am ashamed even to talk about the Russia-India trade.. .what is $ 3 billion expected in 2006"[5].

Defence Trade: Can't Do Without

The Indian defence sector is highly dependent on Russian defence supplies. 12 out of 16 Indian Navy submarines are of Russian origin[6]. Its five destroyer of Kashin II class and three Krivak III class frigates are of Russian origin. The $625-675 million cost giant ship of Russia, ex-Russian-Admiral Gorshkov (Indian designation Vikramaditya), will join Indian Navy in 2008 or later. The Indian Air Force (IAF) is equally dependent on Russia; 32 of the 41 fighter squadrons are of Moscow origin, consisting of MIG-21, 23, 27, 29 and Sukhoi-30 MKI[7]. Rest of the Indian fleet consists of three Mirage-2000s and six Jaguar squadrons. In army, Russian T-72 and T-90 models constitute 60 percent of the 4168 main battle tanks with the various battlefields transport and logistics system. In 2001-05, exports to China and India accounted for 43 and 25 percent of Russian deliveries respectively.

Purchase of Major Arms and Weapons

The following chart provides a description of India's orders of major weapons since 2000. This has been adapted from the SIPRI Arms Transfer Database, 2007.

List of Major Arms and Weapons Purchased by India since 2000[8]

Total Number Ordered	*Weapon Designation*	*Weapon Description*	*Year of Deliveries*	*Details*
1440	9M120 Vikhr/AT-16	Anti-tank missile	2002-04	For Mi-17 helicopters
40	Mi-8/Mi-17/HIP-H	Helicopter	2000-01	$170 million deal
140	Su-30MK/Flanker	FGA aircraft	2004-06	$3-5.4 billion deal. To be supplied till 2014-15
310	T-90s	Tank	2001-05	$600-700m deal in reaction on Pakistani acquisition of 320 T-80UB tanks
3000	NM133 Kornet/AT-14	Anti-tank missle	2003-06	1.5 billion Rs. deal
1	Gorshkov	Aircraft Carrier	Not Yet	Ex-Russian; $625-675 million deal. Indian designation Vikrmaditya; delivery 2008 being delayed further
28	2S6M Tunguska	Mobile AD system	Not Yet	$ 400 million deal
300	NM311/SA-19 Grison	SAM	Not Yet	9M311 (SA-N-11) version for Kashtan CIWS on Gorshkov aircraft carrier
2	Akula-2	Nuclear Submarine	Not Yet	$700 million or $1.4 billion deal. Delivery 2007-09
28	BM-9A52 Smerch	MRL	2006-08	$450-500m deal. Russia refused technology
16	MiG-29SMT/Fulcrum	FGA aircraft	Not Yet	$700-740m deal. MiG&29K version inclusive 4MiG-29 KUB; for use on Gorshkov. Delivery 2007-09. Option of 30 more aircraft
28	3M-54E1 Klub/SS-M-27	Anti-ship missile	Not Yet	$182m deal. For kilo submarines

Total Number Ordered	*Weapon Designation*	*Weapon Description*	*Year of Deliveries*	*Details*
80	Mi-8/Mi-17/Hip-H	Helicopter	Not Yet	$660m deal. Mi-17 version. Delivery 2007-08
18	Su-30MK/Flanker	FGA aircraft	Not Yet	Su-30 MKI version exchanged for 18 Indian Su-30K; replacing original planned modernization of Su-30 K to Su-30 MKI
300	T90s	Tank	Not Yet	$866m deal. Part of $2.5b deal; option on some 700 more; assembled in India; delivery 2007-08-2010
3	Talwar/Krivak-4	Frigate	Not Yet	$1.2b deal. Russian designation type-1135.6; ordered due to problems with Indian production of major warships. Delivery 2011-12.

Source: SIPRI Arms Transfer Database, 2007.

Recently, India signed a deal to purchase 347 more T-90s main battle tanks, 40 more Sukhoi-30MKI air dominance fighters and 80 more Mi-17 medium lift utility and assault helicopters from Russia [9]. India is not only purchasing 40 Sukhoi-30MKIs, with a cost of $ 40 million a piece, but also plans to expedite the production of 140 such aircrafts at Nashik by 2013-14 at a total cost of $ 4,809 million. This was originally scheduled to be produced by 2017-18 but the Cabinet Committee on Security permitted its early production and induction[10]. India already possesses 190 such jets contracted through two big deals in 1996 and 2000. The IAF operates around 50 multi-role Sukhoi-30 MKIs from Pune, Bareilly and Halwara[11]. Sukhoi-30MKIs will have a cruising speed of 3,200 km along with advanced beyond visual range combat capabilities. The Indian SU-30 combat aircraft displayed a surprising superiority over US F-15C aircraft in the Indo-US exercise in 2004.[12]

Indian Air Force brought an international tender for 126 MTAs. Russia is lobbying for its MiG-35 for the IAF's 6.5 billion contract. Other competitors for this are American F-16 and F/A-18, French Rafale, Swedish JAS-39 Gripen and the European Consortium's Typhoon.

Joint Development of Military Aircrafts and Cruise Missiles

The joint development of aircrafts and missiles indicate a significant shift in defence relationship. India and Russia no longer have a buyer-seller relationship and have successfully transformed to a juncture where they are jointly involved in the R&D and development projects. MTA is another area of joint development. Indian Defence Minister, A K Antony also pointed out that MTA would also be developed for the use by both countries and selling them to the third countries for commercial purposes[13]. This shift in relationship has taken place mainly due to the fact that India is no longer interested in just buying the weapons. It wants technology. It can buy weapons from many other countries and Russia is not the only option as it used to be during the Cold War years. Stiff international competition has pushed Russia to offer licenses and joint production mechanism rather than just weapons.

India and Russia agreed for the joint development of the fifth generation fighter plane. This fifth generation project alone may require India to invest around Rupees 5000 crores[14]. India is planning to spend $30 billion in the 11th plan (2007-2012). Russia was especially keen for the funding of its Sukhoi's fifth generation fighter aircraft.[15] Fifth generation of Sukhoi would be comparable to American F-35 Lightning-II Joint Strike Fighter project. It has also been reported that India has taken the final decision and has agreed to fund this fifth generation Sukhoi project which will have a unique configuration of a lethal mix of stealth, beyond visual range combat capabilities, reduced radar tracking signature, super manoeuverability and supersonic cruising capability[16]. The only operational Generation-5 fighter in the world at present is the American F/A 22 Raptor, which comes at $258 million apiece.

The two main competitors for collaborating with India on developing the fifth generation aircraft were Russian corporations. India chose PAK-FA design of Sukhoi Design Bureau against the MiG Corporation which was advocating its own fifth generation design[17]. MiG's Russian competition is the Su-30. The Indian Air Force already possesses 140 Su-30s. Air experts believe that Sukhois outperform MiGs on several counts. While the MiG-35 has a range of about 4000 km, the Su-30MKI, with its refueling capacity can fly up to 10 hours with a range of 8000 km[18]. The Su-30s are also almost three times heavier than their rival. They also have the capacity for air-to-air refueling which MiGs do not have. The MiG 35 is basically seen as a light combat aircraft that could prove useful for ground attacks, air and area defence and point defence while Sukhois are multi-role fighters. By choosing the Sukhoi PAK-FA fighter for the fifth-generation project, India has showed its inclination to go in for a heavier fighter that has the financial backing of Russia[19]. The MiG's own fifth generation is an unofficial one and does not have funding from the government of Russia. The fighter in the 20-tonne class, will have the ability to use beyond visual range weapons and will carry weapons inside it to give it the ability to supercruise fly at supersonic speeds without using afterburners. But for MiGs, as S. Krishnaswamy, the former Air Chief Marshal, says, "you don't need radars to pick a MiG29 in the air-just look for that black smoke"[20]. The MiG 35 is said to be the old wine in a new bottle which uses RD-33MK engine and has an enhanced fuel capacity that gives it a longer range.

The production of BrahMos is being projected as the most successful example of the joint venture in defence between the two states. BrahMos flies at a speed of 2.8 Mach, which is almost three times the speed of sound and the new BrahMos will have a speed of 5 to 7 Mach[21]. All other cruise missiles at present in the world are sub-sonic[22]. According to G. Leonov Alexander, first Deputy Director General of NPO Mashinostroyenia, the Russian partner in the BrahMos Aerospace joint venture, both the countries are planning to sell 1000 BrahMos supersonic cruise missiles to friendly countries like Malaysia, Chile, South Africa, Kuwait and UAE[23]. This export version would be the anti-ship variant of the 290 km range BrahMos, presently inducted into Indian Navy. This will be the first real export of cutting edge military technology from India which has been mainly an importing country.

India itself placed orders worth Rupees 3500 crores for the BrahMos missile. The submarine version of BrahMos missile can also be launched from an underwater depth of almost 60 metres. A test of BrahMos with Russian Amur-1650 submarines, a second line of Indian submarine after the French Scorpenes, showed a promising outcome. Russian Amur is the first diesel submarine to have vertically launched strike missiles, according to BrahMos

Aerospace chief A Sivanthanu Pillai[24]. Rajput class destroyer has also inducted BrahMos missiles. Three artillery regiments of Indian Army will be trained exclusively as BrahMos missile regiments. The work on air-launched version of this missile will be completed by 2008, according to BrahMos board of Directors, A Dergachev Alexander[25].

S. Krishnaswamy, the former Chief of Air Staff, Indian Air Force, however, has pointed out some of the problems in the joint development project. He argues that BrahMos missiles have been inducted in the Indian Navy but there is no clear report on Russian buying this missile for their own purposes[26]. If India is to emerge as a major power in its own right we need to work hard at building capabilities indigenously. The impenetrable Russian walls need to be recognized[27].

S. Krishnaswamy has also expressed some concerns about the actual involvement of Indians in the joint development of the fifth generation fighter aircraft[28]. He argues that "India can at best only be a partner in funding and a partner in risk-sharing. Besides details of the programme have never been shared with India. The term fifth generation has no meaning unless the capability, performance, design, structure and material, sensors, weapon systems, survivability are known.[29]" He further says that in earlier such projects, there have been several bottlenecks. First, Russia objected on the usage of Russian software and electronic subsystems on Indian machines whereas total transparency was demanded on Indian software. Second, similar guarantees given for the MiG-21 BIS upgrade and SU-30 MKI were not fulfilled. Third, Russian security laws prohibit Indians from working in high security projects. Indians are not allowed to participate or work in the laboratories or at flight test and evaluation centres in Russia.

A recent comptroller and auditor general report also questioned the 2000 contract for the licensed production of 140 Sukhoi-30 MKIs by Hindustan Aeronautics Ltd at Nashik[30]. He pointed out that the average cost of a HAL-manufactured Sukhoi-30 MKI is likely to be Rs. 28.60 crore more than that of the same fighter imported from Russia.

Complains of Unreliability and Delay

India has complained about the unreliability of some of the Russian weapons and also delayed product support. The defence ministry complained about the poor performance of Appassionata navigation system for the 10 kilo or Sindhugosh-class 877 EKM submarines and a large number of subsonic anti-ship cruise missiles in the Indian army[31]. The IAF complained about the distortions on the canopies of the Sukhoi-30MKI Phase -3 fighter jets[32]. This comes at a time when India is on the verge of signing a multi-billion deal for the development of the 5th generation of Sukhoi aircraft. There are also concerns about the irreparability of a number of missiles and undue delay in their induction. Again the quality of Russian arms has also been questioned. Only 1 percent Russian arms producers meet the international quality standard ISO 9000, a common standard for western producers[33].

Delay in defence supplies is another concern for India. For instance, it has been reported now that the induction of the Russian aircraft carrier Admiral Gorshkov (Indian designation - INS Vikramaditya) will not be possible before 2010. Initially, this 44,570-tonne carrier was supposed to be ready by August 2008, as per the Rs 6,900 crore deal signed with Russia in January 2004.[34]

Growing Competition for Indian Defence Market

Recognizing the ever-growing arms market, many other countries have joined the race. In recent years, Israel has emerged as the second largest supplier of weapons to India. India subscribed defence products from Israel worth $1 billion every year for the last few years. India registers an annual sale of around $1.5 billion from Russia and according to a senior Israeli official, out of a total Israeli sale of around $4.5 billion in 2006, India bought worth $ 1.5 billion defence goods in 2006[35]. Israel has supplied Barak-I antimissile defence system, Green Pine early warning radars, three Phalcon AWACS (airborne warning and control systems), Searcher and Heron UAVs (unmanned aerial vehicles) and several high-tech systems[36]. A $350 million joint project to develop the Barak next-generation anti-missile defence system with an increased range of about 60 km from the present 9 km range of the Barak-I system fitted on several Indian warships, has also been proposed[37].

Israel has become so important as an arms supplier that the UPA government refused to blacklist IAI and Rafael, two military supplies companies, even after CBI registered a case alleging kickbacks in the Rs. 1,160-crore Barak-I deal, which was signed during the previous Vajpayee-led NDA government in October 2000.[38] IAI is engaged in other projects and the most important include $1.1 billion deal signed in 2004 for three Phalcon AWACS. The Phalcons help in tracing hostile cruise missiles and low-flying aircrafts. The main Israeli companies involved with India are Israeli Aircraft Industries (IAI), Elbit System, Rafael, Tadiran Communications and Orbit Technology Group[39].

Arms Supply to India, Pakistan and China from Various Countries (US $ Million), 2000-2004[40]

Supplier Countries	*India*	*Pakistan*	*China*
Russia	6649	180	11112
France	303	510	33
Israel	179		36
Ukraine	173		409
USA	40	113	

Source: SIPRI Year Book 2005.

Apart from Israel, France, the USA, UK and Ukraine are other major suppliers of the weapons. It is being argued that with the growing proximity of India with the USA, as reflected in the recent 123 civilian nuclear cooperation, the Russian dominance may come under stiff competition. If the USA can supply nuclear fuel and technology to India, there is no reason why will it not supply 5th generation fighter aircraft (F/A 22 Raptor) or other missile technology. Other countries will also open up accordingly. The USA regards India as a strategic partner and is willing to sell large numbers of weapons to India. US engines have been ordered for the Tejas combat aircraft and for the Shivalik frigate. The US engine will be used on the ADS aircraft carrier[41]. There are reports that Lockheed Martin has offered to sell India F-35 aircraft for the future it buys F-16 for its multi-billion bid. But India did not show interest in F-16 because Pakistan possesses the same aircraft. An unfortunate outcome of all this, however, is that the whole of South Asia and China will witness a resurged arms race incurring massive social costs.

Spiraling Arms Race and Social Costs

The region of South Asia is already engulfed in a spiral of arms race. The purchase of arms by India is followed by similar purchases by Pakistan. There is a direct triangular arms race between India, China and Pakistan. India in its ability to catch up with China is investing huge amount of money on military expenditure. China is chasing USA and investing around 50 billion dollars every year. The following list shows the military spending of various countries in 2006.

State's Military Spending in US $ in 2006[42]

Country	*Spending in Billion Dollars*	*Spending Per capita*	*World Share (%)*	*Rank at constant Prices*	*Rank in PPP $ terms*
USA	528.7	1756	46	1	1
UK	59.2	990	5	2	5
France	53.1	875	5	3	6
China	49.5	37	4	4	2
Japan	43.7	341	4	5	8
Russia	34.7	244	3	7	4
India	23.9	21	2	10	3

There are two factors which are pushing India and China for heavy militarization. Both the countries nurture the dream of becoming the super-power in the early 21st century. With their GDP growing steadily, they feel confident that this is possible within the next 30 years. Hence, military modernization has become an important agenda of these governments. Further, both the countries are facing crisis within the territory as well as on the borders. China feels contained by the US presence in Taiwan, South East Asia, Japan and South Korea and thus tries to strengthen its military. On the other hand, India feels threatened, under the shadow of 1962 defeat, as China becomes stronger militarily. The result is more militarization in India. It displays a typical case of security dilemma and if we include the case of Pakistan, the security dilemma takes a triangular shape. The staggering military spending of China, India and Pakistan as presented in the chart clearly shows this.

Arms Purchase by India, China and Pakistan (Million US dollars), 2000-2004

Rank/Recipient	*2000*	*2001*	*2002*	*2003*	*2004*	*2000-04*
1 China	1797	3018	2586	2038	2238	11677
2 India	598	899	1671	2983	2375	8526
10 Pakistan	144	354	559	617	344	2018

In all three countries of China, India and Pakistan, the level of poverty and illiteracy is very high. The health sector is in poor shape. India's FDI in 2006-07 of around $16 billion was much less than the defence expenditure of about $24 billion in the same period[43]. The increase on defence in the budget of 2006-2007 was a huge 7 percent or 890-billion rupee ($US20 billion). This comes on top of a 7.8 percent increase last year and a huge 17.9 percent rise in 2004. This year 374 billion rupees or over 40 percent of the increased outlay is on new military hardware to expand and "modernise" the Indian armed forces[44]. Compared to the planned increase in defence spending, the government's "pro-poor" initiatives pale into insignificance. The combined rise for education and health spending amounts to less than half the defence increase[45]. On the UN Human Development Index, India is placed 127 out of 177 countries for the third consecutive year due to poor education and health standards.

The region of South Asia is in the vortex of complex arms race regionally and globally. The military expenditure increased most in the region of South Asia in 2004 where spending increased by 14.3 percent in real terms[46]. The main factor behind the strong increase in South Asian military expenditure was massive increase in India's defence budget. This increase reportedly reflects India's ambition to play the role of a regional leader rather than being directly connected to the ongoing tensions in Kashmir conflict[47].

Russia's Contribution to Arms Race

Russia's contribution to this arms race can be gauged from the fact that Russia has a near monopoly on arms transfers to China, supplying 95 percent of China's imports and accounting for 41 percent of Russia's export[48]. Russia is being forced to give China its most advanced technologies and it will remain a major supplier of weapons to China at least in the short term. In the period 2000-2004, India was the second largest recipient of major conventional weapons. It constituted 10 percent of the total global import and

25 percent of Russia's export. India's 78 percent of total arms imports come from Russia[49].

Major Russian Arms Export to Various Countries (Million Dollars, Constant Prices), 1997-2006[50]

	1997	*1998*	*1999*	*2000*	*2001*	*2002*	*2003*	*2004*	*2005*	*2006*	*Total*
India	1129	427	796	479	720	1475	2181	1746	956	1225	11134
China	628	166	1446	1718	3037	2429	1996	2697	3593	3114	20824
Pakistan						99		81			180
Iran	241	259	250	330	355	322	336	264	264	816	3437
Algeria			84	253	377	96	143	230	86	105	1374

Source : SIPRI Arms Transfer Database, 2007.

However, Russia is not alone which contributes to arms race in South Asia. The USA, France, UK are other suppliers which are significantly contributing to this arms race directly or indirectly. A detailed description is beyond the scope of this paper.

Conclusion

Indo-Russian defence trade constitutes the most vital component of bilateral relations. The high dependence of Indian defence sector on Russia is likely to continue for at least one more decade. However, this dependence will gradually diminish as other states such as Israel and the USA start claiming a good share of it in the next few decades. India's growing proximity with the USA is likely to result in closer defence cooperation between the two countries. This will pose a serious challenge to Russian defence supplies.

As the USA produced weapons become more accessible to India, the neighboring countries will also look for alternative sources of defence supplies. An inevitable outcome of this whole process would be a regenerated arms race. All the countries in the region, therefore, will have to shell out a huge chunk of scarce resources to maintain parity with each other. Overspending on military at the cost of education, employment and health can be counterproductive.

References

1. Alexander O. Ghebhardt, "The Soviet System of Collective Security in Asia", *Asian Survey,* Vol. 13, No. 12. (Dec. 1973), pp. 1075-1091. Soviet-Indian Friendship and Cooperation Treaty in 1971 was interpreted by the Soviet experts as the most important step of erecting a collective security system in whole Asia.

2. Abhijit Bhattacharya, *The Pioneer,* 15 Feb, 2007.
3. US Census Bureau statistics available at http://www.census.gov/foreign-trade/balance/c5330.html
4. *Times of India,* 26 Jan, 2007.
5. Dmitri Kosyrev, *Pioneer*, 18 Dec, 2006.
6. *Ibid.*
7. *Ibid.*
8. SIPRI Arms Transfer Database, 2007. Available at http://armstrade.sipri.org/. Accessed on August 12, 2007.
9. *Times of India*, January 25, 2007.
10. *Times of India,* 9 February, 2007.
11. *Ibid.*
12. *SIPRl Year Book 2005,* OUP, 2005.
13. *Times of India,* January 25, 2007.
14. *Times of India,* January 25, 2007.
15. *Ibid.*
16. *Ibid.*
17. http://www.my-india.net/n/a/arc3-2002.shtml
18. Manu Pubby, 'Dog Fight', *Indian Express,* February 4, 2007, http://www.indianexpress.com/sunday/story/22423.html.
19. *Ibid.*
20. S. Krishnaswamy, 'Growth Engine', *The Indian Express*, February 4, 2006. available at http://www.indianexpress.com/sunday/story/22423.html.
21. *The Times of India*, Jan 25, 2007.
22. *Ibid.*
23. *The Times of India*, Jan 24, 2007.
24. *Ibid.*
25. *Ibid.*
26. *Indian Express,* January 27, 2007.
27. *Ibid.*
28. *The Indian Express,* 26 January, 2007.
29. *Ibid.*
30. *Ibid.*
31. *Times of India*, February 17, 2007.

32. *Ibid.*
33. *SIPRI Year Book 2005*, OUP, 2005.
34. *Times of India*, August 10, 2007.
35. *Times of India*, February 9, 2007.
36. *Ibid.*
37. *Ibid.*
38. http://timesofindia.indiatimes.com/Israel_sneaks_to_No_2_spot_as_arms_supplier/articleshow/1581346. cms.
39. *Ibid.*
40. *SIPRI Year Book 2005*, OUP, 2005, pp. 402-421.
41. *SIPRI Year Book 2005*, OUP, 2005, p. 426.
42. Available at http://armstrade.sipri.org/. Accessed on 12 August, 2007.
43. For FDI see http://www.ibef.org/economy/fdi.aspx. For military expenditure see http://armstrade.sipri.org/. Both the web-sites accessed on August 15, 2007.
44. Sarath Kumar, India's "pro-poor" budget boosts military spending and market reformshttp://www.wsws.org/articles/2006/mar2006/indi-m06.shtml
45. *Ibid.*
46. SIPRI Year Book 2005, OUP, 2005, p. 309.
47. SIPRI Year Book 2005, OUP, 2005, p. 311.
48. *Ibid.*
49. *Ibid.*, 425.
50. SIPRI Arms Transfer Database, 2007. Trend Indicator Value of Arms export from Russia, 1997-2006.

9

Russia and India : BrahMos Reaffirms Faith

Ranjana Mishra

Introduction

India and Russia have a long tradition of friendship. Russia has been a trusted supplier of weapons and defense systems to India for many years. Both countries share a credible sense that they are rising on the tide of history. When the Soviet Union collapsed in December,1991, both sides became preoccupied with internal economic issues: Russia with its chaotic decline and consequent transformations and India with pursuing reforms to stimulate economic growth by coming out of the socialist shackles that had fettered its own economy. Now both nations have emerged from those transitions stronger and more confident than they have been ever before. Thus they came together to lay the foundation of their future ties. Russia was pitching its MiG-35 and Delhi was diversifying its sources of weapons procurement that marked a significant change in policy direction. Sweden's JAS-39 Gripen, France's Rafale fighter, and the American F/A18 Super Hornet or F-16 planes were all contenders for the contract. In the backdrop of such intense competition to sell fighter planes to India, President Putin's agenda was to ensure Russia's position as India's main arms supplier. With a view to maintaining the Russian status quo, he offered more than just weapons for sale. Russia was willing to transfer to India hitherto inaccessible technology and bring India closer to a strategic partner in many new projects. The Russian Defence Minister Sergei Ivanov had said that should India sign up for MiG-35, India might be allowed to build and maintain the engines for the MiG-35. India would also participate in the production of a new stealth fighter being planned by Russia.

For a long time now, both countries have been working together to make the BrahMos missile system viable, and ahead of President Putin's arrival in 2000, a deal was signed that provided to give India the blueprints to make engines for its existing MiG-29 fighters, and a memorandum on the joint development of a new military transport aircraft. All ambitious plans that were drawn by Russia and India to jointly design, develop and manufacture high-tech weapons systems bore fruit, when India announced that it had conducted a successful test of its BrahMos supersonic cruise missile. The BrahMos derives its name from two mighty rivers in both countries: Brahmaputra in India and Moscow in Russia. BrahMos Private Limited was established on the basis of an intergovernmental agreement signed by Moscow and New Delhi in 1998. And this was the first of a series of joint ventures India and Russia intend to launch for production of military hardware.

G. Parthasarathi senior, who started his diplomatic career in Moscow, and was one of the last three persons alive, who were witness to the final discussions in Moscow of the famous Indo-Soviet Treaty of August 1971 told *rediff.com* that "President Putin has reasserted Russian influence in its neighborhood, rolled back or contained NATO influence in his neighboring countries and made it clear that Russia would act decisively if its vital interests were threatened. He said that Putin had made sure that on the world stage now, Russia could not be ignored. He averred that in the UN and elsewhere Russia was slowly but surely making it clear that whether it was in the Middle East, Iran or North Korea, its role could not be ignored. Putin had shown particular interest in deepening the strategic partnership with India and had resolutely backed India's position on developments in its neighborhood. The joint venture of BrahMos would be a strengthening factor between the two nations[1]. The BrahMos is the only operational supersonic cruise missile in the world and other nations were yet to acquire such a missile. BrahMos was indeed the most important milestone in Indo-Russian cooperation. The project would open up new vistas in our existing relationship with Russia in other areas as well. This was acknowledged by Dr. Manmohan Singh at the BrahMos Aerospace complex in Delhi cantonment. Singh admitted that with successful strategic partnership, a new meaning from this magnificent project had branched out to joint design, development and production between the two countries.[2]

Russian-Indian joint venture BrahMos Aerospace Private Limited, founded in 1998, was engaged in developing and manufacturing of Supersonic Anti-Ship Cruise Missile of the same name. With a joint contribution of $250 million allocated to the creation of this missile-system, Russia shared $122 million, and

India $128 million. The share holdings of the firm were divided in the same fashion in tune with their contribution. The Russian side was responsible for creation of hardware and missiles itself. India created the computerized control systems of this missile. More than ten thousand specialists worked on the creation of BrahMos in India alone. Russian planes Su-30 MKI are being refitted in India for installment of these missiles. A volley of three BrahMos may destroy a Frigate Class ship. And for the first time BrahMos was presented to public in August 2001 within the framework of the International Aerospace exhibition MAKS-2001 in Moscow. The second testing was made in April 2002, the third in February 2003 from one of the Indian military ships in the Indian Ocean. A total of six successful tests were conducted - the last one being in November, 2004 in the Bay of Bengal area. All this shows that the missile fully complies with declared technical characteristics.[3]

A Peep into the Past

Historically, a conjunction of three pillars strengthened the intimacy of Indo-Soviet ties. They are political, military, and economic interests. Friendly relations between the people of USSR and India, established in the common struggle against imperialism, for national freedom, and social progress during the first half of the 20th century, have developed into multifaceted and forceful relationship between the two countries. The relationship flourished in post-independent India. The feudal system was being dismantled and the Soviet Union succeeded in repelling fascist aggressors and compelled the building of a developed socialist society in that country.[4] The Soviet achievements in the midst of under-development were an emulative model for Nehru's India. The USSR had played a pivotal role in helping India establish her defence industry as opposed to American apathy or even hostility in this regard. An analytical review of the historical background would indicate that in the wake of United States military aid to Pakistan, Sino-Russian confrontation, Indo-US estrangement, Sino-US quasistrategic alliance, Sino-Pak strategic nexus, US-Pak military Alliances, and Russia's need to reach out to the Third World through India as a leading nation helped or spurred the forging of the India-Russia relationship.[5] The Soviet Union offered credit lines, technology and experts for establishing and expanding Indian military infrastructure after 1955. From 1959 India had accepted Soviet offers of military sales. Indian acquisition of Soviet military equipment was important because purchases were made against deferred rupee payments: a major concession to India, which suffered from a chronic shortage of foreign exchange in those years. In early November, 1959, the two countries signed the first agreement providing for the Soviet sale to India of eight more AN-12 transfort planes and MI-4 helicopters for the purpose of developing communication system near the Indo-Tibetan borders.[6] The proximity between the two countries led at times to India being labeled as a Soviet satellite.[7] A breakthrough was made in this direction when Moscow agreed to collaborate in the manufacturing of its MiG 21 fighter plane in India in August 1962. A Soviet technical team arrived in India to help the Indian government in setting up the factories for the manufacture of MiG fighters and guided missiles. By the end of the year projects were completed for the airbase factory at Nasik, Maharashtra, an engine factory at Koraput in Orissa and a factory at Hyderabad in Andhra Pradesh to produce air-to-air missiles and radar equipments. That followed the signing of another agreement providing for the Soviet delivery to India of an unspecified number of MiG-21s, light and heavy tanks, heavy artillery suited for mountain fighting and long and medium range guns and missiles for India's defence against China. The Chinese communists bitterly reacted to the Soviet arms aid to India and claimed that "massive military aid to India had now opened a new chapter of collaboration" between the Soviet Union and the United States to ally India against China.[8] Implementation came only a couple of years later. Nehru obtained a Soviet commitment of neutrality on the India-China border disputes and war of 1962.[9] In 1965 clashes between India and Pakistan erupted into full-scale war in August. Moscow stayed officially neutral, but continued to supply arms to India. Washington, like Moscow, intending to unite India and Pakistan against China, encouraged Kosygin to play his role. Soviet Premier Alexei N. Kosygin went further by offering his good offices for a negotiated settlement, which took place at Tashkent on January 10, 1966.[10] When relationship between Moscow and Beijing deteriorated to armed clashes in 1969, Brezhnev called for a collective Asian security system and economic grouping to contain China. As Pakistan-China relations improved, Washington developed a Sino-America détente and India came closer to the USSR.

From the mid 1960s, Moscow emerged as India's most important defence supplier. During 1965-69, the Soviet Union supplied 80 percent of all defence equipments to India. Within the coincidental convergences of their separate interests, Moscow and New Delhi concluded a Treaty of Peace, Friendship, and Cooperation in 1971.[11] By this time, India was on the brink of war with Pakistan, now supported by both China and the United States. When Pakistan attacked India in December 1971, beyond military assistance, Moscow coordinated its support for India in three obvious ways: first, warning China to remain out of the conflict, secondly, deploying Soviet warship in the Bay of Bengal to deter demonstrative force of U.S. Naval ship Enterprise; and thirdly vetoing a resolution in the United Nations Security Council whereby the U.S. called for Indian troops withdrawal.[12] The revolt in East Bengal unleashed pent up forces. The Nixon government brushed aside Mrs. Gandhi's request to halt arms supplies to Pakistan. His policy was vehemently criticized by his own ambassador to India, Chester Bowles as *immoral.*[13] Communist China also gave full support to Pakistan and reminded New Delhi that the slaughter of the East Bengal population was a domestic affair of Pakistan. A few days after the conclusion of the Treaty of Peace, Friendship and Cooperation with India, the Soviet Union witnessed the formation of a Sino-American-Pakistan axis that created an ominous scenario, full of risks and incalculable furies. A few days after the Treaty, the USSR assured President Yahya Khan that the Soviet-Indian treaty was not directed against his country and that it would not bring any change in the Soviet policy towards Pakistan. Mrs. Gandhi somehow did not endorse Brezhnev's 'containment' proposal in view of the sensitive nature of India's defence dependence on the Soviet Union. She tried but in vain to improve relations with China and the United States, decided to detonate a nuclear device in May 1974 and refused to endorse the multilateral Nuclear Non-Proliferation Treaty. Despite the direct conflict, India's military dependence on the USSR continued, although the quantity decreased. In the 1970s, their share fluctuated between 70 percent and 57 percent.[14]

In an effort to stiffen the donor-recipient relationship, Brezhnev gave full support to Mrs. Gandhi's 'emergency'. However, when the Janta coalition defeated Mrs. Gandhi in 1977, Moscow did not dither a bit. Immediately it reaffirmed its friendship with India and signed three new economic agreements. Nevertheless, the new Indian government continued to diversify India's sources of weapons supply, ordering 116 Jaguar bombers and Sea Harrier fighters from Britain, 4 submarines from West Germany and 40 Mirage-2000H aircraft from France[15]. Moscow reacted with additional incentives in the form of the latest weapons and technology. Brezhnev's readiness to permit Indian licensed production of some newer Soviet systems at concessional prices and his willingness to accept payment in Rupees, wooed India to be once again heavily dependent on the Soviet Union. Moscow offered New Delhi generous terms and concessions, granting long-term credit, arranging repayment by merchandise export rather than foreign exchange. Moscow also allowed licensed production of weaponry through some technology transfer. After Mrs. Gandhi was re-elected in 1980, she charted a chary path of political support to the Soviets in view of Soviet invasion of Afghanistan. The government, therefore, attempted to diversify and indigenize defence supplies to its armed forces. Indigenization saw the launch of three DRDO weapons programs: the LCA, which was to replace the Mig 21, the main battle tank Arjun, which was to succeed the Vijayanta and T-55 MBTS; and the IGMDP, which was to replace certain Soviet SAMS, especially SA-2 and SA-6. Despite this diversification, Soviet weapons and aircraft continued to play a lead role in India's military arsenal.

The collapse of the Soviet Union turned out to be a harrowing experience for India's defence setup. India was faced with a difficult task of working anew its foreign policy in relation to the fifteen Soviet successor states. It was initially not clear as to what place India would occupy in the new Russian scheme of things.[16] Besides, due to greater emphasis on relations with the industrialized countries of the west, Russian relations with India got low priority in the early 1990s. With the emergence of independent Central Asian republics, Russia's and India's borders fell further apart. Besides the stand taken by India during the August 1991 coup did not particularly endear the new Russian leaders.[17] The break up disrupted India's most important source of defence supplies. As a result, India was forced to cut down production of some weapons systems and dig deep into its war contingency spares to keep its military machine rolling. Not only production, but shortage of spare parts also seriously affected India's capability to maintain the existing weapons systems. The major worry for India was the servicing, production and upgrading the extant Soviet weapon systems in its armed forces. Since practically all the frontier armor and mechanized units of the Indian army had used Soviet made equipments for several years, lacking the indigenous capability to produce spare parts and supplies for these systems aggravated the situation and India's military faced an immediate crisis. It became an extremely difficult task for India to coordinate supplies from the huge military industrial complex of the former Soviet Union spread over 15 newly independent countries. This situation imposed considerable logistic problems for India. Less than 10 months after the disintegration, India's domestic arms production was badly affected by the disruption in military supplies from the ex-Soviet states. The above situation posed a question mark on the rationale of overdependence on a single source. However, arguments were put forward that resource constraints, Cold War mentality, failure of the indigenous arms industry, and the reluctance of western suppliers to transfer technology left India with no other choice in those ways.

After the disintegration of the Soviet Union, India's 'special relationship', made it almost friendless in the new world order fashioned by the remaining superpower, the US. Its defence modernization plan was halted for almost a decade; its indigenous defence industries clearly lacked depth. Policy makers became increasingly desperate to find alternative supplies for its armed forces. Though the collapse of the USSR dramatically transformed Indo-Russian relations in the new world order, the military-technical cooperation had emerged as the mainstay of a sort of new deal between the two "neo-reformers". By the end of 1990s, the strength of Indo-Russian military cooperation had surpassed even Cold War levels with all three branches of the Indian military involved in procurement of hitherto denied weapon systems such as strategic Mach-2 category bombers (read the $TY22M_3$ backfire for the navy). India bought more hardware from the Russian defence industry than Russia's own military forces and many experts believed that this income source was crucial in Russia's transition to a free market economy.[18] It has been estimated that about eight hundred Russian defense facilities were kept running only on Indian defense contracts. Changing parameters of the relationship helped both sides to move from a buyer-seller interaction to one of joint development and marketing of weapon systems. As a result, one can see progress in some areas, notably the manufacture of T-90S Tanks, Flanker Family Aircraft, BrahMos Cruise Missile, and kits for "new Mig 21 BIS". Significantly, Russia is eager to involve India in the development of a fifth generation fighter, probably based on the S-37 Berkut (Golden Eagle) to meet the air superiority threat posed by the F-22 Raptor.[19]

In October 1992, a summary of the long awaited foreign policy concept prepared by the Russian foreign ministry was made public.[20] In 1993, New Delhi and Moscow worked to redefine their relationship according to post-Cold War realities. President Yeltsin replaced the 1971 treaty, which was extended by V.P. Singh, with a new treaty of Friendship and Cooperation. The new treaty dropped security clauses of the Cold War epoch, directed against the United States and China. A breakthrough was achieved in settling the issue of Indian debt to Russia and the Rupee-Rouble exchange rate. Russia agreed to an exchange rate that automatically subtracted two thirds of the debt to be repaid over twelve years and the rest was to be repaid over a period of forty five years.[21] The whole repayment was agreed to be made through Indian merchandise.[22]

In other areas relations gathered momentum from the mid 1990s itself. Since 1992, more than eleven summit meetings have taken place and about 100 agreements, including strategic partnerships, have been signed between the two countries. Various inter-governmental commissions and committees are working to improve bilateral relations. By the end of the decade, at the diplomatic level, everything seemed on track. The two sides agreed to explore possibilities of synergy in economic areas to provide a framework for the new relationship. However the success was limited. The visits of 1993 and 1994, followed by the appointment of Yevgeny Primakov as Foreign Minister in January 1996 rekindled the desire to work out a strategic partnership. In 1998 Prime Minister Primakov's visit to India provided a fillip to the sagging bilateral relations. The following reasons could be ascribed in this quest for deepening the relations between the two countries.

First, Russia's initial bonhomie with the West could not deliver the expected financial and potential support the former needed to resuscitate its morbid Soviet-era economic and political institutions and their subsequent conversion into thriving institutions of free market economy and democracy.[23] Secondly, ever since the establishment of an independent Russia, its interests in Europe, West Asia, and Central Asia and South Asia have clashed with those of the US. A number of positions taken by Russia showed the areas of divergence. Russia was opposed to the inclusion of the newly independent countries of its former East European satellites in NATO. Russia opposed the US policy in the Balkans, especially the

NATO bombing of Kosovo without the implicit or explicit authorization of the UN. Russia continued to support the governments of Iran and then Saddam-led Iraq. And finally, the West's opposition to Russia's policy in Chechnya caused further frictions. To allay the fear of increasing US unilateralism in the international arena, Russia laid emphasis on multipolarity. Its "Look-East" policy to co-opt China and India in a strategic triangle formed part of this new thrust. Thirdly, Russia was conscious of the Central Asian Republics' vulnerability to the political influence being expected by the Western Europe and Turkey on the one hand and Pakistan, Iran, and Saudi Arabia on the other. It was equally concerned about the US security plans in the Western Pacific to deal with potential crisis relative to Taiwan and mainland China's confrontationist territorial claims in South East Asia. China-India relations grew in importance as factors to balance US strategic postures in the Western Pacific, in arms control and disarmament of the security environment in South East Asia.

Yet another reason was that Moscow's initial policy makers in1992-1995 were anxious to present a new face of a refurbished post-communist nation devoid of previous ideological baggage, and the special relationship with India was seen as a legacy of the past.[24] Strategically, both countries ignored controversial issues like the CTBT; they instead resolved the Rupee-Rouble exchange rate, spare parts supply and cryogenic engine issue. It was also made clear by Russian leaders that India would continue to occupy a central place in Russia's overall South Asian policy. Russia gave its unequivocal support to India on the Kashmir issue, promised to support India in the latter's bid for a permanent UN Security Council seat and made a commitment not to give military-technological assistance to Pakistan. During Chernomyrdin's visit in 1995, Russian officials enthusiastically talked of "Russian-Indian partnership" and referred to India as their 'best partner' in the region. Primakov spoke of India as a 'global power' and a 'priority partner' of Russia.[25] During his Prime Ministerial tenure, Primakov emphasized the need for correcting the imbalance in the country's ties with the west and the east. India was upgraded to the fourth place after the USA, EU, and China in the list of countries with which it was deemed important to develop relations.[26] It was also finalized that India and Russia would sign a strategic partnership treaty in their next meeting.

Relations since 2000

A major breakthrough was achieved, when Russian President Vladimir Putin paid a visit to India in October 2000. Both countries signed a 'Declaration on Strategic Partnership' and ten attendant agreements covering various aspects of bilateral relations. The declaration spelt out in detail the long term nature of Indo-Russian relations in all aspects of mutual cooperation like political, defence, economic, trade, science and technology and cultural spheres. Also the joint statement issued at the conclusion of the bilateral talks affirmed Indian and Russian positions on various bilateral regional and international issues. President Putin's visit was reciprocated by the then Indian Prime Minister, Atal Behari Vajpayee to Russia in November 2001. During the second visit of President Putin to India in December 2002, both countries signed a 'Declaration on further consolidation of Strategic Partnership' between them. These apex visits have resulted in the signing of numerous agreements encompassing all possible areas. As an Indian analyst pointed out, the Strategic Partnership 'broadened the concept of security itself' and 'balanced the earlier relations that gave a privileged position to defence-related security'.[27]

During Putin's visit, India and Russia tried to resurrect some sort of an old Indo-Soviet relationship. The summit declaration proclaimed the "establishment of relations of strategic partnership between them based on mutual understanding and long-term interests in each other" and the "elevation of their multifaceted ties to an even higher and qualitatively new level" while imparting them a "specially close and dynamic character both in the bilateral field and in the international arena". This was however a far cry from the Soviet guarantees of countervailing intervention in the event of Sino-US aggression. This strategic partnership was further consolidated by Prime Minister Vajpayee's visit to Moscow where both leaders - Putin and Vajpayee - sought global cooperation for combating terrorism. During the second visit of President Putin in 2002, the framework for India-Russia relations was firmly set. This was a framework of another special relationship, expanding cooperation, and multiplying contacts in various fields, some of them of critical importance to India. Lately India-Russia relations have been strengthened by the highly successful visits of the Indian Premier to the Russian Federation in 2005. Putin aspired to make Russia a superpower with a substantial role in world affairs once again. His tenure has resulted in a boom in the Russian economy as a consequence of rising price of oil. The fact that the US has been caught in its own problems in Iraq and Afghanistan has helped him indirectly[28].

At the same time, India is emerging as a global power with a booming economy and billions of dollars in foreign exchange. It is a buyer for a large amount of defence equipments to modernize its armed forces and will be a potential buyer for large equipments for building nuclear power plants. Russia, on the other hand, wants to retain its leadership role as the largest and most reliable supplier of defence equipments to India. India also needs oil from Russia, where ONGC is keen to invest in the equity of Russian oilfields. It has already made the beginning at Shakhalin 1 project. Putin aims to go beyond the traditional perimeters of ties by tying up with India not just to supply equipment but also to participate in joint ventures, joint research and joint marketing of various strategic products. Another major area of cooperation identified by the two sides is in the aviation sector. Russia has asked Hindustan Aeronautics Limited to become a joint partner in the manufacture of Sukhoi-30 MKI and the MiG 29 M2 series. The two sides have also agreed to extend their cooperation in jointly manufacturing the supersonic missile BrahMos. With the additional investment of $50 million for the development of the Air Force version of the missile, work has begun in both India and Russia for modifications. The integration aspects have been finalized with the Sukhoi Design Bureau. The Indian Air Force has issued instructions for the fitment and trial of BrahMos on its Su-30MKI. The fitment of BrahMos on a new warship was under consideration. Other high tech areas where further collaboration between defence scientists was envisaged includes stealth technologies for aircraft, aerodynamic technologies such as creation of plasma wing tunnel facility for air vehicle applications and development and testing of submerged air intake models for unmanned aerial aircraft.

The present version of "BrahMos," the product of an Indo-Russian joint venture weighing about three tons, could strike a target located 290 kilometers away. The missile is eight-meter long and carries a conventional warhead, weighing about 200 kilograms. Supersonic BrahMos missile was unique in many parameters. Its maximal velocity was M2.5 – 2.8 (750 meters a second). A two-stage vehicle, the missile's propulsion consisted of a solid propellant booster and liquid propellant ramjet system. Its low radar signature, ability to vary flight trajectories and height of flight from

10 meters up to 14 kilometers made BrahMos practically impregnable for antimissile defense of the opponent. Launching of a missile was carried out from the transport-launch canister. Universal for multiple platforms BrahMos could be installed and launched from the board of a ship, a submarine, from a ground mobile launcher, and also from a plane. Land, sea and sub-sea based missiles are identical. Air-launched version had a smaller booster and additional tail fins for stability during the launch.[29] Various Indian commentaries, meanwhile, noted in the wake of the April 28 test that the eventual deployment of the PJ-10 BrahMos would leapfrog the Indian navy over that of regional rival China, and help to even out the balance of naval power in South Asia. At present the Chinese navy has armed some of its ships with Russian-made "Moskit" class cruise missiles, which had a range of 120-kilometers and which Indian sources described as inferior to the newly developed BrahMos. *The Times of India* contended that the BrahMos should give India the edge it needed in the heavily militarized Indian Ocean and surrounding areas. Not noted in these Indian commentaries, but probably discussed with some satisfaction in Moscow, was the fact that Russia was the major arms supplier to both India and China, and that it stood to gain monetarily not only from the well-publicized tensions afflicting India and Pakistan, but also from a potentially more portentous battle for influence in the region between New Delhi and Beijing.

As for the BrahMos itself, it was being developed and produced in tandem by the Defence Research and Development Organization from India and Russia's Federal State Unitary Enterprise NPO Machinostroyenia with a host of additional Indian and Russian institutions and defense facilities being involved in the effort. Contrary to the Pakistani charges, moreover, Russia appeared to have designed the BrahMos very carefully, to ensure that it stayed within the parameters set out by the MTCR. The regime permits the transfer of missile technologies capable of carrying at least five hundred kilograms to a range of 300 kilometers or more. Primarily an anti-ship missile, based on Russia's own Yakhont missile of the same type, the BrahMos is highly accurate, can be guided by means of an on-board computer and said to have a variety of applications, capable with modifications of being launched from multiple platforms base on land, sea, submarine and air.

According to Indian sources, India and Russia completed testing of the new missile and introduced it into service in both the Indian and Russian armed forces since 2004. Indian sources suggested that New Delhi and Moscow intended to aggressively market export versions of the BrahMos to "friendly third-world countries" to be identified by mutual consent.[30] But success even on a somewhat more modest scale would probably fulfill the hopes of those in India and Russia who pushed for the BrahMos project and who hoped it would serve as a model for broader military-technological cooperation.

Conclusions

The hard reality of India-Russia relations is something more than strategic calculus. It is, in fact, based on strong, lasting relationship, spanning over decades and aimed at strengthening their respective economies through sale and purchase of arms and transfer of technology. Success with the BrahMos would provide both countries the leverage to move toward achieving what they were looking for when they initiated this cooperation nearly a decade ago. For India, that is the creation of a modern defense industrial sector capable of producing high-tech weapons both for the country's own armed forces and for export abroad. For Russia, it is the establishment of a partnership capable of providing a core of the country's still sophisticated, yet cash-poor defense producers with the financial wherewithal needed to remain players in the global arms game. And finally, BrahMos enables both countries to produce the weaponry necessary to return a reformed Russian armed forces to its former world power status.

References

1. India likes to do business with Putin by Sheela Bhatt in New Delhi, Rediff news letter, 25.01.2007, p. 1.
2. http://www.rediff.com///news/2006/jun/28brahm.htm
3. *BrahMos Russian - Indian Enterprise* by Allister Maunk, AIA Indian section, global challenges world, 22.04.2005, p. 1.
4. For details see, Nirmala Joshi, Foundation of Indo-Soviet Relations, Radiant Publishers, New Delhi, 1975.
5. Peter Zwick, Soviet Foreign Relations: Process and Policy, New Jersey, Prentice-Hall, 1990, pp. 316-318.
6. Gibert and Joshua, Guns and Roubles, Soviet Aid Diplomacy in Neutral Asia (American-Asian Educational Exchange, 1970, p. 23).
7. Dr. Subhas Kapila, India-Russia strategic cooperation: time to move away?, marketing @stratmag.com,S trategic Affairs-Analysis.htm, pp. 1-15.

8. Cecil Victor "Indo-Soviet Military Cooperation : Factors for Self Reliance" in V. D. Chopra (ed), Studies in Indo-Soviet Relations, New Delhi, Patriot Pub.,1986, pp. 84 -94.
9. Arthur Stein, "India and the USSR Relations", New Delhi, Allied, 1987, p. 131.
10. Dr. Nisha Saha Achutan, Soviet Arms Transfer Policy in South Asia 1955-81, New Delhi,1988, p. 34. See also, Dr. M. Saleem Kidwai, Indo-Soviet Relations, Rima Publishing, New Delhi, 1985, pp. 55-75.
11. Treaty of Peace, Friendship, and Cooperation between the government of India and government of "USSR" www.meadev.nic.in. New Delhi, 9 August 1971.
12. William H. Mott, Soviet military Assistance An Empirical Perspective, London, Greenwood Press, 2001, p. 226.
13. Heman Ray *op. cit.* p. 277.
14. Sipri Year Book, World Armament and Disarmament, London, Taylor and Francis, 1981, p. 115.
15. Robert C. Horn, Soviet-Indian Relations; Issues and Influence, New York, 1982, p. 160.
16. Nirmala Joshi, India and Russia; Enduring Friendship, India Quaterly, Vol. LVIII, No. 3.4, July-Dec. 2002, pp. 114-118.
17. N. Mehrotra, "Indo-Russian Relations after the Disintegration of USSR" *Strategic Analysis*, New Delhi, Vol. 19, No. 8, November 1996, pp. 1133-1135.
18. Jerome M Colonel, Indo-Russia Military and Nuclear Cooperation, New York, Lexington Books, New York, 2001, pp. 58-59.
19. "Agreement Between the government of Russian Federation and the Republic of India on Defence Cooperation", *Strategic Digest*,Vol. 23, No. 4, April 1993, p. 602.
20. "Yelstin Okays Russian Foreign Policy Concept", The Current Digest of the Post-Soviet Press, Ohio, Vol. 45, No. 17, May 26, 1993, pp. 13-15.
21. Robert Donaldson and Joseph H. Nogee (eds) Foreign Policy of Russia, New York, M.E. Sharpe, 1998, p. 273.
22. Shasikant Jha in Shams-Ud-Din (Ed.) India and Russia towards Strategic Thinking, New Delhi, Lancer, 2001, p. 45.
23. Anita Inder Singh, India's Relations with Russia and Central Asia, International Affairs, RIIA,Vol. 17, No. 1, 1995.
24. Bunn Nagara, Russia India In New Convergence, www.southreview.com.
25. "Documents of Moscow Declaration",Visits of Indian Prime Minister to Moscow, *National Herald*, New Delhi, 5 July, 1994.

26. *The Hindu*, March 29, 1996.
27. Anuradha M. Chenoy, A Defining Moment, *Frontline*, Vol. 17, Issue 21, October 2000, pp. 14-27.
28. *Gulf Times*, Delhi Diary, Article by A.K. Krishnan, Published: Wednesday, 31 January, 2007.
29. Alliste Maunk, *op.cit.,* p. 1.
30. Reuters, AP, April 28-29; *The Times of India*, April 10, 28-29; Brahmos.com, April 30; Interfax, April 11; *Moscow Times*, April 15; *The Hindu*, Express News Service, June 13, 2001.

10

Basic Trends of Indo-Russian Strategic Partnership during Vladimir Putin's Presidency

Ms. Nivedita Das Kundu

Vladimir Putin's last visit to India on January 25-26, 2007 provided fresh impetus to the strategic partnership between the two countries. The visit reinforced the interests of both states in maintaining their traditionally close friendly relationship and in strengthening a multipolar world order.

In recent times, both India and Russia have been pursuing a multi-sector approach in their foreign policies. In a nutshell, both countries do not want to act as members of any bloc, but rather wish to pursue independent and flexible foreign policies keeping their respective national interests and aspirations to become important powers in mind. Ever since India and the US signed the nuclear deal, some quarters have perceived that India is inclining more towards the US and that consequently the Indo-Russian relationship will be strained. But Putin's visit and acceptance of the Indian government's invitation to be the chief guest at the Republic Day celebrations have diluted much of these incorrect perceptions. Russia has never imposed any sanctions on India, nor has it provided arms to Pakistan. Moreover, Russia recently warned China not to install Russian made RD-93 jet engines in the fighter aircraft that China is jointly developing with Pakistan. It is true that times have changed and the old mindset or sentimentality does not exist in today's world. Besides, the policies of both countries are mainly driven by pragmatic and economic considerations. Although differences arise over certain issues on certain occasions, the overall parallelism in the Indo-Russian relationship definitely symbolizes the trust that still exists between them.

Now India and Russia have reached a stage where both their economies are resurgent and also at the same time diversifying. Over the last few years, they have achieved significant rates of economic growth. In the last few years, the Indian economy grew by more than 7 per cent per year, and Russia's at about 6.9 per cent. Overall, both economies are developing significantly to provide a good base for expanding business contacts and promoting new projects.

Nonetheless, in spite of accelerated growth and immense opportunities in each other's economy, statistics show that Indo-Russian trade in 2005-06 was only US$ 2.75 billion. Promises were made by the leaders of both countries earlier as well as this time to boost trade and set the task of reaching $ 10 billion by 2010. But the Indian business community feels that to put these words into practice and strengthen the economic pillar of the relationship, certain practical issues and concerns need to be addressed, like the easing of visa regulations for Indian businessmen, optimising the Indo-Russian shipment route (the North-South Corridor provides the shortest route but it has not been commissioned yet), the expansion of inter-banking co-operation and the issue of utilizing the remaining funds under the Rupee-Rouble debt agreement.

While addressing these issues and concerns, Putin stated that there can be no effective economic co-operation without political support, and suggested that the high level of political trust between the two countries needs to be translated into economic cooperation. Expressing concerns about red-tapism, he stressed upon the need for both governments to cut red tape and provide initiatives to boost economic co-operation. He also articulated the point that both countries are market-oriented economies today and therefore need to make greater efforts to conquer each other's markets. For his part, he promised to put in place the conditions for easing the entry of Indian businesses into the Russian market even in non-traditional sectors.

The last meeting of the Indo-Russian Business Co-operation Council and the Trade and Investment Forum which took place in New Delhi during February 2007, was significant one. But the question that still remains is, whether a fresh impetus was provided to boost trade and economic co-operation between the two countries.

Bilateral trade between Russia and India was severely affected due to the disintegration of the Soviet Union. The break-up of the

USSR in 1991 and India's economic liberalisation about the same time resulted in a drastic reduction in bilateral trade and economic co-operation. An analysis of bilateral trade shows that India's main exports to Russia are not growing at a consistent rate over the past few years, while Indian imports from Russia have remained almost static over the last decade and a half. There is a need to address specific areas to ensure greater trade flows and to reach the target set by the two governments of US $10 billion in total trade by 2010.

The greatest hindrance to trade between India and Russia is the lack of trade routes. The agreement on the new India-Russia Transport Corridor may help in reducing transport costs. The present route, which passes through the Suez Canal and enters the Russian port of St. Petersburg via Kotka (Finland) and Rotterdam (Netherlands), is long and time consuming. The new route-Mumbai-Bandar Abbas-Astrakhan-would comprise sea and land links across India, Iran and Russia and will shorten travel time by as much as ten days. Despite the interest shown by both sides to increase bilateral flow of goods and services, there are still some trade barriers, (non-tariff barriers for instance), that continue to plague bilateral trade. These too need to be identified and addressed, since they hinder market access.

Another issue that needs to be addressed seriously pertains to the remaining funds under the Rupee-Rouble debt agreement. Between 1953 and the collapse of the Soviet Union, bilateral trade was conducted through a specific system of trade and payment called the Rupee trade system based on annual plans. However, after the collapse of the Soviet Union, the Indian and Russian governments renegotiated the entire trading arrangement. After several rounds of discussions, an agreement was reached in 1993, under which rouble credit was denominated in Rupees and a repayment schedule was drawn up. The agreement provided for an annual repayment of about US $1 billion equivalent in Rupees to Russia over a period of 12 years starting from 1994, with smaller amounts for a further period of 33 years. The Rupee debt funds were to be used by the Russian side to import goods and trade related services from India. Since then, bilateral trade has been based on payments in freely convertible currencies. All Russian exports to India follow the new system. But in the last decade, about two-thirds of Indian exports were financed through the renegotiated rupee-debt repayment mechanism.

India and Russia also need to look at other relevant issues including the expansion of inter-banking co-operation. Despite economic policy changes in both countries, the Indo-Russian economic relationship is still dominated by defence/public sector transactions. The military industrial complex (MIC) still stands at the core of strong Indo-Russian economic linkages. India is further expected to continue importing defence equipment from Russia in the coming years.

Macro-economic stability and growth in the two economies continued mainly because of their intensive expansion of internal consumer and investment demand. Overall, the economic policies of both countries aimed at supporting macroeconomic equilibrium and stimulating growth. Today, Russia's ambition seems to be not just limited to becoming a prime supplier of energy to the world market but to eventually re-emerge as a great economic power using petrodollars. Similarly, today's India has a lot to offer to Russia. Sectors in which India has shown high export growth over the last few years are information and communication technology, professional services such as medical health (specifically dental), engineering, travel and tourism, as well as certain financial services. Russia, on the other hand, has demonstrated expertise in, apart from the energy sector, research and development in scientific and technological sectors, transport services, etc. The two countries could also consider building a strong platform for sharing views on innovation and research and development in the above mentioned areas so as to learn and benefit from each other's competence. Both countries could also roll out new initiatives to boost bilateral economic co-operation.

Russia's Economic Report of December 2006 states that it has been experiencing severe shortages of skilled labour due to demographic decline. This has had an adverse effect on its economic growth. In this context, it could be of mutual interest if professionals from India were to be hired to meet Russian requirements. This idea was discussed during Putin's January 2007 visit as well as during the recent visit of Russia's Minister of Economic Development and Trade. Now Russia is looking for alternatives in the form of expatriate labour from Central Asia and the Caucasus, mainly because of the latter's familiarity with and knowledge of the Russian language. If Indian job seekers were to learn the Russian language, it would boost employment opportunities for them in Russia.

Chinese labourers have already started finding a foothold in Russia's Far East, and they might very soon spread to other parts of Russia as well. There is no doubt that Russia will prefer Indians rather than Chinese in this regard.

India and Russia have to exploit their comparative advantages in a globalising world if they wish to expand bilateral trade and deepen economic co-operation. This is imperative to add greater ballast to their strategic partnership in the 21st century.

Areas in which the Russian side showed deep interest in co-operating over the past few years include telecommunications, shipbuilding, and high technology including outer space. In the field of space, both countries have agreed to jointly develop and exploit the Russian global navigation satellite system Glonass. They hope to restore this system through joint efforts and organize its transition to new Glonass-M and Glonass-K space devices. Russia intends to increase (with the participation of India) the grouping of Glonass system to 18 satellites in 2007. The launch of these satellites will be on board both Russian and Indian space boosters. Apart from Glonass, India and Russia have also agreed to jointly develop a 'Youth' satellite for educational purposes.

In the energy sector, the Russian side was keen to construct four new nuclear power units in Kudankulam in Tamil Nadu as well as new nuclear power plants in other parts of India. Of course, these are contingent upon the NSG revising its guidelines and Russia has stated that it will work at that forum to help India's case. Indo-Russian nuclear cooperation would extend to both the fission and fusion processes as well as non-power applications.

In the oil and gas sectors, Russia is interested in joint construction of oil and natural gas production and transportation facilities in India and in the surrounding regions. This is in contrast to recent Russian actions that seemingly seek to deny the hitherto easy access of western companies to Russian energy resources. (Moscow, it may be recalled, recently cancelled the production share agreement with Royal Dutch Shell in Sakhalin II, which has now been taken over by Gazprom). But such a course of action seems unlikely with Indian companies. India's OVL and Russia's Rosneft are jointly bidding for Sakhalin III. But still some ambiguity remains over this issue. Putin had earlier personally intervened to get India onboard in Sakhalin I, but this time he appeared non-committal on Sakhalin III. Nevertheless, India has geared-up its energy diplomacy and is now moving quickly to penetrate the Russian energy market.

Against the backdrop of the Goldman Sachs BRIC report, which states that the emerging economies of Brazil, Russia, India and China will increase their footprints on the global economic landscape in the 21st century, it is evident that the Indo-Russian economic and trade engagement needs a significant boost. Present economic engagements are mostly in the public sector and even here it is narrowly focused on the defence sector. Military ties between India and Russia are developing steadily and today it includes joint research and development, production, marketing, regular cooperation between the different branches of arms and joint training exercises.

One significant example of joint defence production is the BrahMos (Brahamaputra-Moscow) anti-ship cruise missile, which can be launched from submarine, ship, aircraft, and land based mobile autonomous launchers. The most interesting aspect of this joint venture is its commercial angle. It has been developed for a global market and some 20 Indian and 10 Russian companies are involved in its production. Its export will, however, be restricted to friendly developing countries.

The joint development of multi-purpose transport planes is another significant feature of the evolving relationship between the two countries. India and Russia are also expanding the scope of such ventures by agreeing to jointly develop a fifth-generation fighter aircraft. Other important features of Indo-Russian defence co-operation include the Admiral Gorshkov aircraft carrier, which will join the Indian Navy as the INS Vikramaditya after a full refit by the end of 2008 or later, and deliveries of MiG-29 which will take place by the end of 2007. Of late, Russia has also advanced a proposal for selling the advanced Mig-35 fighter jet to the Indian Air Force. All these indicate that Russia will maintain an edge over other countries in supplying military hardware to India's defence sector.

In spite of such notable defence co-operation, there is a need to develop an institutional mechanism that will link Institutions and thereby spur innovation as well as commercialisation of new technologies. Economic and investment projects also need serious information support, which is lacking at the moment. On the whole, it is necessary to publicise the positive experiences and growth of both countries, which will help people in both countries to orient themselves according to present realities and will boost bilateral co-operation in various fields.

The Putin era will be noted as a transformational period for Russia as well as for the Indo-Russian strategic partnership, given that he was the major factor in re-vitalising both after the Yeltsin years. Putin's last visit to India signifies that at present both countries attach considerable value to this strategic partnership, which has reached a stage where any change in the leadership in either country or closeness with any other country would not make much of a difference to the partnership.

11

Indo-Russian Defence Cooperation—Some New Aspects

V.D. Chopra

Any one who has been closely watching how India during the last six decades has emerged one of the major military powers and has been defending its sovereignty and integrity would agree that in this process of building its military strength, the Soviet Union and now Russia have made a valuable contribution. In totality this cooperation between the two countries is incomparable with its cooperation with any country of the world. India's military might was tested on a number of occasions during the last six decades, particularly in 1965 Indo-Pak War and in 1971 India's help to the liberation struggle of Bangladesh. On both the occasions the United States stood on the other side of the fence. It is in this background that an objective estimate should be made about new trends in Indo-Russian defence cooperation.

Indian Prime Minister Dr. Manmohan Singh's visit to Moscow in December 2006 was successful despite the speculations about the outcome of this visit. The two sides unexpectedly signed important agreements. India and Russia signed two space agreements.

One of them is a long-term deal under which the countries will jointly develop and use GLONASS, the Russian designed satellite system that gives spacecraft, marine vessels and ground vehicles, a positioning capability of 5-10 m. For India, its joint use with the U.S. Navstar GPS will mean new opportunities in navigation, cartography and topography. A reliable space positioning capability is crucial to modern societies where it is used for the military such as smart weapons and in many economic and scientific applications.

According to press reports the Indo-Russian arms trade was worth around US $ 9 billion. India expected Russian cooperation of Project ATV (Advanced Technology Vessel) to create India's nuclear powered submarine. Russian Deputy Prime Minister and Defence Minister Sergey Borisovich Ivanov referred to Russia's non-proliferation commitments that experts supposed would keep Russia from selling nuclear reactors of India' planned submarine.

Another deal under which two Russian Akulas being finished by the Komsomolsk-on-Amur shipyard would be leased to India. If it were to be concluded, the deal required a crew training programme that had to start immediately, while the submarines were still in production. In 1988-1991, the Indians, seeing their own SSN effort launched in the 1970s largely stalled, leased the Russian multipurpose Project 670A K-43 Nerpa submarine renamed *'Chakra'* and very soon came up with the S-2 project currently nearing completion. India was breaking ground for the completion and leasing of the two Akulas laid down back in the 1980s and 80% completed but severely under-funded in post-Soviet times.

It is relevant to mention here that a contract worth up to US $ 1.8 billion is under active consideration to reactivate Admiral Gorshkov, already renamed *'Vikramaditya'*. Experts in this area say that the Akulas are bound for India. Indirect evidence of that is the beginning of an extensive training programme. This will take considerable time. The question still open is when the Indian leasing is officially completed, what these two Akulas will be called during the next decade. The two submarines would be a considerable part of the Indian defence.

Both the countries have a great deal of space capacity on the global arms market. Some experts claim that India dominates Russia's arms trade. The country indeed accounts for 40% of Russian arms export revenues up to US $ 2.5 billion a year, and this amounts to 70% of Indian arms imports. Still there is a lot, which can be done by these countries in this area.

Modernisation of the Indian Air Force (IAF) seems to be underway, if media reports are any indication. According to Russian Interfax News Agency report June 2007, which quotes unnamed defence industry sources a multi-million dollar Indo-Russian deal for the modernisation of lAF's fleet of MiG-29 fighters is on the immediate agenda.

Interfax report further points out that "the contract stipulates the modernisation of 64 MiG-29 fighters, including 8 fighter trainers". As part of the modernisation plan, the MiG-29 fighters would be equipped with new Phazotron "Zhuk-ME" radars, which are capable of engaging multiple targets simultaneously. "The modernisation contract would run into "several hundred million dollars" and the lifecycle of the upgraded MiG-29 fighters would be extended from current 25 to 40 years, as a result of this modernisation. The report also says that the upgradation of first two MiG-29 fighters would be carried out in Russia, while the rest would be upgraded at the Hindustan Aeronautics Limited (HAL) facilities at Ojhar near Nasik in Maharashtra by 2010. HAL had also invited proposals from international partners including Russian helicopter manufacturers for co-development of Multi-role Helicopter of 10 tonnes. The Russian side is also interested in bidding for the Multi-role Combat Aircraft of IAF with MiG-35 aircraft. Earlier report around March 2007 had said that India and Russia had signed a US $ 800 million deal with a consortium of Russia's state owned Rosboronexport and United Aircraft Corporation to improve the air combat capability of its MiG-29s.

According to these reports, the MiG-29 aircraft currently deployed with the IAF, would not only receive new phased array radar and long range (beyond visual range) missiles, but would also be equipped with Klimov RD-33 engines with digital fuel injection, an aerial refuelling capability and a modern 'glass cockpit'. These reports had also stated that under a parallel plan, the IAF was in the final stages of negotiating a 1.5 billion euro deal with Thales and Dassault to upgrade its 52 French made Dassault Mirage-2000 H fighters.

Indian Air Force chief had said that the IAF had begun upgrading its combat aircraft fleet over the last few years in order to enhance its operational capability. "While the MiG-21, MiG-27 and Jaguar aircraft have already been upgraded, the upgrade of Mirage-2000 and MiG-29 is being planned." He further said, "The upgrade is essentially on the radar, avionics and weapon systems."

This shows how, despite a zigzag process and hard bargaining both by India and Russia, defence cooperation between the two countries is developing. This is confirmed by the fact that important agreements between India and Russia were signed during Russian President Vladimir Vladimirovich Putin's visit to India in January 2007 on the occasion of India's Republic Day.

The Defence Cooperation between India and Russia got a further boost, when four different documents were signed in New Delhi on 24th January 2007 between the two countries at the conclusion of the Sixth Meeting of the India-Russia Inter-Governmental Commission on Military Technical Cooperation (IRIGC-MTC). The Meeting was co-chaired by the Indian Defence Minister A.K. Antony and the Russian Defence Minister Sergey Borisovich Ivanov.

The first agreement is on License Production and Technical Documents for the RD 33 series 3 Aero Engines, the second is the general contract for RD 33 series 3 Aero Engines and associated products. The two sides also signed a Protocol of intent for the joint development and production of multi-role Transport Aircraft and the Protocol of the Sixth India-Russia Inter-Governmental Commission on Military Technical Cooperation. The Sixth Inter-Governmental Commission meeting witnessed the strategic depth of India-Russia defence relations widening to encompass non-defence strategic areas such as information technology and space research.

In his opening remarks, A.K. Antony said that "Indo-Russian Defence Cooperation is interdependent and mutually beneficial. This has graduated from a simple buyer seller relationship to joint research, development and production. Referring to the Indo-Russian joint venture BrahMos, India would like to have more such joint efforts in the years to come. Both sides are in advanced stage of negotiations in the joint development and production of multi-role transport aircraft and fifth generation fighter aircraft. Necessary measures are being taken to expeditiously finalise the respective intergovernmental agreement in this regard. Russia is the only country with which we have an institutionalised mechanism at the level of defence ministers to monitor our military technical cooperation. The India-Russia Inter Governmental Commission is an effective set up to monitor the progress and give directions for the development of the military technical cooperation". The Minister expressed happiness that the meetings under this Inter-Governmental Commission have been held under the revised format where the subgroups, working groups and it met in a spaced manner with a view to discuss and resolve various issues at appropriate levels.

Referring to the institutionalised mechanism to monitor execution of military technical cooperation programmes, the

Defence Minister stressed the need to monitor the timely implementation of the decisions being taken in these meetings. In this regard he suggested that both sides could work out a mechanism where all concerned – the enterprises, government agencies and the user could join together.

Referring to the round of joint naval exercises in Russian waters in April 2007, the Defence Minister said that "While we have travelled far ahead in our military technical cooperation, there is a need to develop professional military-to-military cooperation between the armed forces of the two countries. This includes exchange of each other's areas expertise, training cooperation, joint-exercises etc. The term of the 1996 Agreement exclusively covering military-to-military cooperation has expired and we could consider signing a fresh agreement duly taking into account the present day requirements. There is also need to impart a greater degree of strategic security dialogue between the officials of our Ministries of Defence and between the Service Personnel of the Armed Forces of the two sides. The current issues of mutual concern such as international terrorism, non-proliferation of weapons of mass destruction and timely delivery of assistance and rehabilitation during and after major natural disasters, are areas where we could have greater exchange of ideas. This would be to the mutual benefit of our countries and with an improved professional military-to-military cooperation. Problems arising in military technical cooperation could also be addressed in an effective manner".

A.K. Antony emphasised that India's ties with the Russian Federation are time-tested and based on continuity, trust and mutual understanding. There is a national consensus in the two countries on the need to preserve and strengthen the fundamentals of Indo-Russian relations and they are unaffected by political developments in either country. The Defence Minister said "we share common concern in the fight against global terrorism and in ensuring peace and stability in our respective regions". He recalled the Declaration on Strategic Partnership between India and the Russian Federation signed during the visit of President Putin in the year 2000, which lays down the contours of India-Russia relations in the 21st century and elevates them to a new level".

Conclusion

"Nuclear submarines, Heavy Battle Tanks, Fighter Jets and Aircraft Carriers - this is just a partial list of the current defence trade items between India and Russia, which is estimated to be worth up to US $10 billion by 2010. For three decades and more, Russia has been and today still is India's largest trading partner. While Russia will continue to be a major partner for India in the coming decades, the Russian industry needs to learn to compete with the West, the Israelis and domestic defence players if it chooses to be dominant in the years to come. The fact remains that the defence market today is a buyer's market and that India is one of the largest defence importers in the world". *(Indo-Russian Ties : Trouble Brewing Underneath,* Srirangan, Defence and Security Observer).

This survey shows how in the changing world situation and entry of new arms sellers into the Indian market, Indo-Russian defence cooperation still stands on a firm and high footing. This implies that despite India's attempts to develop relations with the US in the area of nuclear technology, Indo-Russian defence cooperation still stands on a high pedestal in this country's defence preparedness and modernisation of its defence.

12

Indo-Russian Economic Cooperation : Positing Prospects for 21st Century

Dr. Devidatta Aurobinda Mahapatra

Much of the discourses on Indo-Russian economic cooperation in the 1990s are replete with terms like 'lost decade' and 'decade of lost opportunities', etc. The downward trajectory nonetheless gradually gave way to a steady though slow growth in economic cooperation in the 2000s as the increasing realization in turning the strategic cooperation in political sphere into economic sphere gained ground. In this context the emphasis of Indian establishment that the roadmap for achieving a significant increase in the bilateral trade turnover to the tune of $10 billion by 2010 by diversifying and increasing trade in goods and services and through investment has to be made 'top priority' is noteworthy.[1] With a dismal start the current bilateral trade between the two countries stands below $4 billion. Some of the factors that obstructed the smooth growth of economic relations included Rupee-Rouble controversy, lack of diversification of economy in both the countries, major focus on military cooperation and negligence of other areas such as energy, space, information technology, etc. However of late as the relations in the beginning of the 21st century would reveal the two countries have come to realize the need to boost economic partnership in terms of bilateral trade and commerce alongside the traditional sectors of military and defence cooperation. The present paper focuses on prospects as well as problems of bilateral economic cooperation between India and Russia in the changing world order.

20th Century in a Nutshell

The economic cooperation between India and the Soviet Union could be seen in the background of the Cold War. Attributing the initial success of India in heavy industries to Soviet Union, Marshall, I. Goldman, the noted economist observes that "India's early advocacy of non-alignment would have been impossible without Soviet financial help, for without the availability of such help, India would not have been able to risk a stance that was independent of the West."[2] About the Bhilai steel plant, he writes: "The Bhilai steel mill provided a demonstration of Soviet technological mastery at German and English expense." There was also another aspect of Soviet assistance to India and that was the military aid. India had sought Soviet military assistance because it could not obtain supplies in rupees. Soviet military assistance began even before the India-China conflict of 1962. Since then Soviet military aid to India has been substantial, for example, supply of military planes and assistance to build a MiG factory, the supply of tanks and submarines and other. Normally, military aid involves only the sale of armaments but in India, the Soviet Union showed willingness to not only supply the items but also to create production facilities. The Western world was not ready to do so till the late seventies. The ratios of dependence for Russian spares in India were 40, 64 and 80 per cents for the army, the air force and the navy respectively.[3]

India's public sector was largely a Soviet creation. Before the death of Nehru, Indo-Soviet cooperation had already expanded to heavy engineering items, oil refining, oil exploration, coal, iron ore, electric power generation, power equipment production, antibiotics and pharmaceuticals, precision instruments and aluminum production. The Soviet contribution to the public sector capacity was substantial. According to one estimate, in steel it was over 40 per cent, in power generation over 20 per cent, in the production of heavy equipment about 80 per cent, oil production about 80 per cent, oil refining about 40 per cent, coal over 10 per cent, coal washery over 15 per cent and aluminum over 25 per cent. As for drugs and pharmaceuticals, the public sector medical industry was largely a Soviet contribution in the initial years of Indian economic development.

However, the initial years in bilateral relations aftermath of the Soviet disintegration was not only uncertain but also marked by a high degree of suspicion. It can be mentioned here that both India and Russia launched the policies of liberalization and market reforms in 1991. Both were facing, as President Yeltsin visualized, 'mostly the same problems', and for the solution of these problems the Russian leader suggested, "we are to cope with enormous economic and social tasks, and cooperation between India and

Russia in this area could prove useful and important."[4] As the later developments such as Rupee-Rouble crisis, cryogenic rocket controversy and Russia's attitude on Kashmir revealed, economic relations were not smooth between the two countries. However, within a time frame of about two years, the Russian romanticism with the West came to a halt and it turned towards the old allies.

President Boris Yeltsin's visit to India in January 1993 marked the beginning of a new phase in Indo-Russian relations. The visit ended all speculations regarding the deteriorating relations between the two countries. Major irritants in Indo-Russian relations were resolved during the visit. Restoration of economic relations was among them. Trade between India and Russia almost collapsed in 1991-1992 because of disagreements over Rupee-Rouble exchange rate and the amount India owed to Russia as the successor state to the Soviet Union. This controversy was sorted out during the visit of Yeltsin. The two sides agreed that 63% of the debt would be repaid over the next twelve years at an interest of 2.4%, using the exchange rate of 1 rouble to 19.9 rupees that existed on 1 January 1990. The remaining 37% of the principal would be repaid over 45 years with no interest at the January 1992 exchange rate of 1 rouble to 3.1 rupees. Repayment of debt would be in Indian goods.[5]

The 1990s represented one of the most difficult decades in Indo-Russian relations. Though the initial two years were almost non-starters in bilateral relations, it was only with the visit of then Russian President Yeltsin that the relations gathered momentum. Though politico-strategic relations became strengthened, the post-1993 phase was not much enthusiastic from the point of view of economic cooperation. It was in the decade of 2000s that both the countries realized the imperative of economic cooperation.

Prospects of Economic Cooperation in 21st Century

The mid-1990s witnessed a paradigm shift in bilateral economic relations due to two major reasons. First, the Russian economy after 1998 registered tremendous growth mainly due to high energy prices. According to one estimate, the rate of annual GDP growth of Russia was 6.4 per cent in 1999, 10.0 per cent in 2000, 5.1 in 2001, 4.7 in 2002, 7.3 in 2003 and 6.6 in 2004. According to D. Robinson, "Within a comparatively short time, Russia has navigated a course from default on both external and domestic payments - to bondholders, companies and pensioners alike - to one of the shining stars of emerging markets with a very modest debt level, several years of strong growth, budget surpluses, and a comfortable reserve cushion. By any standard, this has been a successful period."[6] The high natural resource prices especially of the petroleum products sailed Russia through the difficult phase of its transformation from a sagging economy to a vibrant economy. Second, around the same period the mandarins at foreign office, under the leadership of Primakov, charted a new course in foreign policy by turning towards old allies like India.

The visit of Russian President Vladmir Putin to India in October 2000 can be considered a landmark in bilateral economic cooperation. Under the Integrated Long-Term Programme of Scientific and Technical Cooperation (ILTP) signed during the visit, both countries undertook more than 100 joint scientific projects, which could provide relatively cheap technologies in various fields from biomedicine to semi-conductors, computer chips, new materials and energy sources. During the visit of Indian Petroleum Minister Ram Naik to Moscow in February 2001, the Indian Oil Company, ONGC Videsh Ltd. and the Russian Rosneft signed an agreement on the joint exploration of hydrocarbon resources in the Russian Far-Eastern island of Sakhalin. During the visit of President Putin to India in December 2002, both sides signed the Joint Declaration on strengthening and developing economic, scientific and technological cooperation.[7] A document on economic cooperation between Indian State of Karnataka and Samara region of Russia, and another document on telecommunication were signed during the visit.

The last quarter of 2003 witnessed some positive developments in economic relations between the two countries. The Confederation of Indian Industry (CII) opened its office at the Russian Chambers of Commerce and Industry in October 2003 to facilitate the process of economic cooperation. During the visit of Prime Minister Vajpayee to Moscow in November 2003, 85 Indian businessmen accompanied him to study the prospects of investments and joint collaborations with Russian companies.[8] Mani Shankar Aiyar, India's Petroleum Minister visited Moscow in October 2005 to discuss India's energy requirements with Russia. He welcomed Gazprom's (Russian firm) interest in the Iran-Pakistan-India pipeline (IPI). A 10-member high-level delegation of Gazprom arrived in Islamabad in October 2005 to begin formal discussion on the construction of the $7 billion Iran-Pakistan-India (IPI) gas pipeline, and an ambitious project of gas storage in Pakistan. It was the first visit of the Chairman of Gazprom to Pakistan, the world's largest gas producing company with over 20 per cent share in global gas production.[9]

During Prime Minister Manmohan Singh's visit in May 2005, both countries decided to set up a Joint Study Group (JSG) on Economic Cooperation to look into the feasibility of the Comprehensive Economic Cooperation Agreement (CECA).[10] On the Kudankulam issue, the Prime Minister sought to allay fears of President Putin on the nuclear fuel falling into wrong hands and said a bill to prevent its misuse would be introduced in the Indian Parliament. The Indian Cabinet had already okayed the bill. During Manmohan Singh's visit to Moscow in December 2005 to attend the sixth bilateral summit, President Putin said, "We have been successfully cooperating in nuclear energy and Kudankulam nuclear power project is an example. We see India taking necessary steps to build relations with the Nuclear Suppliers Group (NSG)."[11] Prime Minister Singh observed that there was a vast potential for expansion of cooperation in the field of civil nuclear energy given India's growing energy requirements and the importance of nuclear energy as a clean and viable alternative energy source. Some of the most 'significant and promising areas' of cooperation identified during the visit were energy, telecom and transportation.

A major hurdle in Indo-Russian nuclear cooperation has been the restrictions imposed by Nuclear Suppliers' Group (NSG) on both India and Russia. Russia, which is also a member of 44-member NSG, has assured India of easing the restrictions. Sergei Lavrov, Russia's Foreign Minister during his meeting with External Affairs Minister, Natwar Singh in Moscow on 29 October 2005 indicated that NSG could make an exception regarding India in terms of norms observed by the nuclear group so that civilian nuclear energy cooperation could be expanded.[12] Natwar Singh was in Moscow to attend the meetings of the Indo-Russian Inter-Government Commission (IRIGC) and the Shanghai Cooperation Organization (SCO).

Viktor Khristenko, Russia's Energy and Industry Minister invited India to invest in Russia's energy sector, and join Russian companies in exploration and extraction activities in third countries, particularly in Central Asia. In the context of the interest expressed by ONGC and other Indian companies in picking up a stake in Russian energy companies like Transneft, Manmohan

Singh and Khristenko, during the visit of the former to Moscow in December 2005, agreed to promote cooperation between their respective oil companies through 'joint ventures and equity participation.'[13] The Russian minister specifically welcomed India's interest in participating in the Sakhalin-3 oil project in Siberia. India has already invested $2.7 billion in Sakhalin-1 but is expected to have to bargain hard for a share in the even more lucrative Sakhalin-3 venture where Russian and international energy-majors such as Lukoil, Gazprom, Rosneft and Exxon Mobil are all jockeying for position. Prime Minister Singh conveyed India's willingness to consider positively the construction of additional reactors in view of its growing energy needs.

In a meeting in Moscow in December 2005, Prime Minister Singh and Russian businessmen agreed to develop a long-term energy partnership and decided that India and Russia would explore oil and gas assets both in production and explorations in third world countries like the Central Asian region. India also responded positively to the Russian request to construct additional nuclear reactors in view of India's growing energy needs. This was a clear signal that nuclear energy is set to play a pivotal role in India-Russia economic relations since international restrictions on technology transfer to India are expected to be lifted shortly. Referring to India's investment in Sakhalin-I, Manmohan Singh showed interest in Sakhalin-III. The dialogue between ONGC, GAIL, Roseneft and Gazprom, he said, is gaining momentum. Asking the business communities to seize the initiative, the Prime Minister also informed them that India was working on an agreement to permit the utilization of the remaining rupee debt for Russian investments in India as their bilateral trade was moving from the Rupee-Rouble arrangements to becoming a fully market determined phenomenon. Both countries discussed the difficult visa regime, lack of information, weak financial base and lack of transport links.

In the field of Indo-Russian economic cooperation, some new areas can be identified. One area is joint cooperation in Central Asia. India could play a bigger role in Russia's energy strategy such as joint exploration and prospecting for new areas in Eastern Siberia and in the Caspian Sea Basin. Involvement in the construction of the pipeline network, modernizing and upgradation of existing port facilities is another such area. India will have to go in for long-term agreements to buy Russian oil. The transport route in the present situation is via the Black Sea. A new opportunity that has opened up is to directly deal with the vast regions of Russia. For instance, the agreement between Gujarat and Astrakhan, Karnataka and Samara, can prove helpful. The potential for cooperation in diamond processing, development of inland waterways and road construction needs to be explored.

Both India and Russia have already taken steps such as establishment of ILTP, which currently comprises about 130 projects in 18 thrust areas of science and technology and Intergovernmental Commission on Trade, Economic, Scientific, Technological and Cultural Cooperation, signing of MoU between Confederation of Indian Industry (CII) and Russian Union of Industrialists and Entrepreneurs, Indian investment in Sakhalin project, the Russian agreement to explore Bay of Bengal, and involvement in Tehri, Barh and Obra power plant projects, etc. to improve bilateral economic relations. Russian gas sector Gazprom and some of its affiliates such as Stroytransgaz are already working in India, though more synergy needs to be infused in such ventures. India can provide Russia consumer goods such as tea, coffee, tobacco, textiles and some other traditional products. The booming IT industry of India can be another help to Russian economy as it would provide Russian industry the information technology at a comparatively cheaper price than the European counterparts. In the era of globalization, private sector partnerships must be the new cementing force in Indo-Russian relations.

Russian cooperation with India is phenomenal as some of the recent developments would indicate. When the Indian nuclear power plant at Tarapore went into shortage of fuel this year, the Russian Prime Minister, Fradkov declared Russia's readiness to supply fuel to the hungry plant. Among Nuclear Supplier Groups (NSG), Russia has agreed to establish 1000 MW nuclear plant at Kudankulam in Tamil Nadu. Russia has also expressed readiness to support Indian move to waive NSG restrictions on India for civil nuclear cooperation. Both the countries are committed to peaceful nuclear cooperation that is mutually advantageous. There are substantial cooperation in the fields of defence, especially on joint research and development of armaments as in the case of BrahMos. The visit of Indian Prime Minister to EU in 2006 has not been much encouraging from Indian standpoint, at least in one respect. The EU, currently led by Finland could not commit to the Indian Prime Minister to support India's need to waive NSG restrictions so that

India can contact other countries regarding civil nuclear cooperation. Russia has proved itself different in this context.

Following are major areas identified by Confederation of Indian Industry (CII) during its interactions with Russian delegations in January 2007.

1. *Pharmaceuticals*: Russia is the second largest export destination for Indian pharmaceutical products, after the United States. However, while the US market is witnessing a negative growth, Indian exports to Russia have witnessed a 42% growth. India's ranking in Russia's market has fallen from 2nd position to 5th, after France, Germany, Slovenia and Hungary. A McKinsey report suggests that India's pharma market will rise to US$ 25 billion by 2010, of which US$ 11 billion will consist of domestic sales. India is competitive in terms of production costs, setting up plants (it is 40% cheaper to set up plants in India) and clinical research (35% to 40% savings in conducting research in India). Russia is the 8th largest pharma market and the 9th largest generic market in the world. Also, Russian demands for pharma products are rising as cardiovascular, respiratory, etc. diseases are increasing.

2. *Energy*: Indian and Russian companies can expand collaborations and joint ventures in third countries in the energy sector. The security of supply and the security of demand will lead to a stable partnership. India has already invested $2.7 billion in Sakhalin-1 but is expected to have to bargain hard for a share in the even more lucrative Sakhalin-3 venture where Russian and international energy majors such as Lukoil, Gazprom, Rosneft and Exxon Mobil are all jockeying for position. India's energy needs can substantially be met by the Russian reserve in oil and natural gas.

3. *Prospects of cooperation in third countries*: Particularly in Central Asia. Both countries could invest in coal/iron ore and the mining sectors. During Prime Minister Manmohan Singh's visit to Moscow in 2005, both the countries agreed to explore oil and gas assets in production and explorations in third world countries like the Central Asian region.

4. *High technology*: Cooperation with Russia is another area that India should keep pushing for such as in the area of coal gasification. A technology centre is proposed to be set up in Moscow that will help Indian companies to transform their ideas from the lab into a profitable business.

5. *Financial services*: The network of Russian banks is very underdeveloped in India, and even though there are some Indian banks in Russia, much still needs to be done. The CII has already opened its office at the Russian Chambers of Commerce and Industry in October 2003 to facilitate the process of economic cooperation. The Russia-India Business Council may work to smoothen and enlighten the prospective business ventures in each other's country and address issues such as rigid-visa regime and bureaucratic problems. The council would likely open new avenues of cooperation among the business communities of the two countries.

6. *Research and development and the commercialisation of technology*: Both countries can cooperate in this area. The real estate sector Infrastructure, energy and machinery are some of the main sectors that the Russian side can invest in India. Hyper-mechanical equipment is needed by India.

There is also scope for cooperation in areas like mining sector, diamond cutting and polishing, textiles, particularly synthetic fibres, etc. Projects such as expansion of air links between India and Russia can also be undertaken. The announcement in 2006 of direct flight from Amritsar to Moscow is one such step that would enable more accessibility, especially to the businessmen from Punjab to Russia and vice versa.

Prospects of Military and Technical Cooperation

Indo-Russian defence cooperation aftermath of the collapse of the Soviet Union in 1991 got a severe jolt, first due to new Russia's pro-Western tilt, and second, due to poor relations accumulated by many factors, one is certainly the diversion of interests of both the countries. While more than half of the Indian defence requirements were met by the Soviet Union, its collapse suddenly reduced the percentage of supply. As a result India searched for other suppliers. The first half of the nineties were very slow in defence cooperation between the two countries, thus motivating the then Indian Defence Minister, Sharad Pawar to visit other countries such as Ukraine for defence purposes. The conditions later improved, especially with the visit of Yeltsin to India in 1993, and visits to Russia by Indian Prime Ministers, Narasimha Rao and Deve Gowda in 1994 and 1997 respectively. In the current scenario, it can be said that Indo-Russian defence cooperation is the best part of their relations, as Russia has once again become India's largest arms supplier.

In 2003 agreements were signed between the two countries on cooperation in terms of joint research and development ventures, such as the BrahMos missile and the fifth generation jet fighter, in the fields of biomedical and other technologies and joint space efforts, and joint collaborations in Central Asian republics.[14] Among the ten accords signed during the visit of Prime Minister Atal Behari Vajpayee to Moscow in November 2003, there was an agreement on cooperation in space research, which included Russian assistance in an Indian lunar mission. India is the only country with which Russia is engaged in the joint development and production of high-tech and complex weapon systems. Another hallmark in the relationship is the Indian production of the Su-30 MKI jet fighters, under Russian licence, for sale to Malaysia. Russia has expressed willingness to cooperate with India on co-production of weapons systems and platforms, like a fifth-generation fighter aircraft, advanced warships and submarines.[15] Russia's recent offer include joint production and investment-sharing in the development of a fifth-generation fighter aircraft and a medium-class passenger-cum-cargo aircraft. There are negotiations for opening an Amur-class submarine assembly line in India. Russia's sale to India forms 40 per cent of its total sale of military equipment worldwide.

One of the long-hassled defence deals finally came to a settlement after India signed its biggest ever defence deal ($1.5 billion or over Rs. 7000 cr) with Russia for the purchase of the aircraft carrier, Admiral Gorshkov, in New Delhi on 20 January 2004. Defence Ministers of both the countries, George Fernandes of India and Sergei Ivanov of Russia, rightly called the deal a 'historic landmark'[16] in bilateral ties. The Russian carrier would replace India's only aircraft carrier, INS Virat. Its likely induction in 2008 or later would ensure that the navy does not lose its expertise in handling aircraft carriers.[17] A Russian firm, Beriev, is currently building three A-50 AWACS (Airborne Warning and Control Systems) called A-50Ehl. The surveillance aircraft will be the first of its kind to be built in Russia, and combines a variety of systems from Israel, India and Russia.

The Indian and Russian troops held joint military exercises in October 2005. Undergoing familiarization at Agra, paratroopers from both countries moved to Rajasthan and conducted a mock operation to destroy a terrorist camp. At the same time, the navies conducted joint exercises on the eastern seaboard. Some key Indian military and naval personnel underwent a two-month course in

Russian to transcend the language barrier. A joint naval exercise was held in 2003. This is the first time that both wings of the armed forces simultaneously held mock war games. The two countries hoped to make the joint exercises a regular event on the lines of similar exercises with the Western countries. Deepak Sinha, heading the 50th Independent Para Brigade, said the training of airborne forces was being held in two parts. The first was carried out in Agra, while the second was carried out in the Mahajan field firing range in Rajasthan. Five warships from the Russian Pacific Fleet, including a missile cruiser and two amphibious assault ships, took part in the 'Indra-2005' joint naval exercises which were more of anti-terror in nature and have been organized within the framework of Indo-Russian anti-terror cooperation. The exercise is supposed to enhance the capacity of both the countries to counter maritime threats. It was a two-day exercise that ended on 19 October 2005. The exercise was large in scope in comparison to the last one held in 2003 as it focused more on tactical part rather than on using more weapons.[18]

Bilateral defence was one of the major components of Prime Minister Manmohan Singh's visit to Moscow in December 2005. The two sides agreed to shift the main emphasis in their military-technical cooperation to joint development and manufacture of futuristic weapon systems.[19] In his joint press conference with President Putin, Singh observed: "Our perspective goal is to move towards collaborative projects involving design, development and production of the next generation of military products." On 6 December 2005, both countries signed the much-debated Intellectual Property Rights agreement, which opens the way for joint high-tech projects on a large scale. As per the agreement the accord would apply to new deals only, and not with retrospective effect. India agreed to give preference to Russian suppliers, but on condition that they make deliveries within reasonable time and price. The Multi-role Transport Aircraft and the 5th-generation fighter plane have been identified as two such projects. During the visit, both countries also updated their 10-year programme on military-technical cooperation up to 2010 to take into account the new thrust towards joint production of new weapons. The two sides signed a protocol on procedures for making changes in the programme. According to Russian sources, the lease by India of two nuclear submarines is also in the pipeline. Under a \$1.8 billion contract for a 10-year lease of two nuclear submarines,

Project-09710 'Shchuka-B', Russia has resumed the construction of the vessels, which were frozen in the 1990s. Both sides also discussed the plan to jointly use a military base in Central Asia.

As per reports, Russia has offered MIG-35s to India.[20] Each of the fighter planes that the Indian Air Force would buy could cost anywhere between Rs. 150 crore to Rs. 200 crore, while the total contract would well be over Rs. 25,000 crore. There are indications that the Indian government could be issuing the Request for Proposals, finally putting the process for the purchase in motion. The aircrafts are an improved version of the MIG-29s with capabilities that MIG Corporation claims no other fighter aircraft in the world has. The Russian experts have stated that the aircraft has an all aspect thrust vector control; can actually stop mid-way during flight. This quality would not only allow the fighter to get better accuracy in its attack role, but would also help to avoid an enemy fighter chase.

Conclusion

What Prof. Felix Yurlov of the Institute of Oriental Studies, Moscow told the author about four years ago still holds true today in the context of Indo-Russian economic cooperation. According to Yurlov political relations between India and Russia cannot become full-fledged unless accompanied by proportional economic cooperation.[21] It is common knowledge that the level of economic cooperation between the two countries is meagre compared to the huge potential both countries possess. However, there is no denying the fact that the recent years have witnessed some remarkable developments in economic cooperation. While India could fill the vast consumer markets in Russia, the latter could meet India's requirements in the areas of energy, metallurgy, arms and nuclear equipments. One of the important areas of cooperation is energy. Another crucial development is that both the countries have moved from buyer-seller relations to joint research and design of arms and armaments. More concrete steps need to be taken especially in the areas of infrastructure both organizational and geographic, visa, and diversification of areas of cooperation, services and technology. It is true that when the spirit of political bonhomie is infused into economic sphere, the two countries would most likely touch bilateral trade to the tune of $10 billion by the year 2010. The coming years would likely witness rapid developments in bilateral economic cooperation.

References

1. For details see the interview of Indian Ambassador to Moscow, Prabhat Shukla on 24 September 2007 in, *http://www.itar-tass.com/eng/level2.html? NewsID=11898417,* Accessed on 26 September 2007.
2. Marshall, I. Goldman, *Soviet Foreign Aid* (New York: Praegar), 1967, p. 85.
3. *National Herald,* 26 October 1996.
4. Excerpt from the speech of Boris Yeltsin, President of the Russian Federation in the Central Hall of Parliament on 29 January 1993, in *Strategic Digest,* Vol. 23, No. 4, April 1993, p. 592.
5. *Far Eastern Economic Review,* Vol. 156, No. 6, 11 February 1993, p. 18.
6. Quoted in Michael Ellman, "Russian Economic Boom, Post-1998: Illusion, Miracle or Recovery?", *Economic and Political Weekly,* July 17, 2004, p. 3234.
7. For details of the Joint Declaration see, *Strategic Digest,* Vol. 32, No. 12, December 2002, pp. 1430-1432.
8. *The Hindu,* 10 November, 2003.
9. *The Tribune,* 8 October, 2005.
10. *The Kashmir Times,* 10 May, 2005.
11. *Daily Excelsior,* 7 December, 2005.
12. *The Tribune,* 29 October, 2005.
13. *The Hindu,* 6 December, 2005.
14. *Times of India,* 17 November, 2003.
15. *The Asian Age,* 18 October, 2005.
16. *Times of India,* 21 January, 2004.
17. *The Hindu,* 21 January, 2004.
18. *The Hindu,* 19 October, 2005.
19. *The Hindu,* 7 December, 2005.
20. *The Tribune,* 20 November, 2005.
21. Personal Interview, 12 January, 2004.

13

India and Russia : Mismatch of Potentials and Performances in Economic Ties

Sanjay Deshpande

The revolutionary Soviet Union emerged early in the 20th century and had created an economic, political and social system radically different from the widely prevalent then capitalist order. The Soviet Union received recognition during and after the Second World War as a mighty military super power. This new system gave emphasis to education, health and housing for its citizens. Its spectacular achievement in the explorations of outer space and then its collapse in the last decade of the past century will arguably be among the major political events of the tumultuous century that has gone by.

Russia became the principal successor to the Soviet Union. Events in Russia during the last decade and a half remain relatively unexplored. However, there is a vague recognition that from the Soviet Union's centrally planned economy Russia has moved on to a market economy. Russia ventured into a path of structural reforms in early 1992, as part of its programme of transition to market and capitalism. In its transition towards a market economy, Russia did make major progress in structural reforms by liberalizing prices and trade regulations and in privatizing state enterprises. However, Russia did not get the desired goal. Instead, declining economic status, sluggish foreign investment and a growing share of gray economy continued to plague the country. There seems to be no end to misery to be faced by common Russians. It is necessary to understand the condition of the economy at the time of the Soviet collapse in order to get an in-depth knowledge of why the structural reform process was essential in Russia. Economist Gregory Khanin wrote "the economy was in a state of catastrophe when the Soviet Union disintegrated." According to him this situation was worse than a crisis condition.

An economy can recuperate from a crisis state, but from a catastrophe the revival of an economy is made possible as a self-destructive mechanism sets in. In the former Soviet Union, such a self-destructive socio-economic mechanism was rooted during the last years of Brezhnev's regime. In order to revive the economy, it was necessary to destroy this self-destructive mechanism, which was characterized by chaos. The old state economic structures and methods of governing had rapidly lost their grip. The political crisis during the Perestroika period worsened when Yeltsin took over Russian presidency in June 1990. In addition to these general reasons, the following five separate and concrete reasons were responsible for the crisis situation turning into catastrophe: 1. The foreign exchange crisis; 2. The fall in the production of raw materials; 3. The fall in the supply of labour; 4. Decline in fixed capital assets; and 5. The budget crisis.

The collapse of the Soviet Union saw total anarchy in the initial years with near complete breakdown of the administrative system, law and order and increase in crime rate. Untamed privatization of state properties in practically all areas of economy created mass unemployment and disillusionment about the future amongst the Russian people. Russia's reformist Prime Minister Yegor Gaider strongly recommended the shock therapy to improve the situation. This policy was a prescription that promised quick cure. Western economists like Jeffrey Sachs and Anders Aslund, who were advisors to the Russian government argued along with Gaidar that the interdependence among price liberalization, behaviour of enterprise managers and macroeconomic stability - all needed simultaneous action. They propagated shock therapy and structural reforms for attaining economic growth. The proponents of shock therapy felt that since the economy was chaotic, such harsh measures were essential as the only way to quick prosperity. The economists, who propagated economic reforms, advocated gradual but firm control on budget deficits and inflation based primarily on political acceptability. The harshness of the reforms wa to be eliminated because factory closures and a rise in unemployment stretched over a longer period. Smaller aid package that was more realistic was recommended. Both programmes however recommended price decontrol and privatization. This shock therapy proved to be pernicious. It created powerful oligarchs, who were benefited from questionable privatization in the country and gradually evolved as real power brokers. Unbalanced economic development, inexorable inflation, massive corruption, poverty and organized crime were other deficiencies of this therapy. The 'shock therapy' had shocked the very development process laden with deficiencies and lacking in economic transparency. The above factors severely affected Russia's foreign trade along-with India. Traditionally both India and the former USSR had close economic ties and there has been a sustained effort to promote it mutually. This is evident from the agreements reached at the various summit meetings.

Reasoning out the Decline

Among the several causes that affected Indo-Russian economic relations, the following are some of the prime ones that determined the shape of things to come in the aftermath of the Soviet collapse. First, foreign trade was the monopoly of the state during the Soviet Union. After the collapse of the Soviet Union, the state lost domination over foreign trade. The young and inexperienced private organizations were not adequately equipped with or efficient enough to manage foreign trade. Under the prevailing chaotic conditions, dodgy and mafia elements affected Russian economy in general and foreign trade in particular. Secondly and coincidentally, India embarked on the path of economic liberalization in 1991. However, India did not introduce shock therapy. In order to get profits from liberalization policy, many Indian trade operators were active in trading activities. They were motivated only by short term perspective for Indian goods. They did not pay attention to the quality products being exported to Russia. Such type of businessmen and traders were not interested in cultivating the huge untapped Russian market from a long term perspective for Indian goods.

Thirdly, uncertainty arose out of transition coupled with defunct system of annual trade protocols that landed Indian exporters of agricultural and consumer products in heavy loss. Fifty percent of them constituted India's export and they incurred heavy losses due to non-payment ability on the part of the Russian importing agencies. This situation discouraged many exporters who were involved in trading with former Soviet Union. As a result, trade between the countries slumped to a new low of less than one billion dollars in 1992.

Fourthly, after the Soviet dissolution, Rupee trade was terminated and India's debt to the USSR amounted to Rs. 36,000 crores which was converted into debt Repayment Funds payable to Russia in Indian merchandise. In May 1992 a fresh Indo-Russian Trade and Economic Agreement was signed during the official visit of Russian Secretary of State, Gennady Burbulis. It was agreed that the bilateral trade would henceforth be carried out only through hard currency transactions, and India would repay its debt to Russia, it being the successor state of the USSR. Transition from rupee to hard currency trade, the objective does not seem to have materialized for a variety of reasons. This has created confusion in India's trade with Russia.

Fifthly, during the last decade, the multiplicity of payment methods in trade has prevailed - DRF, hard currency, Escrow and barter created some element of misunderstanding and a large amount of confusion in bilateral trade. The lack of stable mechanism for imports from India starting with the allocation of Rupee funds, changing over to auction of rupee funds at discounted rates, the lack of consistency and transparency in payment had also added to the complexity of India's trade with Russia. Sixthly, in the process of liberalization of the economy, both India and Russia declared economic reforms to open up their economies. Russia had radically changed its priorities in favor of the US and the West to establish good economic relations with the capitalist world. Finally, there were problems of transportation of goods involving a long period of 12 weeks for delivery of goods from Indian ports to Russian cities. The traditional export route through Odessa port was not accessible as it had become a part of Ukraine. Now they have to find a new trade route, which was more time and cost consuming.

Economic Relations under Yeltsin

Notwithstanding the relatively less impressive performance of India's trade with Russia and problems facing bilateral trade, there are wide potentialities for promoting trade and economic relations between the two countries. Cordial relations prevailing between India and Russia and the political goodwill built and sustained over the last several decades forced the two countries to expand the trade relations. The Indian and Russian governments renegotiated the entire trade understanding in 1993. Therefore, old traditional participants like the public sector units and foreign trade enterprises of both sides were left insignificant. This change allowed private sectors to get a free run. They were involved in non-regulated and incorrect and often illegal business practices. Hence, the private sectors ruined the trade instead of strengthening it. This further eroded the consumer and supplier confidence in both the countries. Russia looked towards West to carry out economic reforms while India continued to work towards enhancement and stabilization of relations with Russia by moving ahead in the ongoing projects committed since Soviet years, especially in the area of defence cooperation. India was also bound to adopt such policy as nearly 80 percent of her armed forces are equipped with Russian weaponry and hardware.

During the late 1990s, the then minister of economy, Alexander Livshits, admitted while stating that "had it not been for the contracts and new orders from India and China our defence industrial establishment would have completely crippled down, therefore we should value our old trusted allies." Dynamic changes in global economic conditions and the ongoing transformations in both India and Russia forced to enhance trade relations. There is a need to emphasize on strong economic essentials such as high quality and competitiveness in trading practices. Russian policy makers stated that Indian businessmen and exporters have not clearly comprehended changes in Russia's market and economic status. They have failed to make impressive gains in the rapidly changing market situation in Russia and faced tough quality and price competition from other competitor countries. For over four decades, they closely depended on both with the Soviet Foreign Trade Organisations and Government of India departments and banks to secure contracts. They executed the contracts without knowing the ground realities like consumer preferences, quality of the goods/services traded with. In brief, they never faced a real market competition and were not prepared to adjust to the market realities. Inflation and cumbersome custom procedures and tax laws, deteriorating security system, political uncertainty, criminal mafia and unreliable banking system during the 1990s further complicated their trade. The August 1998 fiscal crisis in Russia led to total bankruptcy of thousands of foreign companies including many Indian firms which blunted their confidence making them reluctant to do business with Russia.

During the visit of Gennady Burbulis to India in 1992, it was agreed by both sides to accord most favoured nation status to each other and to set up an inter-governmental commission on trade, economic, scientific and technical cooperation. Russia renewed export of oil, newsprint and military equipments. In response, India opened $285 million technical credit line to Russia for importing traditional items like tea, coffee, leather, tobacco and spices. The trade had slightly gone up to $1.32 billion including India's exports of $750 million and imports $569 million in 1993.

During President Boris Yeltsin's visit to India in January 1993 both the sides fine tuned their relationship in post-cold war realities. At that time, on the economic front a new emphasis was laid on investments and joint ventures in areas of mutual interest. Four documents were exchanged on the settlement of India's debt to erstwhile Soviet Union. They covered modalities of debt repayment, i.e., purchase by Russia of goods and services from India under Indian credit line, reimbursement by Russia to Indian exporters for goods already exported but not paid for and counter-trade and other internationally recognized norms of trade. Though considerable attention has been paid by the Indian and Russian leaders to cooperate in the field of trade and economic relations, bilateral trade has not increased as expected for various reasons. The volume of bilateral trade has been below $2 billion all through these years. India's exports to Russia showed a general northward trend during 1992-1993 and showed some decline in 1997-1998. The value of trade has been fluctuating annually between 31 billion to 41 billion rupees. There has been a general declining trend since 1999-2000. However, India's imports from Russia have increased significantly during the last decade. It may be mentioned that this trade data do not include India's imports of defence equipments from Russia and also shuttle trade with Russia. In the first half of last decade shuttle trade accounted for a significant quantity of total exports from India. The quantum of this shuttle trade has declined over the years. According to unofficial estimates, at present the shuttle trade could be around $10 billion in the total imports of Russia. This trade originates mainly from India, Dubai, Singapore, Hong Kong and Saudi Arabia.

Improved Relations Under Putin

The new millennium saw a change in leadership of Russia when the present president Vladimir Putin, assumed power in May 2000. He had the Herculean job on hands inherited from his predecessor. The vast state was diseased with vices like massive corruption, organized crime, deflected industry, high inflation, bankrupt factories, unemployed youth, and a society where majority were robbed of their savings by the state and deprived of basic needs. These problems had created a massive gap between the haves and the have-nots. The only beneficiaries were *Novie Russkiye or the neo-rich,* who had acquired industrial gems of state property through fraudulently and illegally conducted auctions under the garb of reforms and privatization. This group of Russians familiarized as Oligarchs who had become oil barons, media tycoons, wood lords, metal giants and big bankers. They not only wielded economic power but also made self-favoring economic policies. The state was virtually under their diktat. During the Yeltsin regime huge state funds were being illegally transferred from Russia to European banks. Putin went about carefully with the process of strengthening the vertical power concept of the Russian state so as to eradicate the rot in the local administration system and the regional authorities. This was being done to stop further disintegration of Russia as a state.

Indo-Russian relations including trade and economic ties have acquired a new status when President Putin assumed the office of presidency in the Kremlin. Putin first visited India in October 2000 and the declaration on "Strategic Partnership" was signed. Since then there have been eight annual summits between the Russian President and Indian Prime Minister, and about 40 important bilateral documents have been signed. These summits have enabled to review the status of bilateral relations in all spheres including trade and economy. The 2004 summit noticed the areas in which the future of the Indo-Russian relations needs focus. India recognizes Russia as a market economy; hence supports its entry to WTO. A substantial and new emphasis on economy including the field of energy and banking has been made. While giving the Nehru Memorial Lecture in New Delhi, president Putin stated: "I believe that the future of Indo-Russian economic ties lies in the spheres of investment cooperation and the implementation of major strategic projects." The December 2005 summit set the target to move away from a declaratory stage to a constructive phase of action. Both sides jointly earmarked goals to expand trade in hi-tech products, to improve forms and methods of investments, to bolster scientific and technological partnership in priority areas such as space exploration, IT, software parks, communication and advanced and alternative technologies. A Joint Study Group was formed in 2006 to enhance Indo-Russian trade relations to understand how Russia and India can engage with each other in order to achieve the $10 billion target. The JSG submitted its findings in February 2007 at the time of the meeting of Indo-Russian Trade and Investment

Forum. Putin's last visit to India in January 2007 was yet another landmark in the history of India-Russia relations.

The Indo-Russian relations have for the first time been divested of ideological baggage under Putin's leadership. In the Soviet era, bilateral ties were cast in the paradigm of Cold War compulsions, whereas during Yeltsin's presidency, Russia looked at India through the prism of Moscow's short-lived honeymoon with the west. But Putin has put partnership with India on the solid base of what he described in 2000 as "the concurrence of long-term national and geopolitical and economic interests of Russia and India." It is Putin's deep conviction that both countries stand to gain from each other's strength and it is in Russia's interests to help India gain more regional and global clout. Hence the invitation to president Putin as the chief guest of 2007 Republic Day celebrations serves not only to reaffirm the value India attaches to strategic partnership with Russia, but is also a tribute to the Russian leader's personal role in cementing the partnership between the two countries.

It has been the mantra of every bilateral summit held on an annual basis since 2000, to deplore the low trade, which lags far behind the excellent political and defence relations between the two countries, and to call for tapping the "vast potential" of two way commerce. Last year the two countries set a target of boosting trade to $10 billion by 2010. Similar promises had been made in the past but were never fulfilled. The low volume of bilateral trade between India and Russia requires urgent and close attention. The trade has increased only marginally from $1.5 billion a decade ago to $2.75 in 2006. Trade has stagnated despite the fact that the Indian and Russian economies have been dynamically growing at 7-9 per cent annually, and moreover often described as mutually complementary. By contrast, India's trade with China has soared from $2 billion to $18 billion in recent years, and so has Russia's trade with China, crossing $36 billion last year and still growing more than 30 per cent a year.

Possible Areas of Cooperation

Though the volume of bilateral trade is low, there are wide potentialities for promoting trade and economic relations. Indian exporters and traders can look forward to expanding market opportunities in Russia, it being a huge market. President Putin stated "Indian entrepreneurs should make use of wide opportunities available in Russia." There is considerable scope for intensive cooperation in the energy sector that includes nuclear energy and nuclear security and is emerging as the key dimension of Indo-Russian future economic partnership. The sides agreed "to promote and assist Indian investments in Russian energy sector," says the joint declaration signed by leaders of both the countries. The ONGC-OVL's investment of $2.7 billion in the Sakhalin-I project is the precursor to other mutually beneficial investment in this vital sector. OVL is expected to further expand its activity to Sakhalin-III in future. ONGC-OVL, Gazprom and GAIL are jointly developing a block in the Bay of Bengal shelf. India is one of the rapidly growing consumers of oil and gas to promote its booming economy. Its transport from Russia to India via various routes is easily achievable as Russia is one of the leading producers and exporters in the world. Russia can play a major role in ensuring India's energy security in terms of exploring newly discovered oil and gas fields as well as modernizing the existing facilities and expanding the infrastructure including pipelines, refineries and gas distribution networks. In 2006 leaders of both countries met in St Petersburg during the G-8 summit. Bilateral energy cooperation was highlighted in their talks. The Prime Minister, speaking about energy security, had emphasized that "extreme volatility and instability in hydrocarbon markets can affect the global economy's chances of sustained growth. Therefore, we would like to see arrangements worked out at the global level for more predictable supply and demand, so that the goal of energy security becomes a reality." From the Indian perspective, diversification of energy supplies and moving away from dependence on fossil fuels is important.

It is essential to note that Indo-Russian cooperation should be directed even more effectively in the use of nuclear resources, for which large potentiality exists to meet the growing demand for energy in India. Kudankulam project of $2.6 billion, which has been coming up with Russia's assistance, might partly solve the energy crisis in South India. The share of nuclear energy in India's total energy production is relatively less. Therefore more nuclear power plants are to be set up in various parts of India, incorporating advanced and innovative technologies ensuring energy security. Both the governments should encourage and assist companies to invest in the energy sector. Indo-Russian nuclear energy cooperation as an overall component of ensuring India's energy security with tremendous economic bearing must receive focused attention in both countries. Russia could easily provide a counter weight to Indo-US nuclear deal in the offing.

Besides the energy sector, there is wide scope for cooperation in the field of information technology. Putin's visit to India's IT capital, Bangalore, is an indication that Russia would like to gain from our experience in this field. Putin was keen to set up an information park in Russia. Collaboration between the two countries will be for mutual advantage. The metals industry is one of Russia's key economic sectors. India will become one of the major centres of ferrous metals production in the next few years. Russia exports ferrous and non-ferrous metals to India. VSMPO-AVISMA Corporation is delivering titanium products to India for the needs of aircraft-building, chemical and engineering industries. Some of the Russian enterprises, including Rusal, cooperate with the Indian side in the production of aluminum in India. Some joint large scale Russian-Indian projects in power, metals, civil aviation and space studies are being developed or implemented.

Pharmaceuticals is another area that needs to be noticed. Russia is the largest export destination for Indian pharmaceutical products after the US. Indian exports to Russia have witnessed 140% growth in post-Soviet years. In last few years India's ranking in Russia's market has fallen. India is competitive in terms of production costs, setting up plants and clinical research; yet falls short of quality and standard. Yet, India does have very few plants and research laboratories in Russia. Russian demands for pharma products are rising as cardiovascular, respiratory, cerebro-vascular diseases are increasing; but Indian companies are unable to cater to their demands. Another problem Indian exporters face in this area is registration of the products. The Russian Pharmacopoeia requirements are difficult to find. If found they are mostly in Russian. To comply with RPR, one has to spend extra time, energy and money to prepare a dossier. Russian authorities take 2-3 years to register a product. By the time the registration has been completed, the market scenario changes and product producers have to file for new products. Russia follows European Union norms for registration, but EU takes a maximum one year to register the new product.

Both sides should have intensive cooperation in mining, textiles, synthetic fibers, nanotechnology, biotechnology, communications and financial investments in infrastructure projects and state protection to investments in strategic sectors. FICCI, CII have intensified their contacts with their Russian counterparts by holding Indo-Russian buyer-seller meets. It is necessary to intensify interaction between the representatives of business, academic community and policy makers and also among the private companies in the regions through chambers of trade and commerce and other business promotion organizations. In augmenting bilateral economic cooperation both countries encounter a series of obstacles. They include :

- It is difficult to acquire visa to travel to Russia for business. However it is easy to get it if there is an invitation by a Russian company. Moreover, a lot of paperwork is needed. There is need that Russia should simplify visa rules for businessmen. An introduction letter from the Chamber of Commerce and Trade of the country should suffice for the embassy or consulate to issue one time visa for a stipulated period. Many entrepreneurs cannot travel to Russia to see the business environment and make enquiries. Russian authorities have been demanding that India sign the re-admission treaty with Russia in order to minimize illegal immigrants to Russia via third countries.
- Language is one of the biggest barriers in dealing with the Russian market. There are few directories or information books about Russian companies in foreign languages. Foreign businessmen face difficulties to find out their counterparts in the country if they do not have local partners.
- The local staff in all fields of Russian business has to be trained with international business standards. India has offered Russia to train their staff and bring them to international standards.
- Rupee-Rouble debt is still the hurdle for expanding the trade between the two countries. Russia is still left with huge Rupee funds to utilize through trade of Indian commodities, while India's trade with Russia has shifted to dollar parity transactions.
- Lack of ready information has also added to some problems. No separate website on Indo-Russian trade is available to facilitate online interaction between businessmen.
- The North-South corridor represents the shortest route to Europe and Russia. Although this route is already in use, major choke point is the Astrakhan customs port. At the

moment, they use an alternative route to Russia not through Bander Abbas in Iran. However, the corridor does represent the shortest link to Russia from India and must be strengthened.

Conclusion

In the 1990s the relative positions of India and Russia have dramatically changed. Both countries began to pass through tough economic transformations. In the past, the Soviet Union played an important role in India's industrialization. It had a comparative advantage in steel sector and that was central to the needs of India. After the Soviet disintegration, the urgency of economic reforms and changing global political scenario has brought both countries even closer. Now India has to assess, where Russia has a comparative advantage. So far India has been able to identify only defence production and oil and gas sector. But India can have cooperation in mining, heavy engineering goods, synthetic fibers, and biotechnology. Similarly, India can help Russia restructuring and modernizing through its expertise in Information Technology, Communications, and Pharmaceuticals, banking and financial services. Future bilateral economic relations will depend on Russia's importance to India's developmental needs and vice-versa. Two factors will determine the future of Indo-Russian economic relations: sustained growth of the Russian economy and competitiveness of Indian industry. The strong political will and annual high level summits between the two countries have to improve bilateral economic relations that can be converted into real economic gains. The present relations are certainly not proportionate to the existing potential. Some bold concrete policy initiatives are needed not only to improve these relations but also to provide a new fillip to bilateral ties. According to the Strategic Partnership document, both the sides will explore joint ventures in third countries. However, nothing has happened so far on this front. Both economies are growing at an average of 7-9 per cent every year. So this is the right time to give a new direction to Indo-Russian economic relations.

14

Offshore Energy Cooperation

Kishore Kumar

Abstract

Russia is today one of the biggest hydrocarbon resource holders of the world. A large amount of their oil is likely to be produced from western Siberia and Volga-Ural basins. The development of new oil and gas basins in the Arctic offshore, East Siberia and Far East will further replenish the existing resource base. On the other hand, a developing country like India has seen, in recent years, substantial rise in energy demand due to population growth and economic development. However, the country has long suffered 'energy poverty' due to excessive dependence on West Asian source. The need of the hour is to diversify the sources of energy supply.

From an Indian perspective, fluctuating relations with some countries in the neighbourhood have impeded progress in accessing energy sources on our doorstep. As a result, we have started looking to our extended neighbourhood, like Russia, who have shown remarkable keenness on cooperation and partnership on energy security. Russia's growing production of hydrocarbons and India's expanding market are sought to be matched through dedicated joint ventures. State backed companies of both the countries have come together to cooperate on both upstream and downstream energy projects. India's recent economic performance, growing energy market and technical capabilities make us one of the most reliable partners in the quest for energy security.

The G-8 Outreach Summit on June 6-8, 2007 at the German resort of Heilingendam had the Indian Prime Minister, Dr. Manmohan Singh put forth the Indian stand in clear terms: "..due care must be taken not to allow growth and development of developing countries be undermined while dealing with greenhouse gas emissions". The pointer was towards the emission of global warming gases (GWG) which are increasing at a rate faster than the worst scenario built by the Intergovernmental Panel on Climate Change (IPCC). The Indian view was articulated just before the meeting with G-8 leaders, when the Outreach-5 (O-5) countries comprising India, China, Brazil, South Africa and Mexico met to outline their position on global economy, climate change, protection of intellectual property rights, energy and environment.

It may be recalled that the US refused to sign the Kyoto Protocol in 2001 arguing that "its economic interests will be threatened".[1] What does it imply in terms of energy consumption and economic growth? With 35 per cent of the carbon dioxide emission, the USA does not appear to take any responsibility for the consequences so long as their business is not affected. Asian and European nations strongly criticised the decision of US President Bush on the Kyoto Protocol, the UN Treaty on Climate Change, which commits 27 industrialised nations to cut greenhouse gas emissions, their 1990 level of greenhouse gas emissions, by half by the year 2050. The main US concern was that the cut down would put their firms at an 'unfair disadvantage' to Chinese and Indian ones[2], which are termed as future big emitters of carbon dioxide.

In the midst of all the wrangling over global warming and greenhouse gas emissions, the bottom line remains the role of energy (fossil fuel) in a nation's economic development. Though much larger in scope, the energy security for a nation is often considered synonymous with oil security, keeping in view the growing oil imports and the widening gap between demand and supply of petroleum. India's first Prime Minister, Jawaharlal Nehru, while inaugurating the Committee for Power and Energy Survey, said (December 29, 1962)[3]:

'There are various ways of writing history, the history of the world. One such way can certainly be the growth of power and energy used by human beings. I suppose one could form some idea of the state of development of any country, without knowing anything in detail about it, merely by knowing how much power and energy it produces and consumes, nothing else".

However, limited access to and overwhelming dependence on imported energy sources (oil and gas) constitute a significant obstacle to social and economic development of developing countries.

Energy Demand and Supply

The present trends and available data indicate that energy consumption is expected to continue to increase very significantly over the next few decades. According to research by International Energy Agency (IEA), China, South Asia, East Asia, Latin America, Africa and West Asia will account for 68 per cent of the increase in world energy demand between 1997 and 2020.[4] Hydrocarbons (oil and gas) account for about 65 per cent of world energy requirements (43 and 22 per cent respectively). They increased 95 per cent over the past 30 years and are expected to rise by another 50 per cent by 2030. On the other hand, the growth rate in energy consumption in the developing countries is 3-4 higher as compared to the industrialised world.[5] The member countries of the OECD currently use 54 per cent of the world's energy, but this is expected to decline to 44 per cent by 2020 while that of developing countries may rise to 45 per cent from the current 34 per cent. The Asian demand has gone up significantly, mainly in China and India, due to high population growth and economic/industrial development.

India too registered a rapid rise in energy consumption since the 1990s due to economic liberalisation and accelerated pace of economic growth (over nine per cent GDP growth rate in 2005-06). Transport and power have been the two fastest growing sectors in energy demand. [6] Our energy mix has been dominated by coal and hydrocarbon (50 and 45 per cent respectively), but the poor quality of coal and the lack of infrastructure to clean it have made the government slowly switch from highly polluting coal-fired power plants to those using natural gas. Hence, the demand for petroleum products may increase substantially in the next two decades, and become the primary fuel outstripping coal.[7] India is today the world's fifth biggest energy consumer, and is projected to surpass Japan and Russia to take the third place by 2030. Along with an ascendant economy comes a mounting hunger for energy, and the level of growth cannot be sustained without continually boosting the country's energy supply.

It is estimated/projected by experts that Indian oil resources may dry up by 2020 and reserves may also run out in another 7-8 years even if only 30 per cent of the demand is met through domestic production. So, with the growth in demand and almost no growth in production, the bulk of demand in energy (hydrocarbons) will have to be met by imports. The major reserves of oil, almost 70 per cent, lie in the Persian Gulf—Saudi Arabia, Iran, Iraq, Kuwait and the United Arab Emirates (UAE). Other significant sources are the Caspian Sea, Western and Central Africa (Nigeria, Sudan, Angola, Ghana, etc.). The principal sources of gas lie in Asia—27 per cent in Russia, 15 per cent in Iran and 14 per cent in Qatar.[8]

On the other hand, India is impeded by rising oil prices in the face of unprecedented growth levels, reliance on energy, heavy industries and lack of energy-efficient technologies. While China is, in the words of Prime Minister Manmohan Singh, ahead of us in planning for its energy security... India is still plagued by power shortages (energy poverty), undermining the confidence of investors.[9] Our quest for energy security is further impeded by our sometimes tense relations with energy suppliers, energy transit countries and energy competitors. Nationalism and oil are proving to be a volatile mix, which requires to be resolved through 'energy diplomacy'.

Quest for Energy Security

There is no escaping the fact that energy is the essential input for economic development and also for improving the quality of life. However, the growth of its requirements the world over has been accompanied with energy poverty, especially in the developing countries of the South which have fastest population growth. The avowed responsibility of the government is essentially two-pronged: development of conventional forms of energy (mainly fossil fuel) for meeting the growing need of the society at reasonable cost, and also non-conventional (renewable) forms of energy (solar, water, air, bio-energy, etc.) for sustainable development.[10] This is the essence of energy security, and safeguarding this interest depends entirely on oil diplomacy!

The policy makers have taken numerous initiatives to address the country's growing energy requirements, viz. creating 15-45 days of emergency reserves, augment production, regime deregulation and diversifying beyond hydrocarbon sources. Nevertheless, in the short to medium term, the country will have to rely on an increasing amount of imported oil and gas, as has been spelt out in the *Hydrocarbon Vision 2025* (1999). In the present scenario, the

Indian economy has become increasingly sensitive and vulnerable to international oil market. Hence, the thrust is more for active overseas engagement for sourcing as well as exploration and production (E&P) of hydrocarbon.[11] For the purpose, the Oil and Natural Gas Corporation (ONGC), the Indian Oil Corporation (IOC) and the Gas Authority of India Ltd. (GAIL) have formed a consortium—ONGC for E&P IOC for marketing and GAIL for transportation and marketing of gas.

As mentioned earlier, oil diplomacy is essentially the need to advance energy sensitivity to the realm of foreign policy. The issue of diversifying the sources of supply, along with building strategic reserves and storage facilities, is the main concern of energy security today. India has a huge market for Bangladesh gas due to their proximity to the industrial area of Kolkata (close to the border). Some progress has been made as the energy ministers of India, Bangladesh and Myanmar have recently issued a joint statement for the construction of a 900-km gas pipeline from Myanmar's offshore *Shwe* field to Kolkata, passing through Arakan state (Myanmar), Mizoram and Tripura, and Bangladesh.[12] Another MoU was signed with Iran in 1993 for a 1,700-km pipeline from Iran's South Pars field with 700 km passing through the Pakistani territory.

However, the future of this project at times becomes doubtful due to periodic violence across the line of control in Kashmir and tensions in Pakistan's Baluchistan province. Similarly, the Indo-Central Asian cooperation in the sphere of energy, the US backed Turkmenistan-Afghanistan-Pakistan (TAP) or Trans-Afghan Pipeline, have also been delayed by instabilities in Afghanistan and poor Indo-Pakistan relations. So, a limited progress in accessing energy resources on our doorstep due to fluctuating relations with neighbours has led to continuing efforts to access energy resources further afield.

Extended Neighbourhood

India has the geographical advantage of having a key location between the Persian Gulf and East and Southeast Asia, along with substantial market depth in respect to energy products. This is why Japan has expressed the desire to engage India in a strategic partnership on energy, and so has the United States, with the Gulf nations also welcoming an increased role for India.[13] On its part, India has organised a few Round Table Conferences between oil consuming nations and energy producers in order to identify commonality of interests and specific areas of cooperation. The first was held in January 2005 between four principal oil consuming countries (China, Japan, Korea and India) and oil producing countries of West Asia and Southeast Asia. Another Round Table was held in November 2005 between the same oil-consuming nations and the producer nations of North and Central Asia (Russia, Kazakhstan, Uzbekistan, Azerbaijan and Turkmenistan). The specific areas of cooperation discussed in the two regional Round Table Conferences were reforms in the market, development of strategic reserves, crisscross investments between producers and consumers, R&D and technology transfer, and energy conservation, efficiency and environment friendly fuels.[14] There was also an agreement on developing energy interconnections through LNG and transnational pipelines as well as other transportation networks (both by land and sea) for integrating the energy market.

The Indian Ministry of Petroleum and Natural Gas has encouraged oil sector public undertakings to venture abroad to access exploration blocks and oil producing properties for equity oil either on their own or through strategic alliances and joint ventures. The ONGC Videsh Ltd (OVL) has signed a JV with PetroVietnam (1999) for gas production, transportation and power generation from Lan Tay and Lad Do fields in Vietnam.[15] Another contract was signed by the OVL with the Sudanese government for the construction of a 740 km petroleum pipeline from Khartoum refinery to Port Sudan.[16] Some of the supplier countries, like Iran, Myanmar and Sudan, are sought to be isolated by the West on political grounds, but they are still sought to be engaged by China and India which are competing in the energy market as well as collaborating in Iran, Sudan and Russia.

Target Russia

In recent years, discoveries of new energy sources have established Russia is one of the biggest hydrocarbon resource holders in the world. The oil and gas bearing areas are found on about 90 per cent of all Russian shelves, but they are located mostly in remote areas characterised by severe climatic conditions (the Arctic and Far East)[17];

(*a*) Two giant oil and gas bearing basins found in the West Arctic (shelves of the Barents and Kara seas) cover an area of 2 million sq. km and contain potential resources of at least 50-60 billion tons of oil equivalent. Exploration and drilling revealed the existence of ten prolific oil and gas fields — two of them, Rusanovskoe and Leningradskoe, in the Kara Sea, are estimated to have 5 trillion cubic metres of gas (worldwide gas production at present is only 2 trillion cubic metres a year).

(*b*) Exploratory and production development on the offshore oil and gas fields of the Caspian, Black, Baltic and Asov seas have been in progress, albeit on a smaller scale, for a relatively long time. The shallow shelf of the northern part of the Caspian Sea has recoverable hydrocarbon resources estimated at about 2 to 3 billion tons.

(*c*) Shtokmanobskoe gas field in the Barent Sea is perhaps the world's largest known gas field with about 3 trillion cubic metres of gas and more than 20 million tons of gas condensate. The Prirazlomnoe oil field in the Pechora Bay is known to contain over 200 million tons of oil reserves.

(*d*) On the northern shelf, the Jamal gas condensate field is estimated to produce up to 80-100 billion cubic metres of natural gas a year.

(*e*) On the shelves of Far East and Eastern Siberia, there are reserves (excluding Sakhalin shelf) in the sea of Okhotsk and the Bering, Chukchi and East Siberian seas. There have been discovery of more than 20 oil and gas bearing basins in the region.

(*f*) The shelf of Sakhalin had its rich oil and gas resources discovered a long time ago and they have been intensively explored for more than 20 years. By a conservative estimate, they contain 14 billion barrels of oil and 96 trillion cubic feet of gas.

The Sakhalin reserves (Sakhalin 1 & 2) are being developed under production sharing agreement contracts involving international oil companies like ExxonMobil and Shell. These include big investments to upgrade the island's infrastructure—roads, bridges, airports, railways, ports and communications system.[18] Other participants in the project are two Russian companies Sakhalinmorneftegas - Shelf and RN - Astra, the Japanese company Sakhalin Oil and Gas Development Co. Ltd. and India's ONGC Videsh Ltd (OVL). In addition, Sakhalin 3-through-6 are in various stages of development.

Indo-Russian Partnership

Cooperation with Russia in the energy sector is not a new development, it is rooted in history. India was severely short of energy after gaining independence in 1947 when the then Soviet Union helped us not only to prospect for oil, drill wells and produce it, but also to construct oil refineries at Barauni, Mathura, etc.[19] Along with the energy sector, cooperation in other areas (including defence, steel, etc.) made them one of India's biggest trade partners. Today, Russia has the world's second largest reserve of oil and perhaps the biggest reserve of gas which have spurred enhanced Indo-Russian cooperation in this sector. In one of the Indo-Russian Business Meets in December 2005 at Moscow, the Indian Prime Minister, Dr. Manmohan Singh expressed this growing sentiment thus:

> "The energy sector is a key area of interest... we are keen to diversify our engagement in this sector. Russia's position as the world's second largest producer of energy and India's growing demand for energy resources spell out a natural complementarity between us in this sector."

Both Russia and India have endorsed the concept of energy security envisaging a balance between the security of demand and supply. In view of their corresponding resources needs, capabilities and potentials, both the countries have agreed to further enhance direct dialogue between their oil and gas companies aiming at commercial ventures in India, Russia and even third countries.[20] In October 2000, both the countries signed a bilateral strategic partnership which revived the idea of large scale energy cooperation. Due to President Putin's initiatives, Russia involved the ONGC Videsh Ltd. (OVL) in the Sakhalin-1 project, with 20 per cent stake for the Indian partner in its oil fields. The arrival of the first shipment of oil from Sakhalin-1 in December 2006 and the MoU between the ONGC and Russia's Rosneft oil company (on both upstream and downstream activities) have confirmed the viability of Indo-Russian cooperation. Both ONGC and Rosneft (a part of the Russian gas giant Gazprom) are planning to expand this cooperation in respect to joint oil exploration, production, transportation and export in Russia, India and even third countries.[21]

A major cause for increasing Russian oil exports in recent times has been the speed of economic growth in China and India. Both the countries have been increasing oil demand at an annual rate of nearly 4 per cent, more than twice the average global rate.[22]

State backed companies in both the countries are dealing with Russian companies for a series of cooperative ventures in both upstream and downstream sectors. The Rosneft set up a joint venture, with the Chinese company Sinopec and India's OVL to develop sections of the Sakhalin-3 fields as well as the Vankor deposit in the Krasnoyarsk territory. The President of Rosneft, Sergei Bogdanchikov, expressed this sentiment of cooperation in the words: "It would be ideal to match Russia's growing production of hydrocarbons with India's growing market through dedicated JVs." On his part, the Indian Prime Minister Manmohan Singh expressed the readiness to offer Russian companies to take part in the distribution of oil and gas products, including in adjacent regions (Iran-Pakistan-India gas pipeline). The Russian behemoth Gazprom is ready to take part in the project both as contractor and invester—beginning of a Gazprom-GAIL strategic partnership. The Indian Petroleum Minister, Murli Deora, on a visit to Russia for "Moscow Energy Dialogue" in October 2006, extended invitation to Russian companies to participate in refinery project (Paradeep) and product pipelines. All this shows Russia's resolve to veer its energy policy towards Asia and, more importantly, India.

Conclusions

There have been studies all over the world showing that, in the long-run, energy consumption acts as an engine of economic growth and employment generation (applying the techniques of co-integration and causality).[23] Hence, the need for energy security which is a part of national security policy. Experts aver that energy security is a dynamic concept pursuing national growth and development. However, it can only be attained in a cooperative framework that is founded on engagement with other countries. From the Indian perspective, there is dire need to diversify energy sources, as dependence on the Persian Gulf sources may tend to become onerous. Our extended neighbourhood provides an opportunity to diversify energy dependence. Also, India's geographical location and growing market potential, along with economic resilience and technical capabilities, do provide additional stimulant to the economies of supplier nations like Russia.

References

1. *http://www.vexen.co.uk/USA/pollution.html;www.cnn.com/SPECIALS/2001/globalwarming*
2. "Struggling to Save the Planet", *The Economist,* June 2-8, 2007, p. 57.

3. S.K. Chopra, *Energy Policy for India: Towards Sustainable Energy Security in India in the Twenty First Century,* New Delhi, Oxford & IBM, 2006, p. xiv.
4. ESCAP Secretariat, " Household Energy Consumption in the Asian and Pacific Region: Analysis of Development Trends and Policy Implications", *http://www. unescap.org/esd/energy.trends. htm*
5. *Ibid;* see also Talmiz Ahmad, "Asian Cooperation in Energy Security", *Journal of Indian Ocean Studies,* Vol. 13, No. 3, December 2005, pp. 385-86; "SCADPIus: Energy Cooperation with the Developing Countries", *http://europa.eu.scadplus/leg/en.htm*
6. Bani P. Banerjee, *Handbook of Energy and Environment,* New Delhi, Oxford University Press, 2005, pp. 8-10.
7. Carin Zissis, "India's Energy Crunch", *http://www.cfr.org/publication/12200/,* December 8, 2006; S.D. Muni and Girijesh Pant, *Energy Security: Prospects for Cooperation with Extended Neighbourhood,* New Delhi, Rupa & Co., 2005, p. 14.
8. Ahmad, n. 5, pp. 386-87.
9. Chietigj Bajpayee, "India Recovers Lost Ground in International Energy Game", *Power and Interest News Report* (PINR), *http://www.pinr.com/report.php,* March 16, 2005.
10. Ministry of Information and Broadcasting, Government of India, Publication Division, *India 2006,* p. 255.
11. Muni and Pant, n. 7, pp. 16-17.
12. Bajpayee, n. 9.
13. Muni and Pant, n. 7, p. 25.
14. Ahmad, n.5, pp. 395-96.
15. Muni and Pant, n.7, pp. 199-203.
16. Chietigj Bajpayee, "India, China Locked in Energy Game", *Global Economy, www.atimes.com/Asian Economy...html*
17. Stanislav Patin, "Russian Offshore Oil and Gas Resources" (Tr. by Elena Cascio), *www.offshore-environment.com/russianoil.html*
18. *www.sakhalin1.com/en*
19. "Russia-India Energy Dialogue:Traditions and Prospects", *http://en.rian.ru/analysis...html,* January 30, 2007.
20. *Ibid; Tribune,* January 26, 2007.
21. Andre R. Mihailescu, *"Energy Watch", Middle East Times, www.metimes.com,* May 31, 2007.
22. "Russian Oil Production Skyrockets", *www.rncos.com,* May 14, 2007.
23. Chien Chiang Lee and Chun-Ping Chang, "Structural Break, Energy Consumption and Economic Growth Revisited: Evidence from Taiwan", *www.sciencedirect.com,* October 14, 2005; Anjum Aqueel and M.S. Butt, "The Relationship between Energy Consumption and Economic Growth in Pakistan," *Asia-Pacific Development Journal,* Vol. 8, No. 2, December 2006, *www.unescap.org/drpad/publication.*

15

Indo-Russian Cooperation in Science and Technology

V.D. Chopra

Indo-Russian cooperation in science and technology, particularly nuclear and space technology is of far reaching importance than what appears on the surface. Soviet Union and now Russia have been making available to India their expert knowledge in this sensitive area without any strings. When India during the Nehru era embarked on the path of developing science and technology, various institutions were set up. Jawaharlal Nehru had a clear vision about it. He also started looking abroad to get know-how in this strategic area for its rapid growth. Before we analyse India's cooperation with the Soviet Union and now Russia in this area, it will be pertinent to recapitulate that some of the important institutions of science and technology were set up during the Nehru era and later developed when Indira Gandhi was the Prime Minister. However it was Rajiv Gandhi who took a series of steps to develop scientific technologies in India particularly in the area of information technology (IT). That India today is one of the most important countries, which is developing IT and it has already made information technology available to large sections of the Indian population, this is primarily due to the perspective of Rajiv Gandhi. India has now begun to export IT to other countries. Let us now turn to some aspects of Indo-Russian cooperation in this area.

New avenues and areas of economic scientific and technical cooperation between India and Russia are being explored. A renewed Integrated Long Term Programme (ILTP) for Indo-Russian cooperation in science and technology was evolved nearly two decades ago. The ILTP signed by Mikhail Gorbachev and Rajiv Gandhi in Moscow in 1987 lasted till the year 2000. It perhaps was the biggest exchange of technology in the world. This programme is a reflection of the close cooperation in science and technology that has developed between India and Russia over the last 20 years. The programme had facilitated exchange visits of over 2,500 scientists and generated a close to 300 development projects in India and Russia. Moreover, India and Russia had entered into an agreement to expand their cooperation in nuclear physics. A Memorandum of Understanding (MoU) was signed in July 2000 between the Department of Science and Technology of the Government of India and Russia's leading nuclear research institute, the Kurchatov Centre. The three-year agreement signed by the officials of India and Russia was automatically renewed unless one of the sides decided otherwise. Nuclear physics has thus become one of the thrust areas of Indo-Russian cooperation under the 20 year ILTP, which has been renewed. The two countries had planned setting up a satellite link between the PARAM 10000 in Moscow and supercomputer at Centre Developing of Advanced Computing (C-DAC) in Pune. The C-DAC and the Institute for Computer Aided Design (ICAD) prepared a joint work document identifying applications and areas of requirements. Putin's visit to New Delhi in October 2000 led to further vistas in Indo-Russian cooperation in the peaceful uses of atomic energy.

In Joint Declaration in January 2007 during Putin's visit to India, it was stated' "India and Russia recall with satisfaction their wide-ranging bilateral cooperation in the field of science and technology that has been successfully and jointly steered and conducted in the framework of ILTP. India and Russia affirm to jointly commemorate the 20th anniversary on 3 July 2007 of the establishment of the ILTP. As a major initiative both the sides welcome the decision to set up an India-Russia Technology Centre in Moscow to facilitate and channelise commercial/industrial applications of new jointly developed technologies. Both the sides recognised that this new facet to science and technology cooperation would also provide a stimulant effect to the overall scope of joint work. The signing of the relevant Joint Work Document would enable the Centre to begin concrete work". This agreement is very significant for Indo-Russian joint cooperation in science and technology in the coming period.

Multifaceted scientific cooperation has been thriving between India and Russia. The most important cooperation is in nuclear realm. As the culmination of this process has come, Russia has reaffirmed its support for India acquiring peaceful nuclear technology. Russia has agreed to provide India four 1000 MW generating capacity nuclear reactors at the nuclear power plant in Kudankulam in Tamil Nadu and build more reactors at new sites. "Memorandum of Intent between the Department of Atomic Energy, the Government of the Republic of India and Federal Atomic Energy Agency, the Russian Federation on development of cooperation in the construction of additional nuclear power plant units at Kudankulam site as well as in the construction of Russian design nuclear power plants at new sites in the Republic of India. The Sides also expressed satisfaction at the progress in the ongoing construction of two nuclear power plants in Kudankulam with Russian participation." (Joint Statement on the outcome of the Official Visit of H.E. Mr. Vladimir V. Putin, President of the Russian Federation to the Republic of India, 25.01.2007).

Nuclear cooperation with Russia permits reprocessing of spent fuel from these reactors and receiving uninterrupted fuel supply. The project (Kudankulam Nuclear Power Plant) is located at Kudankulam in Tamil Nadu. The power plants with two sophisticated reactors are described as the VVER type having 1000 MW generating capacity, incorporating the most advanced reactor technology in Russia and rated among the best in the world. Design and project documentations of the plant were prepared by the Russian side and scrutinised by a team of Indian scientists appointed by the Atomic Energy Commission. The Indian Atomic Energy Regulatory Board (AERB) carried out an extensive review of the project documentation and cleared the design. In accordance with the agreements signed between International Atomic Energy Agency (IAEA) and the Government of India, concerning the application of safeguards in connection with supply of nuclear power plant from Russia, KNPP is under IAEA safeguard. India and Russia noted with satisfaction their ongoing cooperation in construction of nuclear power plants at Kudankulam. In this context, the two sides also signed an agreement on cooperation in the construction of four additional power units at Kudankulam.

The Kudankulam project is being implemented under the intergovernmental agreement signed between the Government of India and the erstwhile USSR in November 1988, which was subsequently amended through a "supplement" in June 1998. In the initial phase, a detailed project report for the project was prepared with the help of premier Russian design organisations and institutes, a contract for which was signed between Nuclear Power

Cooperation of India Ltd. (NPCIL) and the Russian organisation, Atomstroyexport in July 1998. Putin's visit to New Delhi in October 2000 led to an agreement on Indo-Russian cooperation in the peaceful uses of atomic energy. The project entered the second phase of construction - that of civil works - with the ground breaking for the project works carried out on 7 October 2001.

It may be relevant to recall that "the collapse of Soviet Union in 1991 had delayed the implementation of the agreement that was signed in 1988. Also wrangles over costs to be paid in foreign exchange and American objections raised after the Gulf War in 1992 greatly delayed implementation of the agreement. The Indo-Soviet cooperation for the peaceful uses of atomic energy came to the front in September 1976 when Soviet heavy water was supplied to the second unit of the Rajasthan Atomic Power Station (RAPS II) in lieu of Canada stopping all supplies of heavy water, because India had conducted a peaceful nuclear explosion in May 1974. The agreement with the Soviet Union took two years to negotiate as Moscow was insisting on stringent safeguards to ensure that there was no clandestine diversion to non-peaceful activity. The successor state of Soviet Union - The Russian Federation has continued this cooperation and as a result four units are in place at RAPS and the last of them has attained criticality only in October 2000." *(Indo-Russian Nuclear Cooperation, Dr. R.R. Subramaniam, IDSA).*

The Kudankulam project has several distinguishing features. Its design and technology and its impact on Indian atomic reactor design technology, are outstanding features of Indo-Russian cooperation in this strategic area. It is relevant to mention here that strong pressures were built by nuclear weapon powers, particularly the US, on Russia to block the implementation of the Kudankulam project. These pressures were built by the London Club of which Russia is a member.

To take the financial aspect first, one should note that the soft repayment terms of the Russian loan for the project set new parameters that facilitate implementation of this massive nuclear undertaking without financing terms of the project, completed in recent negotiations between the entire design of the project and supply all the equipment and machinery from the Russian organisations shall be covered under the State Credit extended by the Russian Government for the project. The total amount of credit for the project from the Russian side will work out to about 50 percent of the total project cost. The credit utilised for the project is to be repaid in 14 equal instalments, beginning with the commercial operations of the plant. This will enable loan repayments largely from earnings of power generations.

The scientific and technological aspects of the Russian reactor design have a special bearing for India, for induction of the light water reactor design, based on low enriched uranium as fuel will mean a departure from the existing pattern of atom and power plants in India. These have pressurised heavy water reactors that use natural uranium as fuel and heavy water as moderator and coolant. The view of the scientific establishment is that far from being a technological slowdown, it is the induction of the Russian reactor technology. The Kudankulam project will be based on the latest WER, reactor design of pressurised water type (PWR), which is rated as the leading type of nuclear power reactors worldwide.

A joint statement on cooperation in the field of peaceful uses of atomic energy, said : "India undertakes that the reactor facilities and nuclear fuel supplied by Russia shall remain under the IAEA safeguards during the entire period of their actual use in accordance with the agreement on safeguards, which shall be concluded between the Republic of India and the IAEA. It will also inter-alia take into account measures relating to physical protection and other issues as may be mutually agreed."

"It said as states possessing advanced nuclear technologies and as responsible states, India and Russia shared an objective of ensuring non-proliferation of weapons of mass destruction and their means of delivery, including possible linkages with terrorism".

"The two sides recognised the importance of research and development (R & D) for development of innovative technologies for reducing the risk of nuclear proliferation to further facilitate the wide scale development of nuclear energy. They expressed their willingness to further expand and strengthen their bilateral civilian nuclear energy cooperation by broad-basing cooperation covering both power (fission and fusion energy) and non-power applications in areas of mutual interest to be identified by both sides. The Department of Atomic Energy, India and the Federal Atomic Energy Agency, the Russian Federation will work out in 2007 a comprehensive programme of cooperation in the field of peaceful uses of atomic energy between India and Russia." *(Tribune News Service,* 25.07.2007)

This shows that Indo-Russian cooperation on peaceful uses of nuclear technology is not only in place but is progressing. It is important to note that during Putin's visit to India in January 2007, Indo-Russian cooperation on space technology too was on a high priority. Three agreements were signed by Madhavan Nair, Chairman, Indian Space Research Organisation (ISRO) with the Director of Federal Space Agency of the Russian Federation. Of the three, two were connected with the Russian Global Navigation Satellite System, GLONASS and the other was on cooperation in the joint satellite project, YOUTHSAT. This has assumed importance in the context of some developments in this region such as Chinese test of anti-satellite weapon.

"Under the latest agreement, Russia and India plan to jointly use GLONASS. The system is expected to be fully operational by the end of 2007 with 18 satellites in orbit for military and civilian purposes. By 2009 there will be 24 satellites in orbit. The Russians are even talking with the US and the European Space Agency on using GLONASS jointly with GPS and Galileo Satellite Navigation Systems. The other agreement concerns a youth satellite for education purposes. This is not the first time that India has collaborated with the Russians in the arena of space. India's only astronaut, Ramesh Sharma, had visited outer space, courtesy the Soviets". *(Watch This Indo-Russia Space, Ajey Lele, Research Fellow, IDSA, posted online, Indian Express,* 30.01.2007).

However, Indo-Russian cooperation in space slowed down because of internal developments in Russia, primarily US pressure on the ruling elite. Nevertheless, the situation has changed and once again Indo-Russian cooperation in space and technology has started developing. Indain space technology is making rapid progress.

This perfunctory survey on the course of Indo-Russian cooperation in science and technology clearly reflects that after 15 years of disintegration of the USSR, Indo-Russian cooperation has begun to take a new turn.

16

International Terrorism and Indo-Russian Relations

Kalim Bahadur

Indo-Russian relations go far back into the history of the two countries. When India entered the comity of nations as an independent entity the world was divided into two camps. The western camp was led by the United States and the socialist camp by the Soviet Union. Many newly independent nations joined either of the two camps. India opted to follow the nonaligned course which meant that India would join neither of the two military alliances though it would continue to have economic and political relations with both the groups. However, at the height of the Cold War Indian stand was not received with sympathy and understanding by the western countries. They equated non-alignment with communism. This led to their policy of non-cooperation with India in its efforts to develop its economy. The Soviet Union and later Russia came forward to help India in its economic development specially in setting up of heavy industries and in the fields of defence, space and nuclear energy. India was greatly helped by cheap credits which could be repaid in rupees at a time when India was facing shortage of foreign exchange. One cannot forget that India's heavy steel plant at Bhilai was set up with the help of the Soviet Union at a time when western countries had refused to help. It can be safely asserted that the present economic resurgence of India is largely due to the assistance of Soviet Union/Russia. Indo-Soviet relations were not confined to the economic field, but soon developed a strategic dimension. Russia has rendered important political, diplomatic and strategic help to India whenever it was needed at critical junctures. The famous 1971 Indo-Soviet Treaty of Friendship came to the help of India when it was faced with the crisis in East Pakistan and war between the two neighbours loomed large on the horizon.

At present both India and Russia have been facing the threat of terrorism during the last two decades. India has been the victim of the terrorist attacks from across the border for the last 25 years. The terrorist threat in the Russian Federation is linked to the separatist movement launched by some Chechen groups. The terrorists in Russia have killed hundreds of innocent people in Russia and now constitute a threat to peace and stability of the country. There has also been a rise of the Islamic extremist movements in some of the states of Central Asian Republics which can spill over to Russia and its other neighbours. The organizations like the Hizbul Tehrir and the Islamic Movement of Uzbekistan and Taliban in Afghanistan and similar extremist organizations in Chechenya constitute a threat to peace and stability in the region. The Dagestan Liberation Army was also an Islamic extremist group that emerged in 1999 with the objective of fighting for the independence of the Republic of Dagestan. Dagestan and the Republic of Chechnya which have a majority of Muslim population, are located in Russia's northern Caucasus region. The Chechen rebels who adhere to Islamic fundamentalism, sometimes claim Dagestan to be a part of Islamic Chechnya. In fact, in August 1991, Chechen-led rebels declared that Dagestan was an Islamic state. Both Chechen and Dagestan terrorists have carried out violent attacks in Moscow which have killed hundreds of innocent citizens. The group frequently targeted apartment buildings and other civil installations in Moscow. According to the terrorist group, the bombings were in retaliation of military action within the regions of Chechnya and Dagestan by the Russian air force. The Dagestan Liberation Army like the Chechens claims that Russian rule on Dagestan and Chechnya is illegal and these regions should be free.

Like the Chechen conflict the dispute about Kashmir goes back sixty years when India and Pakistan became independent from the British colonial rule amidst controversies and violence following the partition of India. Pakistan claimed that Jammu and Kashmir being a Muslim majority state should have gone to it. Kashmir's accession to India had been ratified by an elected constituent assembly. It was about Jammu and Kashmir that Pakistan had gone to war with India thrice in 1947, 1965 and in 1999. Having failed to seize Kashmir through wars, the rulers in Islamabad decided to get it through a terrorist campaign in the name of Jihad. In this war Pakistan has used Islamic extremist groups, several of whom have international connections including links with the terrorist groups active in Chechnya. The fact that Osama bin Laden in now located somewhere in the Pakistan-Afghan border area and al Qaida which is an international terrorist group makes the war in Chechnya and Kashmir pose the same threat to both countries. The terrorists in the state of Jammu and Kashmir have been trained and armed by the agencies in Pakistan and they are pushed into the Indian territory. Most terrorists have linkages with international terrorist groups. Many terrorists, who include Chechens, were trained by the US agencies during the war in Afghanistan, who, after the withdrawal of the Soviet army, were transferred by the Pakistani agencies to Kashmir. Terrorists in Kashmir have also killed hundreds of people in Jammu and Kashmir. Some of these elements have been fighting in Chechnya. The breakup of the Soviet Union was followed by the independence of its constituent republics and also by outbreak of terrorism in some areas. In the present phase of India-Russia relations, the common threat of terrorism is a factor that brings the two countries together to cooperate in the struggle against it. The 1971 Treaty of Friendship and Co-operation has been renewed but it has not lost the relevance that it had in the era of the cold war.

The Yeltsin years saw some cooling off of India-Russia relations as the latter was facing serious economic problems in the post Soviet era. In the new situation, the most important task for the Russian leadership was the revival of economy. An economically weak Russia would have lost its importance in world affairs. The Russian security was linked with the western powers where India did not play any significant role. Russia had always been the main supplier of military material to India. With the emergence of President Putin, the Indo-Russian relations have been given new direction. The security dimension was restored which had been omitted from the 1993 renewed version of the Treaty of Friendship and Cooperation. The Vajpayee-Putin Declaration of Strategic Partnership signed during the latter's visit in 2000, spelt out a new perspective of Indo-Russian relations. Now both the countries include political, economic and scientific cooperation alongwith defence and geo-strategic factors as part of the security partnership. The document proposed cooperation in the fight against terrorism and separatism, an issue which deeply concerned both India and Russia. The declaration clearly referred to the problems of Afghanistan, Taliban Jihad, Kashmir and Chechnya. The two sides were clear that India-Pakistan relations could be normalized only if the cross border terrorism stops. Both the countries have blamed the Taliban for supporting insurgencies and terrorist groups. The meeting also intensified political cooperation and holding of annual Summit meetings and Ministerial meetings was initiated. In 2001 Prime Minister of India Atal Bihari Vajpayee and President Putin in their joint declaration in Moscow reiterated their stand on terrorism saying it was against the multi-ethnic and democratic countries such as India and the Russian Federation that violent actions have been perpetrated under the slogan of self-determination. In reality these represent acts of terrorism, which in most cases have strong international links. "India and the Russian Federation support the adoption on the basis of international law of decisive measures against all States, individuals, and entities which render support, harbour, finance instigate or train terrorists or promote terrorism. It is essential that all States, without exception, should pay particular attention to the prevention of access of the terrorist and extremist organizations and groups to financial resources on the basis of international law." The two sides believed that Taliban had become a breeding ground of international terrorism and extremism. In the joint session of India's Parliament, President Putin had stressed that the same extremists organizations that were creating problems in Jammu and Kashmir were also behind terrorism in Chechnya and the Northern areas of Russian Federation. Both sides stressed the need for an early finalisation of the Comprehensive Convention on International Terrorism and further urged nations to pass law domestically that "makes all acts of terrorism for political purposes," unjustifiable irrespective of political, philosophical, ideological and racial considerations.

A joint statement issued at the end of the three-day visit of the Prime Minister, Atal Bihari Vajpayee, to Moscow, in November 2003 urged Islamabad "to implement in full its assurances to prevent infiltration of terrorists across the Line of Control" and "to dismantle the terrorist infrastructure in Pakistan and Pakistan-controlled territory as a prerequisite for a purposeful dialogue between the two countries." Russia has registered its appreciation and support for India's peace initiatives and hoped that Pakistan will come out with a positive response. The Ministers noted that international terrorism continued to pose a grave threat to all nations and expressed concern about the new and evolving forms of the menace. They agreed that under central and coordinating role of the UN and within the framework of its Global Counter-Terrorism Strategy, collective action must be strengthened further by taking into account the mutating character of terrorism and its networks. They further agreed that an early entry into force of International Convention for the Suppression of Acts of Nuclear Terrorism and the earliest possible adoption in the UN of the India-sponsored draft Comprehensive Convention on International Terrorism would lead to further consolidation of the international legal basis for combating terrorism. The sides underlined the substantial potential of their counter-terrorism cooperation in regional organizations. They agreed that there can be no justification for any act of terrorism, irrespective of motivations and wherever and by whomsoever committed. They stressed that selective approaches in counter-terrorism cannot yield sustainable results and it should be combated in a consistent, sustained and comprehensive manner without any double standards. The two sides also agreed to coordinate action against all factors that feed international terrorism, including its financing, illegal drug trafficking and trans-national organized crime'. There is no doubt that Indo-Russian cooperation in the struggle against international terrorism will play an important role in world peace.

17

Challenges of Terrorism in India

Major General Afsir Karim, AVSM (Retd.)

Defining terrorism in precise terms presents serious problems as national interests of various countries of the world, religious and ethnic affinities defy all attempts of reaching an agreement. It has, therefore, not been possible to find an acceptable definition of terrorism at the international level. It is also not been easy to discover the root causes of terrorism, because attempts of forming a composite picture of this complex phenomenon is not easy. Terrorism has become the most dreaded threat to the world order as it has taken the form of a specialized and highly lethal politico-military campaign.

Terrorism that is launched across international boundaries with predetermined political objectives employs lethal force and brutal violence against innocent bystanders. Assassinations of political leaders, massacre of innocent people, creating environments for fomenting inter-religious, ethnic conflicts and socio-economic unrest, is an integral part of their strategy. International terrorist organizations based in some countries have acquired the capability to wage low intensity conflicts in targeted countries and pose a serious threat to their national integrity and economic progress.

It has not been possible to identify specific strategies to combat terrorism though terrorism is an age old phenomenon that has been used as a substitute for direct warfare for centuries. In the past the weapons available to the terrorists were not lethal enough to cause extensive devastation, but the methods now available to terrorists can cause fear and panic on very large scale affecting the ruling classes and public alike. The targets of influence and the victims of terror are not necessarily the same. With the availability of new technology and more sophisticated weapons, terrorists have started using indirect terrorism in that the target of terror and the target of influence were different. The real targets are the larger audience and the people watching the horror. The ability of terrorism to affect the morale of a very large target without exposing a large number of terrorists makes it an efficient weapon to disrupt and destabilize a society or a political system. Threats of attacks or even a perceived threat of terrorism is enough to force a state to curtail civil liberties, divert essential resources from constructive tasks.

In the 1970s and 1980s, a majority of radical Islamic groups focused their violent activities on destabilizing and replacing the moderate Islamic regimes of their own countries. A radical change came after winning the war against the Soviet army in Afghanistan. After this victory thousands of Muslim volunteers from divergent backgrounds forged close links across the globe to internationalize the terrorist movement. Jihadi fighters returning home after the war motivated people in their own countries to organize radical Islamist groups. Many were trained to join terrorist groups operating in Kashmir, Bosnia, Chechnya, Kosovo and the Philippines. Some others merged with militant groups in Indonesia and Africa.

Islamic terrorism assumed the shape of an organized international movement in 1990s when some prominent extremist leaders who were exiled from their countries settled in western countries. Some such fundamentalist leaders who settled down in Western Europe, the United States and Canada, soon discovered that democratic freedom enjoyed by them in these countries facilitated establishing of secret cells and networks to sponsor international terrorist operations abroad. They found that many groups of the Western Muslim communities were ready to finance them and help in acquiring new technologies. They were able to acquire the wherewithal and establish important links to coordinate their efforts that eventually led to 9/11 attacks.

India needs to take special notice of the resurgence of Islamic terrorism in its immediate neighborhood because of highly complex equation of Muslim and non-Muslim populations within its own borders. To take a long term view of terrorism and its management it is important to understand the rapidly changing form of Islamic terrorism. Assessment of the future course of terrorist activities accurately is difficult, because we have yet to develop a suitable methodology of doing so.

Jihadi Induced Terrorism in India

India has been facing the challenge of terrorism since independence but it assumed a more dangerous form after Pakistan adopted sponsored-terrorism with the help of international Jihadi groups as an instrument of its foreign policy. The fundamentalist groups in Pakistan, gradually acquired arms and finances and trained armed cadres to carry out trans-border terrorist operations initially in Kashmir. Later, other parts of India were also targeted. India now faced asymmetrical threats to its territorial integrity and national unity in which guerrilla warfare, terrorism and subversive activities were combined for political and territorial gains. Terrorist groups like Jesh-e Mohammad and Lashkar-e-Tyyaba, carried out sustained operations against India, later some Jihadi elements started operating from safe bases in Bangladesh, Myanmar and Nepal. Till recently terrorist organizations operating in India were supported directly or indirectly by ISI, Pakistan army and religious-based parties of Pakistan. It is not possible to counter Pakistan supported terrorism effectively without severing the link between these groups and their base areas in Pakistan. Indications are that many groups in Pakistan will continue to assist cross-border terrorism regardless of the peace process now underway.

Some groups are sent to J & K with specific purpose of killing and torturing innocent people for spreading fear and panic with a view to overawing them to follow their dictates. Some other groups are specially tasked to attack minorities and places of worship to disturb communal harmony in various parts of the country. India has yet to formulate an effective policy to deal with this situation.

Pakistan's surrogates in J & K and terrorist cells in some other parts of India have acquired weapons to launch lethal attacks. The main features of Pak-sponsored terrorism and proxy war with the aim of destabilizing the state of J & K were :

1. Terrorism and violence through Jihadi groups, who have also been armed and also trained to carry on Jihadi propaganda for recruiting people.
2. Arming and launching of domestic terrorist groups, who are ready to act against their government and countrymen.
3. Encourage allied groups to generate violence and attack economic infrastructure in various parts of India.
4. Supplying arms and providing training facilities to insurgent and separatist groups in Northeast India.
5. Create communal tensions in sensitive areas to disturb communal harmony, spread disorder and lawlessness in various parts of India.

Terrorism in The Northeast India

Northeast India has major geo-strategic importance for India, and continued internal problems here can gravely endanger India's security especially in view of Chinese territorial claims in this region. The area has a tenuous connection with the rest of India through the narrow Siliguri corridor.

The region has diverse warlike tribal populations, which spill over, into various states of the region and across international borders into Myanmar and Bangladesh. The unrest and insurgency in Nagaland, turmoil and violence in Manipur, tribal violence in Tripura, separatist threats in Assam, pose great danger to the integrity of the country. All these separatist movements, who use terrorism against the people and the state, have cross-border connections.

Naxalite Terror

A well-coordinated Maoist-Naxal effort is in the offing to create administrative chaos and widespread public disorder in India. They have taken recourse to insurgent - terrorism to press their demands and this has created new problems for the country. According to reports they want to establish a 'Compact Revolutionary Zone' in India in collaboration with certain foreign organizations. They seldom attacked common people till establishing contacts with 'Friends of Indian Revolution' and the 'Coordination Committee of Maoist Parties and Organizations of South Asia'. These international connections have resulted in a sharp rise in violence and terrorism in Naxal infested areas. Thus a new face of domestic terrorism assisted by outside agencies interested in spreading violence and chaos in India, has become conspicuous.

Countering Terrorism

A series of new measures are required for maintaining peace and stability in our country :

- A federal agency that can operate in any part of the country to counter terrorism should be created without delay.
- Countering terrorism is much more complex than ordinary policing; importance has to be given to a wide range of non-conventional methods. Counter-terrorist operations do not prove very effective where the terrorists operate from safe bases across international borders. Use of air mobility, sophisticated technologies combined with innovative and

daring tactics can, however, greatly help in attacking the terrorist safe havens and reducing their capability to carry out cross-border operations.

- Adequate measures required for countering Jihadi propaganda have yet to be evolved by us; the consequences of terrorist strikes that raise anger and create distrust among various segments of our population must be managed more efficiently.

- The increasing political clout of religious extremists in Pakistani military establishments and their close connections with the international Jihadi network increases the possibility of Jihadi terrorists acquiring and using Weapons of Mass Destruction. Countering threats of chemical or biological weapons that can cause havoc in any of our metropolitan or medium sized towns must be evolved and tested.

- Political, economic, social and military measures have to be meshed together for countering terrorism effectively. A combined effort can greatly help in preventing terrorist attacks and destroying their support bases.

No one country can combat international terrorism single handed. The threats of international terrorism can be substantially reduced if :

1. Coordinated regional efforts are made to meet the threats of transnational, cross-border, domestic, cyber, chemical, biological, nuclear and radiological terrorism.

2. Joint efforts are made to track down terrorists operating in various countries of the region.

3. Permanent organizations are created to coordinate regional programmes for countering terrorism at the regional level.

4. Assets and financial resources for countering terrorism are pooled at regional level.

5. Pacification schemes and protection of common people and vital establishments should be given special importance.

6. Access to the human and material sources is denied to the terrorists and their active supporters by cooperative efforts of various agencies of the region.

7. People are made aware of the sensitive predispositions of the populations in various countries of the region in keeping with their religious and cultural ethos.

International cooperation to strengthen regional institutions, enlarging and developing security networks will be necessary; the present status of international cooperation in countering terrorism is not particularly encouraging because strategic interests of countries take priority over countering terrorism.

Summation

It appears that future environment will lend itself even more to Jihadi-induced violence; it may attain frightening dimensions if weapons of mass destruction become freely available to terrorist groups. The rise of radical elements in Pakistan and acts of terror committed by them recently foretell escalation of violence in the entire region, India must take suitable measures to safeguard its interest in view of these new developments in its neighborhood. The most effective response to counter Jihadi terrorism would be dismantling the fundamentalist networks in Pakistan, who promote radical ideologies that provide recruits for terrorism. We need to make concerted efforts to convince Pakistan to dismantle terrorist organizations that are operating from its soil.

Inordinate show of force by security forces can lead to conflict escalation. Comparative studies regarding relationship between harsh measures and escalation of conflicts show that there is need for evolving methods of using force that would not hurt non-combatants. New techniques and weapon systems should be introduced to limit collateral damage.

Adequate strategies required for countering Jihadi terrorism must be evolved. We have yet to develop special techniques to offset the psychological impact of the Jihadi propaganda or effectively manage the consequences of terrorist strikes that raise anger and create distrust among various segments of our population.

The future course of Terrorism in India is not clear. Is it a passing phenomenon or has it come to stay as a new weapon of war against us because we now possess superior military capabilities? The question is: can terrorism demoralize or destabilize India or only increase violence and bloodshed? If the attacks on America and its allies and suicide attacks on Israel are any indication, it will be evident that terrorism can neither defeat a stronger adversary nor achieve the political objectives of the sponsors.

18

Rise of Terrorism and Muslim Fundamentalism

V.D. Chopra

In this study we have examined historically the growth of Muslim fundamentalism. However during the last three decades terrorism has been raising its ugly head and now in the beginning of the 21st centry it has assumed a global dimension. Before we examine this problem it will be relevant to recapitulate certain harsh facts. The fact of the matter is that the Mujahiddin movement was created, nursed, financed and trained by the United States by making Pakistan its launching pad to oust pro-Soviet regime of Najibullah in Afghanistan who had the backing of the Soviet Union in the 80s of the last century. There are some historians who are of the opinion that the attack of the Mujahiddin and then of the Taliban movements in Afghanistan and 'Solidarity Movement' in Poland were planned to disintegrate the Soviet Union. In their assessment, Taliban Movement against Afghanistan and 'Solidarity Movement' in Poland on the one hand and Soviet leader Gorbachev's internal policies developed like a pincer movement. This led to the disintegration of the Soviet Union and was the beginning of the end of one of the most powerful countries of the world. This is not the place to discuss this conclusion. However what is relevant is that the fight of well trained and well equipped Taliban militants against the Soviet troops and the support given to them by the various tribes of Afghanistan and finally the withdrawal of the Soviet troops from Afghanistan gave them a new self-confidence and authority in the Muslim world. It is in the midst of this development that Taliban terrorists today have become a very powerful factor. They have carved out a place for themselves on the borders of Pakistan and Afghanistan and virtually created a state within these two countries. They plan, organise and execute their terrorist activities from this centre and have built a network in a large number of countries including India and Russia. This is how the monster created by the United States and built by Pakistan has now begun to hit them. The various terrorist actions in the United States and England should be seen in this context.

In the beginning of the 21st century, it has become abundantly clear that secessionism and terrorism have assumed a dangerous proportion. A large number of countries are facing this menace which threatens their integrity and stability. This indicates that in the beginning of the present century, this ominous development will be a challenge to the international community. Though terrorism did manifest itself in various forms in the twentieth century, the nature and content of both secessionism and terrorism have undergone a basic change.

In a period of globalization of economics and polity and when the concept of one world based on equality and social justice has begun to emerge, secessionism and terrorism have raised their dangerous heads to undo this process. It will, therefore, be incorrect to trace this trend only to Islamic fundamentalism. It has different variants—Islamic, Jewish, Hindutva and ethnic. This point needs to be emphasized because the western scholars and political elite look at this problem merely in terms of Muslim fundamentalism.

The rise of secessionism and terrorism particularly in multi-cultural, religious and multi-ethnic societies has deeper roots than what appears on the surface. That explains why the western world has a narrow view about this danger and, therefore, in actual practice takes a partisan stand.

At the moment there are three hot spots of secessionism and terrorism, namely India, China and the Russian Republic.

There is hardly any doubt that Jammu and Kashmir has always been the target of terrorism and secessionism. How seriously the United States and the Western political elite take this threat to India's unity and integrity is anybody's guess. The fact of the matter is that the Pakistan-trained terrorists have been active in this strategic state for decades. Now this danger has assumed a new proportion.

According to one estimate nearly forty training camps have been set up on Indo-Pak border and at least thirty-five of them are in Pakistan occupied Kashmir. There are thirtyfive to forty thousand trainees in these camps. What is most disturbing is that a section of political elite in this state is making a shrill cry that the army and other security forces should be withdrawn from the state. This dangerous development speaks for itself and needs no comment.

It is also pertinent to mention here that the terrorist activities in North Eastern region have also increased. What is more alarming is that these terrorists are either trained in Pakistan or Bangladesh.

This shows that when India is emerging as a global economic and political power, the threat to its unity and integrity is assuming a menacing proportion. Besides this, one should not ignore the rise of Hindu revivalism in the country. This is the paradox which India faces in the end of first decade of the 21st century. Now, let us look at the rise of terrorism and secessionism in Russia.

Russia's Chechnya territory has been witnessing a rise of terrorism and secessionism for a long time. Nonetheless, the Russian political leadership has been following a dual policy of dealing with the situation firmly on one hand and democratising the political system.

Along with this it has taken a series of measures for the welfare of the people. This has paid rich dividents to it. Moscow's military operation against secessionist forces in Chechnya has raised a new controversy in the West. Russian political leadership has accused the United States of trying to undermine the integrity of the country. It has not left at that. It feels that by indirectly giving moral support to the secessionist forces, attempts are being made to oust Russia from the Caucasus.

The moral of the situation is that both India and Russia are facing a common problem of defending unity and integrity of their respective countries.

It may also be mentioned here that political circles in the western world have never taken a clear stand that Jammu and Kashmir is an integral part of India. Significantly the Soviet Union and now Russia have always considered this strategic state as a component of the Indian Republic.

To understand the social, economic and political factors which have boosted Muslim fundamentalism since 1990, one must take into consideration certain aspects of Muslim population in various countries. In the developing world where the Muslims are either in absolute majority or constitute a substantial minority, the process of modern nation-state building began only since the end of World War II and the dawn of the era of decolonisation. In fact, most of them are yet to start building a democratic structure.

Outside Europe, modern nation-states have developed in three ways. One was the authoritarian political structure with bourgeois economic values. Examples of this can be found in Latin America and a few of them elsewhere, and one can only hope that these state structures will evolve themselves into more liberal regimes. And the third was the Indian way.

No developing nation has been able to overnight become a democratic state, reduce income disparities and launch on a path of economic development based on liberal democratic values. For quite some time after independence, there were strong hopes of building India into a modern democratic nation-state and, with centralised planning, also of reducing income disparities. That dream has not materialised, and a significant portion of our population (around 30 per cent or more) still remains below the poverty line while income disparities have grown wider. On the political side, the growth of healthy political traditions has been disappointing. Parties have fragmented on the basis of personality cults; inner-party democracy is missing, as revealed by the absence of intra-party elections, while black money and corrupt practices dominate elections.

The lack of assertion of autonomy of the judiciary, dominance over it by the executive, tyrannical abuse of power and authority and inadequate protection to citizens against such abuse have become the order of the day.

Population and Poverty

Out of nearly 120 developing nations, about 55 are estimated to be ruled either by the military directly or have military-dominated regimes. The majority of the rest have various forms of authoritarian governments, some of them laying claims to being native to the genius of the country or the people, which very often is a euphemism for tribalism. All of them—kings, sultans, military rulers, chieftains or single-party rule—claim they are practicing their own particular brand of democracy.

Estimates of world Muslim population at the end of the third quarter of the 20th Century vary between 600 and 900 millon[2].

The distribution of population as presented reveals that while two-thirds, (548.5 million) of them live in Muslim-majority countries, one-third (244.9 million) live as a minority in several non-Muslim slates. Among those Muslims who live in Muslim-majority countries, more than 92 per cent (506.2 million) enjoy a majority status of over 80 per cent in their national population. On the other hand, among Muslims who live as minorities in non-Muslim states, 202 million constitute a minority of 12 per cent or less of their national population. It is thus apparent that most Muslims enjoy either a dominant majority status of over 80 per cent or a small minority status of 12 per cent or less in their countries of residence.

Countries in which the Muslims constitute at least 80 per cent of the population are Afghanistan, Albania, Algeria, Bahrain, Bangladesh, Morocco, Niger, Oman, Pakistan, Saudi Arabia, Somalia, Sudan, Syria, Tanzania, Tunisia, Turkey and Yemen Arab Republic.

Countries with 50 to 79 per cent Muslim population are: Benin, Ethiopia, Ghana, Guinea, Ivory Coast, Lebanon, Liberia, Malaysia, Mali, Sierra Leone, Togo and Upper Volta.

Countries with 13 to 49 per cent of Muslim population are: Cameroon, Central African Republic, Chad, Cyprus, Malawi, Mauritius, Mozambique, Nigeria and Zaire.

Thus there are 26 countries where the Muslim population is at least 80 per cent, and another 12 where the Muslim population is between 50 per cent and 79 per cent, there are 6 countries which have a Muslim population ranging between 13 and 49 per cent. These figures bring into sharp focus the concentration of the Muslim population in the developing and the least developed countries on our planet.

In the following countries the Muslim population is up to 12 per cent of the total population: Bulgaria, Burma, China, France, Greece, Israel, Madagaskar, Philippines, Sri Lanka, Thailand, Uganda, the erstwhile U.S.S.R., Vietnam, Yugoslavia and Zambia. In India the Muslim population is more than 16 per cent, which implies that every sixth Indian is Muslim. Above all India has the second largest Muslim population in the world now. As such, there are 44 countries where the Muslim population constitutes the overwhelming majority of the population. Thus, these Asian and African countries, stretching from the Atlantic Ocean to the Pacific, across North and Central Africa and South Asia, constitute an important geopolitical factor. Of the estimated total world Muslim population of about 800 million, the Sunnies, one of the two main branches of Islam, constitute 80 per cent. The remaining 20 per cent are Shi'ites.

Political Structure and Orientations

The Muslim countries differ greatly in terms of their political structure and orientation, as well as their level of social and economic development. There are states possessing huge amounts of petrodollars (e.g, Saudi Arabia, the UAE, Kuwait), and also those which are counted among the world's poorest (Bangladesh, Zambia, Guinea, Mali, Niger, Sudan). A certain lack of uniformity, even a degree of internal contradictoriness, is typical of Islam itself which, to a certain extent, stems from the absence of any centralised organization.

Unlike, the Roman Catholic Church, Islam has no single religious or political centre. Nor does it have a single globally organised church hierarchical system. Saudi Arabia is considered the most authoritative political centre of Islam, and close relations with that country enable the United States to use its influence in the Islamic world to promote its own aims. However, Saudi Arabia, despite all efforts made by its regime, does not enjoy undisputed authority among the Muslim states. In general, Saudi influence is determined not so much by religious or political hold, but by economic factors.

However, despite all their differences, the Muslim countries are united by Islam, which is not only a religion, but also a code of conduct and repository of rules for everyday life and a code of ethics and philosophy. There are two very contradictory aspects in Islam: one, that is conservative, opposed to new trends and social progress, almost desiring to push mankind hundreds of years back in time, to the situation that existed during the emergence of Islam itself; and, the other, an inherent protest against a system that dooms the people to poverty and ignorance.

Centuries of domination of these countries by colonial powers had kept them economically most backward. The measure of dietary energy supply, as expressed in per capita kilo-calorie consumption per day, indicates that most countries in Africa and Asia, have a per capita consumption ranging between a low of 1,800 and a maximum of 2,500 kilo-calories. And over two-thirds of predominantly Muslim population countries fall far below the 1975 world's average of 2,470 kilo-calories per person per day. Only Turkey has per capita consumption level of over 3,000 kilo-calories. The gross national product (GNP) is low in almost all predominantly Muslim countries which do not have oil revenues. The high GNP of $4,090.00 in Kuwait reflects principally the recent wealth from oil. About half of the 27 Muslim countries have a GNP of less than 200.00, and two-thirds are under the 400 figure. Furthermore, it is widely recognized that these figures tell us nothing about how income is distributed among the people of a given country.

With the exception of Lebanon and Malaysia, countries with Muslim majorities of between 50 and 79 per cent are all in Africa. Excluding Ethiopia, the other eight countries are in West Africa, which is the region of overall high fertility and low levels of socio-economic development. The average birth rates for the 1970-75 period were around 50 per thousand in six of the nine African Muslim countries. The death rates were also high, generally over 22 per thousand. Only Lebanon and Malaysia have birth rates in the 30s and death rates as low as 10 per thousand and both have achieved relatively high levels of development in their group.

Iranian Revolution and After

It is in this socio-economic background that the hold of the religious fundamentalist forces in the Muslim word needs to be examined. While Islam is common to all the states; the stress laid on it by political establishments varies. By and large the ruling elite in these countries emphasise Islam, but this is more assertive in societies where tribal values are predominant - states of the Arabian peninsula - than elsewhere. Only in recent years, in some oil rich Arab countries, have a secular-minded modern elite begun to emerge.

Egypt under the leadership of Nasser, Syria and Iraq under the leadership of the Arab Baath Socialist Party and Algeria were the first among the Arab countries to embark on the path of modern nation-states. The Palestinian Liberation Organisation and its various components also made a valuable contribution in creating a secular consciousness among the Muslims in the Arab countries.

That being the position, to paint all Muslim countries with the brush of Muslim fundamentalism would be historically wrong, and a very unfair conclusion.

The view that Islam had a key role to play in the social and political processes in a number of Eastern countries became widespread in the USA after the victory of the Islamic revolution in Iran. The revolution was regarded as the biggest ever defeat for the USA not only for its geopolitical reasons but most specifically because what had collapsed in Iran was a whole system of social development intensively imposed by the USA on a number of developing countries.

The theoretical basis of this US approach to Islam has become the notion of the "Islamic revival". At the same time it is maintained that on the world scene Islam could be a link capable of ensuring a certain degree of unity among the nationalist ideologies in the developing countries with a predominantly Muslim population. On this basis, certain US officials conclude that it is possible to work out a common approach to the Muslim countries. Much has been written and said with particular concern in the USA about the "explosion of Islamic neo-fundamentalism". The term is understood in the USA, first of all, as close adherence to the precepts of the *Quran* i.e., proclaiming Muslim institutions unshakable and in opposition to any form of modernisation.

According to American analyses, the growing fundamentalist trend in Islam, which is the reaction of the Islamic clergy and the poorest sections of the population in the Muslim countries to the Western model of "modernisation", is an attempt by the centrists and some conservative sections to get away from it, and find their own "third" way of reshaping the society. The men in Washington consider all these as negative. In addition to some other negative aspects of Islam, US analysts emphasise that Islam, as a religious and political movement, is hampering the development of capitalism in the Eastern countries. Islamic ideas, with emphasis on the "equality" and unity of all Muslims, hold back development and the spread of the individualistic psychology inherent in capitalism. The Islamic dogmas oppose the establishment of an effective credit system, and in general, modern capitalist relations in production.

As the 21st century begins, the African and Asian countries dominated by the Muslims are witnessing a new awakening to the Islamic beliefs and its moral and ethical value system. Though much has been written about Islamic justice, equality, tolerance and free-will by the scholars of the *Quran and Sunna,* it is not yet clear whether the Muslim masses have been positively affected by the framework of Islamic morality.

Genesis of Religious Conflicts

What most exponents of Hindu revivalism in India fail to understand is that the political map of the contemporary Islamic fundamentalism is largely the product of European imperialism. When Europe finally established its political superiority over the Islamic world, it posed threat to its cultural traditions and social institutions in the same manner as it did to other people under colonial bondage, including the Hindus. In the Indian sub-continent, the plight of the Muslims was at its lowest at the turn of the century, because of the final collapse of the Mughal Empire, and its replacement by the British imperial authority. It brought the downfall of the Muslim privileged classes and the *ulema* who performed religious, judicial and administrative functions under the Mughal courts.

This is how a section of the Muslim leadership joined the national mainstream, while another section consisting of feudal aristocracy and obscurantists became the props of the British rule. It also becomes necessary to distinguish between the communal divisions and the special political forms it assumed following the development of the Muslim League and the demand for Pakistan. The so-called "communal" problem, or the question of relations between different religious communities,- Hindus (two-thirds of the population), the Muslim (one-fourth of the population) and other minor religious groupings (about 10 per cent of the population) had special significance for pre-independent India.

Under certain conditions, the mingling of diverse races or religions in a single country can give rise to acute difficulties, some time leading to riots and bloodshed. Orangemen and Catholics in Northern Ireland, Arabs and Jews in Palestine under the Mandate, Slavs and Jews in Tsarist Russia, the so-called "Aryans" and Jews in Nazi Germany; these are familiar issues of the twentieth-century world. Anti-semitism in Europe in the 30's was the sharpest expression of this type of race-religion division and antagonism. Even today racial conflicts are taking place in the most developed countries.

Under what precise conditions do such types of problems arise? In Palestine before the British Mandate, Arabs and Jews lived peacefully together for centuries. Since the British rule was established, and since the forcible introduction of Zionist immigration by imperialist armed power with Western finance capital, violent conflicts have arisen. These are at times described as racial or religious conflicts, but in reality are national struggles for independence against invasion and alien domination.

In Tsarist Russia, especially during its decline and eventual fall, pogroms of the Jews blackened the pages of its history, and sickened the conscience of the world. These pogroms were widely attributed to uncontrolled outbreaks of the ignorant and savage Russian masses. Only subsequent publication of secret police record finally proved that the government and the "Black Hundreds" or the hooligan "patriotic" organisation, had a tie-up and that the pogroms were directly inspired, and initiated by the government. The day the Russian people became their own masters, the pogroms completely ceased and in the Union of Soviet Republics most diverse races and religions lived happily together.

In Germany under the Weimar Republic, Germans and Jews lived peacefully together. But under the Nazi Germany, the pogrom regime transferred its old base from Tsarist Russia to Central Europe. Thus, there is no inevitable difficulty for the cohabitation of differing races or religions in a country. The difficulties arise from socio-political conditions, in particular wherever a reactionary regime endeavours to maintain itself against the popular movement. However, these are also the surest signs of the impending downfall of such a regime.

The Indian Scene

Prior to the British rule in India, there was no trace of the type of Hindu-Muslim conflicts seen in later years. There had been wars between states, which might have had Hindu-Muslim antagonism. But Muslim rulers freely employed Hindus in the highest positions of their set-ups and vice versa. This traditional character of pre-British India could be traced in the Indian states, where the Simon Report had the occasion to refer to "the comparative absence of communal strife in the Indian states today". What had occasionally been attributed as "communal strife" in certain cases, as in Kashmir in 1931-32, had been misdescription of an entirely different struggle. In Kashmir, the issue was that of popular uprising of a four-fifths Muslim population against a rulèr who happened to be

Hindu; and the British Press was compelled to admit of a "paradoxical position"of a "communal rebellion in which not a single Hindu has been killed" (*Daily Telegraph*, February 8, 1932).

As far back as 1821, a British officer writing under the name of "Carnaticus" in the *Asiatic Review* of May 1821 was declaring the *"Divide et impera* should be the motto of our Indian administration, whether political, civil or military". Lieutenant-Colonel Coke, Commandant of Moradabad, laid down the principle in the middle of the nineteenth century:

"Our endeavour should be to uphold in full force the separation (for us fortunate) which exists between the different religions and races, not to endeavour to amalgamate them. *Divide et impera* should be the principle of Indian government."

In 1888, Sir John Strachey, a leading authority on India, wrote:

"The truth plainly is that the existence side by side of these hostile creeds is one of the strong points in our political position in India.'"[3]

Gandhiji has related how Hume, the joint founder of the Congress, frankly confessed to him that the British Government was "sustained by the policy of Divide and Rule."[4]

In 1910, J. Ramsay Mac Donald wrote with reference to the foundation of the Muslim League:

"The All-India Muslim League was formed on December 30, 1906. The political successes which have rewarded the efforts of the League... have been so single as to give support to a suspicion that sinister influences have been at work, that the Mohammedan leaders were inspired by certain Anglo-Indian officials, and that these officials pulled wires at Simla and in London and out of malice a forethought sowed discord between the Hindu and Mohammedan communities by showing the Mohammedans special favour".[5]

Subsequent evidence has since become available which more than confirms the "suspicion". In the post-war period, particularly after a large number of the Asian and African countries liberated themselves from the colonial rule, the "Muslim Policy" of the West underwent certain basic changes. It is in this period, that the religious revivalist movement became an important political and ideological instrument in the hands of the imperialists to subvert the newly-liberated countries.

Factors of Western Anxiety

A new movement of Afro-Asian solidarity had begun to unfold itself. This new feature of the developing world was illustrated at the Bandung Conference of the Afro-Asian countries on April 18, 1955. As many as 29 Afro-Asian countries attended the conference with 340 delegates from countries totalling 30 million square kilometres in area-about a quarter of the world's land surface with about two-thirds of the world population. Jawaharlal Nehru, supported by other heads of government gave a new sense of direction to the Afro-Asian nations at the meet, laying down a basis for unity and solidarity among them.

The need then arose for a new policy of the West, of the American administration in particular, to make "Asians fight Asians". The various military alliances of that time had this as one of their objectives, though they were also directed against the so-called threat of Communism from the erstwhile Soviet Union.

All these factors have been at work for quite some time. However, from the second half of the 1970s did Washington begin to show a special interest in Islam. This, to large measure was caused by the unprecedented energy crisis of 1973-1974. The Muslim countries of West Asia, and North Africa at that time provided as much as 75 per cent of the oil exported. Another important factor was that these Muslim countries had built up huge financial reserves from sale of oil, which enabled their ruling classes to exert greater influence on the economy of the entire capitalist world. The USA also took into account the growing political and economic weight of the Muslim oil-producing countries in the non-aligned movement, among the developing countries in general, and in international organisations and the world as a whole.

In January 1979, Zbigniew Brezezinski, then Assistant to the US president for National Security Affairs, had even instructed the relevant departments to arrange for an intensive study of Islam and its political role in the world, and prepare a detailed report on the situation in a number of Muslim countries vis-a-vis their religious movements. Thus in the 1970's and 1980's the problems posed by Islam figured prominently in the activities of the US government, its institutions and scientific circles, and Washington began to integrate the Studies as important parts of its foreign policy.

In the mid-sixties, Saudi Arabia initiated a move to set up an Islamic Alliance with a view to uniting all the Islamic countries and sponsored a programme for the revival of orthodox Islam at home and abroad. Simultaneously it accelerated the process of expanding and modernising its armed forces and intelligence in active cooperation with the West. Thus a new power centre opposed to Nasser's Egypt began to take shape.[6]

This has to be seen in the context of the fact that Nasser had become the hero of the Arab masses, particularly after his involvement in North Yemen's civil war against British imperialism. In West Asia the Saudi monarch hit back at Nasser with the announcement that Saudi Arabia had concluded an arms deal with Britain and America worth 360 million US dollars.[7]

In the early eighties, the Carter Administration decided to establish a joint task force of 50,000 for safeguarding the Gulf oil supplies and to build up the America fifth feel, operating from the Island of Diego Garcia near Mauritius, in the Indian Ocean. Soviet intervention in Afghanistan and the proclamation of the Carter Doctrine added urgency to the newly-formed force, called Rapid Development Force. Plans were laid to expand it to 300,000 by the mid-1980 's and increased efforts were made to secure American military bases in and around the Gulf.

The Reagan administration went a step beyond Henry Kissinger's public recommendation: it tried to involve its allies in its military plans for the Gulf. Addressing a conference of military experts in Munich in late February 1981, American Deputy Defense Secretary, Frank Carlucci, asked NATO allies to "station troops in the Gulf". He secured the immediate support of the British Under Secretary for Defense. Early next month, during her visit to Washington, British Prime Minister Margaret Thatcher backed the idea of a multinational RFF. "There is an urgent need for a new defence policy beyond the North Atlantic", she said. "As a loyal ally, Britain will help (the American RDF) to the very maximum of her ability." Her statement coincided with a report that the Reagan administration was seriously considering placing the RDF under its European Command, with its headquarters in Brussels, which is also the headquarters of NATO. A few days later, the US Secretary of Defense publicity called for permanent American military bases in Egypt and Saudi Arabia.

The outbreak of the Iraq-Iran war in September 1980 gave additional urgency to these proposals. Prince Navef, the Saudi

Interior Minister, toured the Gulf States later in the year to win support for the plan, and discuss the structure of the proposed Gulf organisation. The third Islamic summit, held under the auspices of the Organisation of the Islamic Conference in Saudi Arabia in late January, 1981 provided a chance for the heads of the six Gulf states to meet. The result was a decision to form the Gulf Cooperation Council. A meeting of the Gulf foreign ministers, held a week later in Riyadh, decided *inter alia* to establish a coordination committee to unify "the military potential of the Gulf region" by recommending ways of rationalising arms procurement, and developing inter-Gulf cooperation in "training and the use of weapons"[8].

These historic developments establish the fact that the so-called resurgence of Islamic revivalism was not an autonomous development. In the past, colonial rulers had used religious revivalism to subjugate the Asian and African people; in the recent years, this instrument is being used to retard the process of modern nation-state building in these countries. That is why some of the leaders of the Muslim revivalist movement have always had moral and material support of the West.

Carter's Adviser on National Security Brezezinski declared during a visit to Islamabad: "We in the United States neither fear nor deplore Islamic resurgence, we see in it a new element of strength and a new contribution to the cause of peace". The sudden US support to Islamic resurgence may appear surprising, particularly in the background of American hostility to Khomeini's revolution in Iran. In the post-cold war period, the US and the West did get upset about the rise of Muslim fundamentalism, particularly when it took anti-West turn, but they also had something to welcome the revival. These two conflicting approaches surface again and again, depending the way Muslim revivalism asserted itself in the global geopolitical situation, especially after the disintegration of the Soviet Union and East European countries.

Muslim revivalist movements have been there in the past too. But the current phase arose when the Muslim countries were confronted by the challenge of not only the imperialists, but its domination over their economy. The situation was further compounded by the Western cultural invasion. A significant section of the Muslims, including in India, felt the need to return to Islam. They wanted to unite under a big Islamic confederation, and this movement was called Pan-Islam. However, this Pan-Islamic movement could not gather momentum because every Muslim country was passing through a different stage of development, and because of national characteristics, including traditions, history, culture and ethnicity.

The Indian Trend

In India, for instance, this movement took the form of an anti-British movement, and many of its leaders later played important roles in the anti-imperialist campaigns. Maulana Azad was one of the most eminent leaders of this Pan-Islamic movement. Later, in the 1920's he moved to the ideology of the Indian National Congress even as the revivalists accused him of 'betraying' Islam. There were other streams of Muslims too who joined the national movement, such as Ahrar leaders in Punjab and some leading Ulemas from other parts of the country.

It would be a mistake to attribute that the Ulema or their organisations before or after independence were associated with the Islamic revivalist movement. On the contrary, Ulema, in spite of the nature and character of their theological background, disagreed with the revivalists and opposed them. The Ulema have made a contribution second to none in the struggle against British imperialism in India. They have adhered to secularism and democracy in spite of fierce attacks from communal and revivalist parties and groups.

In independent India, Islamic revivalist movement has been represented mainly by the Jamaat-Islami-Hind. The attraction for Islamic revivalism is much greater in a country with Muslim majority than in a country where Muslims are in a minority. That is the reason why the Jamaat-i-Islami could attract greater attention in Pakistan, the Muslim Brotherhood in Egypt and the Islamic revolutionaries of Khomeini in Iran, than in other countries.

The basic premise of Islamic revivalism is to convert the state into an Islamic state; and this appears possible in a country where the majority is of Muslims. This is apparently impossible in a country like India, whose constitutional and political set-up is based on secularism and democracy. Whereas in Pakistan, the Jamaat emphasizes the need to Islamise the state and its laws, in India it confines itself only to purification of the Muslim society and building of an Islamic personality.

Jamaat-i-Islami was born in 1941, almost a year after the famous Pakistan Resolution of the All India Muslim League. The

Jamaat was opposed to both the Indian National Congress and the Muslim League. The Congress, according to it, believed in 'one nation', which would mean the absorption of the Muslims into the Hindu nation. The Muslim League, wanted a Muslim national state, which would not as such be an Islamic state. The founder of the Jama'at-i-Islami, Maulana Maududi, was opposed to nationalism based on territory, race, language, colour or economic factors. All the Muslims were one nation, irrespective of country, caste, colour or race, according to him. His 'Islamic nationalism' was different from 'Muslim nationalism' represented by the Muslim League.

Actually, the Muslim League and its leaders had never spelt out what policy Pakistan would adopt. They had used Islam as a slogan to mobilise the Muslims behind the demand for Pakistan. When Pakistan actually came into being, the Muslim League leaders did not know what political system to adopt. The League leadership consisted mainly of feudal landlords, bureaucrats and the urban rich, and they were satisfied with running the country on the British colonial pattern.

This was an opportunity for the revivalist Jamaat-i-Islam to jump into the field by claiming that since Pakistan had been achieved in the name of Islam, the Islamic state, as understood by them, must be established.

In India, Muslim revivalists have not been able to create a mass base for themselves so far because of the democratic and secular character of the political system. Nevertheless, the emphasis of the Muslim revivalists on Islam as a "complete code of life" governing all aspects of human life, its unique character and exclusiveness, creates a gulf between the Muslims and other communities. And the activities of Hindu revivalists, their slogans, also reinforce the chasm.

On social problems, Muslim revivalists defend the Muslim personal law. Though in theory they are against the formation of political parties within an Islamic state, in actual practice they participate in political activities to strengthen the Muslim revivalist forces. Their economic outlook being most conservative, the revivalist ideology and programme is hardly relevant to the problems which the Indian Muslims face today. Still, the revivalists keep on nursing-the minority consciousness among the Muslims and their economic backwardness becomes a political instrument in their hands. Thus, Indian secularism cannot be talked about in abstract terms. The genuine grievances of the Muslims, their economic backwardness, their low percentage of representation in the services, the neglect of the Urdu language, protection of their places of worship and above all the growing aggressiveness of Hindu revivalism, all these issues need to be dispassionately examined by all those charged with ensuring secularism in India.

Conclusion

It is naive to believe that all the Muslim countries are today witnessing what is called "Muslim Fundamentalism". Secularisation of politics, political superstructures and the consciousness of a modern nation-state are emerging in all the developing countries, and Muslim-dominated countries are no exception. However, this process has its own variants. Hindu fundamentalists in India are playing up the so-called rise of Muslim fundamentalism for their narrow political gains, forgetting that with globalised politics and economy, and the specific Indian conditions the process of modern nation-state should not be thwarted in the national interest.

Most religious philosophies are being given two diametrically opposite interpretations, and Islam is no exception. On the one hand Islam is being given an orthodox and reactionary interpretation, and on the other a liberal and modern one. Periodically, these are cited as ideological guidelines for action to pull up the believers from socio-economic decline. The first set of interpretations emphasizes in varying degrees, reconstruction, renovation, *tajdid* and adaptation[9].

The intensity of the Hindu fundamentalism to bring about synthesis between religion, nationalism and Indian nation-state matches in degree its counterparts in Pakistan. Any synthesis of traditional religion and modern polity, and a blend of religion and science on the intellectual plane, is a formidable challenge, if not an impossible task, for several reasons. First, construction of a viable and dynamic social order requires an adequate command of the modern natural and social sciences and their related methods and techniques of application, in competition with a powerful and fast developing international industrial society. Second, linking the social order and science to a religion with a strong medieval tradition tends to impede original thinking and progress of both science and society, because any idea or practice 'repugnant' to religion is to be shunned and what is repugnant to religion is difficult to define and open only to the arbitrary judgement of the ruling classes and their apologists[10].

Like other religions, Islamic theology has been interpreted differently by people. The traditional literature of Islam relates to various historical periods—the pristine period of the Prophet (peace be upon Him) and uprightly-guided Caliphs. The Muslim community of that time was a cohesive fraternity of believers and their Islam was a revolutionary social principle. Later, under the Umayyads and Abbasids, Islam developed as a part of general social formation in the context of a feudal mode of production. All institutions, ideas and theories elaborated during these later periods bear a deep imprint of the feudal epoch.[11]

There are Islamic scholars who do not hesitate to describe Islamic ideology, in its theory and history, in a historical category in the social institutional sense. There are Muslim scholars who have examined Islam in its historical context, though they, underline that in essence, the *Quran* is a 'Book of Action', a declaration of war against all exploiters of the weaker human beings, and against all vested interests.

This study clearly brings out that historically speaking Great Britain and the United States have been following a policy of dominating the third world countries including the Muslim world. Their objective was to exploit their natural resources, the oil wealth in particular. To perpetuate their domination, the exponents of 'Muslim fundamentalism' became their allies, notwithstanding the fact that Islamic teachings expounded building of a society based on equality in tribal ridden areas. What clearly stands out is that Russia before the October Revolution, later the Soviet Union and new Russia again did not follow this policy. As a matter of fact Russian scholars and political elite took keen interest in the developments of these countries. It is a fact of history that the erstwhile Soviet Union took keen interest in the economic and social development of Central Asian Republics, which at that stage were part of the Soviet Union. It goes without saying that in the modern nation state building, in Central Asian Republics, Russia makes a rich contribution.

Now in the beginning of the 21st century both India and Russia are engaged in a struggle against religious fundamentalism, secessionism and terrorism.

The moral of the situation is that in the new historic situation Indo-Russian relations continue to develop and deepen and are revealing new trends. The rise of religious fundamentalism and the fight against it has become the sheet anchor of the policies of the two countries. In this sense their stand on religious fundamentalism has a commonality of approach and understanding. This stands as a complete contrast to the policies of some other global powers.

It will be a lopsided understanding if we ignore the new ferment which is unfolding itself in the Muslim world. In some of major countries of this region including Egypt, Iraq, Syria, Lebanon and Algeria the movements for building democratic state structures have been developing. Nasserism in Egypt, the Palestinian liberation movement, the Arab Baath Socialist Party in Syria and Iraq, Kamal-Zamalat party in Lebanon and Progressive Party in Algeria are some of the outstanding examples of this trend. Moreover in some of the countries which have authoritarian regimes, around movements for building a democratic system such as in Yemen are gaining strength. According to some experts even in Saudi Arabia this movement is growing. That explains the presence of American military forces in this oil rich country. This graphically illustrates that in this strategic region of our planet, a wind of change is blowing. Pakistan too for the first time is undergoing a process of change, if the recent developments are any indication. What is common in all these movements is that in these areas forces are growing for liquidation of vestiges of colonial period tribalism and above all distortion of Islamic Religion.

References

1. K. Subrahmanyam: India's Unity and Security, p. 63 and 64.
2. Journal of Institute of Muslim Minority Affairs, King Abdulazziz University, Jeddah, Vol, No. 2.
3. Sir John Stracey, "India", 1888, p. 255.
4. J.T. Sunderland, "India in Bondage", p. 232.
5. J.R. MacDonald, The Awakening of India, 1910, pp. 283-4.
6. Dilip Hero : Inside The Middle East, p. 81 and 82.
7. *Ibid.*, p. 254.
8. *Ibid.*, pp. 346-348.
9. Hassan Gardesi: Pakistan Roots of Dictatorship, p. 354.
10. Ziaul Haque: Pakistan: The Roots of Dictatorship, p. 367.
11. *Ibid.*, p. 368.

19

Rise of Hindu Revivalism in India

V.D. Chopra

There are clear indications that the General Elections to the Lok Sabha are round the corner. These elections may be held either in 2008 or on schedule in 2009. As in the past Hindu revivalists have once again become active to broaden their mass base or at least check the decline in their popularity. The crux of the problem is that there is a sharp division in the masses following the Congress and those who are the followers of the secular parties, the Left parties in particular. The political elite of these political formations have not been able to overcome this division. To say this does not mean that one should underestimate the strength of these political formations. The Congress is still the strongest political force in the country despite a steep decline in its influence in the Hindi speaking belt. The fact of the matter is that the Congress is multi-religious, multi-caste, multi-class party of the country and, in the conciousness of the people, it inherits the glorious traditions of the national movement, the Gandhi-Nehru framework of the policies as updated and revised in the new historical conditions. On the other hand the influence of the Indian left though is confined to West Bengal, Kerala and Tripura, it has pockets of influence throughout the country. There is something more to it. The Indian left relatively has a better political image than any other political party. That being the situation, if the leadership of these two political formations objectively estimates the ground reality, they can become a rallying center for the unity of all the secular parties and groups including some of the regional parties. Wh it is happening in India today is that the decline in the influence of the Congress even in its stronghold is being filled by communal, casteist and parochial parties. Nevertheless what is important is to make an objective study of rise of Hindu communalism. The recent controvercy on Ram Sethu has given a handle to Hindu communalism to rehabititate itself. But there is something more to it. This controvercy is creating a new divide between North India and South India. If all these developments are pieced together, it becomes clear that as India is emerging as a global power and an Asian giant, it is facing serious challenges from communal, castiest and parochial forces. Seen in this context, it is relvent to make an objective estimate of the rise of Hindu communalism in the 21st century.

In an ancient country like India, religious-belief system is multidimensional, and has exhibited a remarkable capacity to captivate the minds of the people for centuries. It has a distinctive character, which not only influences ethical value-system of the Hindus, but has a direct bearing on their political behaviour pattern too.

The phrase, "resurgence of Hindu revivalism", implies the existence of a state of torpor or decay from which Hinduism is supposedly arising to a new life. Therefore, it is pertinent to ask what that antecedent state was, and how it has been changing. Unlike other great religions of the world - Christianity, Islam and Buddhism - the Hindu religion has no single founder, no single basic book. It has no Christ, Mohammad, or Buddha; no Bible, no Quran and no Buddhist canon. In a manner of speaking, it has no prophet as such. But has *rishis, munis, avtars* and recognised historical figures like Shankaracharyas, as also other saints, as its religious authorities. With all the revealed nature of the most ancient *Vedas,* the *Smritis* the *Geeta,* the *Mahabharata* and the *puranas* are no less authoritative scriptures of Hinduism than the *Vedas.* In fact, it will not be incorrect to say that *Vedic* Hinduism was very different from that of the *Brahamanas* and the *Upanishads,* and later again from that of the *'smritis',* the *Geeta,* the *Puranas* and the *Mahabharata.* The difference, indeed, is so great that a *Rig Vedic rishi,* if he were to be reborn today, would not be able to recognise today's Hinduism as his religion! There is no *Atma,* no *Brahma,* no *Moksha,* no idol worship in the *Rig Veda.*

This aspect of Hindu religion is being re-called to explain that Hinduism has its own peculiarities and has been undergoing change and transformation from time to time.

Some philosophers claim that Hinduism as a religious philosophy does not reflect the aspirations of the most downtrodden sections of the population, which, according to them, stands in complete contrast to other religions. However, it is a historical fact that the origin of Christianity was in the misery of the slaves in Rome. The roots of Buddhism lay in Buddha's compassion for the downtrodden castes. Islam arose as a movement for uniting the warring tribes by assuring equality to all who recognised only one Allah, and Mohammed as his only Prophet.

Whatever may be the element of truth in this comparison, one thing is certain: that no other religion in the world has succeeded in synthesizing a profound faith in the oneness of God with the actual worship of a myriad of deities, as Hinduism has. It will also not be incorrect to say that the entire superstructure of Hindu religion has not experienced any significant qualitative reforms like, for instance, Protestantism in European Christianity. The social structure of India would have been very different if the envelope of ideas surrounding its existence had taken some other shape, or if Hinduism had experienced its own profound reformation.

Attempts at Change

This is not intended to mean that Hindu religion did not undergo any changes. In the late nineteenth century, reformist movements in India succeeded in attracting widespread popular support, primarily because the various reformist leaders generally spoke in an idiom and utilised philosophical concepts and symbols, which were widely understood. Reformist leaders like Bal Gangadhar Tilak, Sri Aurobindo Ghosh, Swami Vivekananda, Swami Dayanand and others brought into focus that India's decline could be traced to the Hindus' separation of spiritual enlightenment from society's welfare. Aurobindo Ghosh, in the spirit of such European nationalists as Mazzino, saw a divine expression of God in the nation. Nationalism for him was not merely a form of patriotism, but "nationalism is a religion that has come from God", as he said. Both Aurobindo and Vivekanand believed that national rejuvenation would come only when Indians tapped their potential source of power and directed their energies to the service of Mother India. This reformist movement unleashed a new popular mass upsurge, and revolutionary activities increased significantly in Bengal, Maharashtra and Punjab. Gandhiji carried forward this process and gave a new sense of direction to the entire nation. Gandhiji, for instance, was the first to perceive that the specific feature of the Indian village community was that its social division of labour was caste-based, and hence hide-bound and unalterable. That is why he awakened the "dumb millions", and in the process developed a charisma. Then, Jawaharlal Nehru gave a new content to this nation-state concept. He knew more than anybody else that not all religions permit any separation of spiritual and temporal affairs. Nehru and Gandhiji created a new mass psychology in the country that religion and communalism should not be allowed to weaken and break the dialectical link between the "spiritual value system" of various religions and the social responsibilities of the followers of these religions. This was the single biggest factor which finally led to the political independence of India. And in this furnace of the national movement, the concept of the Indian nation-state became part of the popular mass consciousness. That also explains why anti-communalism was inscribed on the banner of the Indian patriotic forces. Not to oppose communalism and not to stand for secularism was considered to be downright unpatriotic.

Here, another aspect needs to be underlined which is specific to India. For centuries Indian village had remained almost isolated from the outside world, and developed as an autonomous entity. This kept our rural masses economically and culturally backward in a caste-ridden society. This explains the historical reasons for the hold of Hindu revivalism in the Hindi-speaking belt of the country. Like Prussia in imperial Germany. The Hindi heartland is by far India's largest region. Its seven states, including the two largest ones - Uttar Pradesh and Bihar - have provided most of Indian Prime Ministers so far, with 43 per cent of Parliamentary seats, it occupies more political clout than any other region. Its definition as a 'political region' starts with the common Hindi language; and extends to its heartland characteristics of cultural parochialism and social and economic backwardness.

During the Nehru era, and partly in the early seventies during the Indira Gandhi period, the success of the Congress in the elections depended on this region. The Congress won disproportionate share of its votes and seats from this region. However, a close analysis shows that this disproportionate electoral support was, in turn, based on the bloc support by India's principal disadvantaged minorities and scheduled castes and tribes, who came to believe in the nationalist era and during Nehru's time, the Congress was their friend and protector. Since 1967, however, a steady decline in the influence of the Congress has been taking place, though this was reversed in 1971, 1980 and again in 1984.

Significantly, except for Bihar, the Indian left did not succeed in making any headway in this region; even in Bihar, the CPI lost considerable mass base particularly after the "Mandalisation" of politics. Therefore, the exponents of "Mandalisation" and communalism are waging a political struggle to dominate this region. One likely reason for this development is that this region is economically and culturally most backward, and those who wield the weapon of religion and caste are succeeding in creating a mass psychology in their favour. Even if this is a simplistic conclusion, it cannot be dismissed lightly.

The conclusion is that we cannot expect our rural masses to be genuinely enthusiastic about radical economic policies and the concept of a secular state without at the same time weeding out from their minds the concept of karma, which for generations had told them that their miserable lot was the result of their misdeeds in the previous births rather than because of their current economic backwardness. It has to be recognised that feudalism, caste loyalties and economic backwardness mould the consciousness of the people, and keep on feeding their minds. Those who claim to be secular and builders of modern nation-state cannot be indifferent to these causes.

Indian intelligentsia too has been brought up in an atmosphere of communal identity which must have influenced its moorings. This, in turn, also promotes veneration for communal identity and caste origin. Let us not overlook the fact that even today in the most sophisticated and modern social gatherings, cast affiliations do play a major role. To try to be critical of these tendencies entails the risk of incurring great social displeasure. But truth is not necessarily what we have become accustomed to imagine as true for centuries; and something that is time-honoured is no sufficient reason for its total acceptance. Were not the institutions of *sati,* of prohibition of widow-remarriage and untouchability time-honoured in the country? Yet, the circumstance of waging a relentless war against these made Raja Rammohan Roy, Vidyasagar and Gandhiji the greatest among our leaders.

Birth and Evolution of Caste System

The Vedantic metaphysical concept of Brahma as the ultimate, form-less, eternal, unchanging, unthinkable, *nirguna* developed *pari passu* with the concept of *Brahma* as the creator and regulator of the social system of *'Chaturvarna'*. Still, further down the line, the theory that every member of every *varna* attains *Moksha* (merging into the Brahma through a series of rebirths, by strictly performing his *varna* duties called *Karma* in Hindu scriptures) was worked out by the Brahmin-Kshatriya establishment in its own interests, though it is difficult to establish as to when this concept emerged. Nevertheless, the fact remains that the development of *Chaturvarna* was not only as a religious institution, but clearly a socio-economic system. It is this theory which gave birth to not only the caste system, but also to the exploitation of the lower castes by the upper castes. The key to the self-propelling nature of Hinduism in this sense lies in the self-propelling character of the caste system born out of *Chaturvarna,* with its occupational endogamous basis.

The historical evolution of the Indian society from the primitive stage to the modern has taken place in a manner in which tribes of the hunting and food-gathering stage evolved into that of settled agriculture, artisanship and handicrafts with the caste system intact. That is why Babasaheb Ambedkar thought that it was not possible to destroy caste division in a short period of time because it was based not only on economic factors, but also because it has its basis in religious dogma. Having studied the effects of religion on the social status of the scheduled castes in Hindu society, Ambedkar brought into focus the mechanism of exploitation in the caste system, and how the caste system was the prime impediment in the way of unity of the exploited.

In his assessment, caste for a Hindu was a certain state of mind. The Hindus clung to the caste because they were deeply religious; therefore, Ambedkar's ideological fire was directed against the Hindu religious philosophy.

Criticising Hinduism as a religion that justified untouchability, Ambedkar wrote:

"The religion which teaches man to behave with man in an inhuman manner is not a religion but infamy. The religion which does not recognise a human being as human being is a curse."

Dr. Ambedkar also pointed out that the struggle against discrimination was made difficult because discrimination itself was supported and sanctified by religion. The common Hindu looked upon scheduled castes as part of his religion, and his behaviour with the scheduled castes proceeded "more from a feeling of attachment to his religion" than due to any premeditated cruelty. When a Hindu for some reason could not meet the demands of the observance of untouchability, he only retreated a little, but never gave them up entirely, as this would mean renouncing the basic religious postulates of Hinduism in the form in which they existed in the minds of the Hindus. Therefore, in his assessment discrimination against the scheduled castes would remain as long as Hindu religion did not undergo any transformation. He, therefore, concluded that it was not possible to destroy caste division in a comparatively short time, because it had its basis in religious dogma. That is why he did not share the perception of the Indian Marxists on this central question.

To say this, does not mean that the role of Ambedkar in the national movement and his contribution to the national consciousness was not significant. The greater part of his political life was spent in the anti-imperialist struggle of the Indian people. On the question of independence of the country, Ambedkar and his supporters occupied patriotic positions. At the same time, as Prof. Hiren Mukherjee writes, "the bitterness of Ambedkar's own experience" on the question of improving the condition of scheduled castes often threw him into a desperate position..."

Ambedkar, therefore, directed his struggle against the "exploitative essence" of Hinduism and the caste system, and did not treat the struggle of all the sections of the downtrodden as an integrated whole. Therefore, the demands for guarantees for the scheduled castes and reservations that Ambedkar had demanded were considered a temporary measure by him. Nevertheless, he still continues to symbolise the aspirations of the scheduled castes, as even after six decades of independence the scheduled castes have not been fully integrated into the national mainstream. Therefore, they again and again assert their separate identity.

There is another aspect of this problem. Almost half of the total number of scheduled caste people live in the five states of the Hindi-speaking belt—Uttar Pradesh (23.5 million), Bihar (10 million), Madhya Pradesh (7.3 million), Rajasthan (5.8 million) and Haryana (2.5 million). In the South, they are concentrated mainly in Tamil Nadu (8.8 million) and Andhra Pradesh (7.9 million), and in the East in West Bengal (12 million). The highest ratio of the scheduled castes in the total population is in Punjab (27 per cent), in Himachal Pradesh (25 per cent), in West Bengal (22 per cent), in Uttar Pradesh (21 per cent) and in Haryana (19 per cent). These figures are indicators of the changes which have been taking place in the political superstructure of India during the last two decades.

Congress and the Minorities

Minority support has always been central to the strength of the Congress. The minorities-scheduled castes, scheduled tribes and Muslims - in the past voted disproportionately for the Congress. The minorities supported the Congress in Hindi-belt *en bloc,* though the Congress enjoyed good support from the upper castes too. The process of erosion in the mass support for the Congress among three minorities began in 1967, but in 1971 this trend was reversed when Indira Gandhi's slogan of Gharibi Hatao (eradicate proverty) gripped the minds of the people. In 1977, after having fallen victim to the excesses of Emergency, they again deserted the Congress en masse. In 1971, the Congress won 65 per cent of seats reserved for the scheduled castes in the 17 large states, but in 1977 the Janata Dal almost reversed the process and captured 58 per cent of these seats. In 1980, the Congress again re-established its 1971 relationship with the scheduled caste voters by winning 61 per cent seats. Except for 1984, after the assassination of Indira Gandhi, the Congress has been gradually losing ground among the scheduled castes and the scheduled tribes, in a zig zag manner as was confirmed by state assembly election results of 1993 end. The fact that in the two biggest states of the country, U.P. and Bihar, the Congress has been voted out of power needs to be studied objectively.

The scheduled castes and scheduled tribes strata today no longer provide the essential support to the Congress in the party system. At the same time, centrist, ethnic and casteist parties and, above all, the religious revivalist Bharatiya Janata Party (BJP), are making efforts to emerge as alternatives to the Congress. In the Hindi-speaking belt, the main struggle to capture power is between the Congress and the BJP and now the Bahujan Samaj Party. The other centrist formation, the Janata Dal, is disintegrating and the Indian left - the CPI (M) and the CPI - have become marginal factors. However, there is another dimension to the changes which are taking place in India's political superstructure.

The Muslim Factor

In the post-Nehru period, a process of alienation of the Congress from the Muslims has been taking place, though both Indira Gandhi and Rajiv Gandhi with their own political styles had partially succeeded in halting this process.

The main reason for this decline phenomenon was the religious Muslim revivalism in the countries around India and Hindu revivalism within the country, which increased the minority consciousness among the Muslims. A study has suggested that the special relationship which the Congress had developed with the poorest strata of Muslims in India began to weaken after Nehru's death.

A significant aspect of Jawaharlal Nehru's perception was the language issue: to him even more important than the status of Hindi or English, was the future of Urdu, particularly in the Hindi-speaking belt. He knew that future of Urdu was an important component of the Muslim consciousness. He, Maulana Azad and Dr. Zakir Hussain knew it well that if the Urdu language was not given its rightful place in the language policy of India, the Muslims will learn it in *madarsas* run by Muslim revivalists. With its multilingual, multicultural and multireligious composition, it is essential in India to give constant attention to the needs and complaints of the minority community. Nehru, therefore, initiated many steps to give the Urdu language its proper place in the Urdu-speaking areas. He, for instance, drew the attention of the Chief Ministers as early as in 1958 that Urdu was being gradually eased out even in places like Delhi, where Urdu had once enjoyed a place of pride. He instructed the Chief Minister of Uttar Pradesh to declare Urdu as a regional language.

Whenever and wherever Hindu-Muslim riots took place, Jawaharlal Nehru took a firm stand. In his speeches and letters to the Chief Ministers and Congressmen, he time and again underlined that the "communal-mindedness of the Hindu majority" was clear manifestation of their backwardness. Secularism, or the acceptance that a citizen's religion was private matter, had been explicitly formulated in the Indian Constitution, but had not been generally accepted. It was in this context that he once confessed that for this reason, he felt a sense of darkness creeping over him.[2]

Nehru was clear in his mind that the question of Kashmir was part of the general problem of the political consciousness of the Muslims in India. In fact, Pakistan's Kashmir policy, its attempts to destabilise the Jammu and Kashmir state and its organised efforts to incite separatist forces by sending armed infiltrators, have all been strengthening Muslim revivalist forces in India. Jawaharlal Nehru was clear in his mind that any weakening of the secular edifice of the country would give a handle to Pakistan. To compete with Pakistan in hatred and barbarity was to accept defeat, and sink below the human level.[3]

What Nehru regarded as the chief problem of Indian unity was the need to foster among the Muslims the feeling that they were not "second class" citizens in India. For this purpose he made secularism the national policy. There was to be no official religion and religious belief was a private matter for each individual. Secularism was the cement of a new social contract binding together the inhabitants of India into one single political community, with religious faith having no bearing on civic rights. This, of course, was the only civilized position possible for any state in the twentieth century: and Nehru strove incessantly to ensure implementation of this policy. The need, for example, to recruit to the civil services a sufficient number of Indians belonging to faiths other than Hinduism was one of his perennial concerns. The rejection of the outrageous thesis that a good Muslim cannot be a good Indian, featured even in his foreign policy and strengthened his resolve not to hand over Kashmir to Pakistan. But a secular society had not become firmly established in India by the time of his death. Communal riots still had not become a phenomenon of the past. Sachar Committee report has highlighted the backwardness of Indian Muslims.

Paradoxically, in his efforts to make the Muslims feel at home in India, Nehru declined to enact a common civil code and insisted on monogamy and rights of divorce, property and inheritance for all Indians of whatever faith. Nehru prided himself on what he had done for the emancipation of women, which was to him the test of civilization; but he had to reconcile himself to the denial of equality, proclaimed by the Indian Constitution, to Muslim women. In the interest of unity and integration, this vital aspect of the social revolution, on which Nehru laid great store, was deliberately held back.

All these and other facets of Nehru's policies, including the manner in which he built friendly relations with Muslim-dominated countries, however, had a deep impact on the Muslims, both in India and abroad.

In the Indian political system, the scheduled castes, the scheduled tribes and Muslims will continue to play a key role in the electoral process as long as its existing secular edifice remains intact. There are around 207 parliamentary constituencies, where Muslim voters are concentrated though the percentage of their concentration varies from constituency to constituency. These constituencies can be divided in three categories:

(I) Constituencies where the Muslim population is 10 to 20 per cent;

(II) Constituencies where the Muslim population is from 20 to 50 per cent; and

(III) Constituencies where the Muslim population is above 50 per cent.

However, the voting pattern in these constituencies has been different. The secular national parties get their support in the first category; while in the second, the pattern is almost the same except for the fact that if a secular party puts up a Muslim candidate, the Muslim electorate votes for that party. In the case of the third category, a Muslim candidate with pronounced pro-Muslim bias gets the support. Higher the proportion of Muslim population, the more likely they will vote for the secular parties with orientation to defend the rights of the Muslims as a religious minority. Herein can be the strength of the Left parties and the Congress, in that order.

Communalised political formations, including Bharatiya Janata Party, have no other option but to rally the entire Hindu population on a Hindu revivalist platform. The BJP can only gain power through this route; any other course will force it to adopt a political platform more secular and radical than that of the Congress.

Rise of Hindu Revivalism

The reality, against all pious expectations is that with all their variants, Hindu, Muslim or Sikh communalism are not showing any signs of withering away with the passage of time. In fact, communalist political formations are playing a see-saw game, reinforcing each other. Hindu communalism is on the ascendency, confirmed by the following table:

Year	*Percentage of Votes Polled by Jana Sangh / BJP*
1952	3.1 Percent
1957	5.9 Percent
1962	6.4 Percent

(Contd.)

Year	*Percentage of Votes Polled by Jana Sangh/BJP*
1967	9.4 Percent
1971	7.4 Percent
1977	41.3 (BLD)
1984	7.4 Percent
1989	11.2 Percent
1990	19.9 Percent

Same trend continued in the subsequent elections.

From the cold statistics, it is clear that a change has come about in favour of Hindu communalism.

Though on the surface there is no "wave" for or against any political party in the Hindi-speaking belt, the demolition of the "Babri Mosque of 6 December 1992 by some " volunteers" gathered at Ayodhya in Uttar Pradesh at the call of the BJP, the Vishwa Hindu Parishad, the Bajrang Dal and several other organisations associated with the Rashtriya Swayam Sewak Sangh (RSS)—collectively called the "Sangh Parivar"—marked the beginning of a new phase in the Indian polity. Now the controversy over Ram Sethu has provided new platform to Hindu revivalism.

There is sufficient evidence to prove that the demolition of Babri Masjid had a grand design behind it and was undertaken with long-term objective of driving a permanent division between the Hindus and Muslims of India, and between the upper caste Hindus and those scheduled castes which were drifting away from the concept of "Hindu Rashtra".

Such a development is a clear proof that the process of modernisation of our socio-economic structures and great expansion the technical and scientific education have not made any basic change in our outlook. What has been most disturbing is that since the midsixties, secular political formations had been entering into political alliances with Communal parties in varying degrees in the game of power politics. This tendency was not confined to the non-Congress secular parties: it had its powerful exponents within the Congress itself. In the late sixties, for instance, a powerful section of the Congress leadership had made determined efforts to come to some understanding with the Jana Sangh and the Swatantra Party, leading to a split in the Congress. However, this is not the place to analyse this development here. What needs to be understood today is that the wobbly stand on such a central issue created a mass psychology, which strengthened communalism, parochialism and casteism. Again, as political consciousness rises and each stratum of the population begins to search for its identity and asserts itself, religious and sectarian beliefs become an effective channel of social communication. At the superstructural level, as the Indian state marches towards economic development, and in the process is emerging a new political elite, various political formations have begun to mobilize the masses through communal, regional and casteist slogans. This trend became more marked in the post-Nehru period. In the initial stages, communal, regional and casteist political formations directed their fire against Jawaharlal Nehru and his thought structures. Anyone who claimed that he or she inherited Nehru's legacy became their target. And there were reasons for this.

Jawaharlal Nehru knew more than anybody else that not all religions permit separation of spiritual and temporal affairs by agreeing to render unto Caesar what is Caesar's, and giving unto God what belongs in Him.

He was also aware of the fact that very majority of the votaries of Hindu, Muslim and Sikh religions did not understand that by giving a new "political" orientation to their religions, the communal leadership was undermining the social values of the teachings of the various religions, thereby destroying their moral and theological base. Communalism was breaking the relationship between what is known as the "spiritual value system" of various religions and the social responsibilities of their devotees. That is why religion, as Nehru saw it "practiced, and accepted even by the thinking minds" did not attract him. He believed that religion was closely associated with superstitions and practiced, and dogmatic beliefs, and behind all this lay a method of approach to life's problems which was certainly not scientific. Yet, he did not impose this rational approach on others, though he practiced the philosophy in his personal life in letter and spirit. Nehru was clear about the fact that religion merges into mysticism and metaphysics, and yet believed that metaphysics and metaphysical philosophy had greater appeal to the mind.

His close associates were never seen performing *'Yagnas'* or consulting *Tantriks* and astrologers. Alas! Today most political, including Congress leaders, draw their inspiration from mysticism and mystic figures, both dead and alive. They, naturally cannot inspire the new generation to follow modern and scientific outlook or look afresh into the Indian heritage, including in the realms of metaphysics and philosophy.

On the other hand, political formations based on religious loyalties are not only political religion, but using every opportunity to rouse irrational emotions to the exclusion of social responsibilities *vis-a-vis* the national mainstream. This has given boost to hypocrisy and obscurantism. Externalised religiosity, therefore, provides a defence mechanism for the new Indian rich to insulate themselves from the growing indignation of the people against social and economic problems faced by them. This new linkage between religion and contemporary Indian polity has its own variant - one in Jammu and Kashmir, another in Punjab and yet another in the Hindi-speaking belt of North India. The common factor of all these variants is that all of them are objectively creating an atmosphere of instability in the country, which in turn, is making our nation state vulnerable to external pressures. Thus, the rise of communalism and intertwining of politics with religion are posing new threats to India's independence and sovereignty.

RSS - The Saffron Brotherhood

Over the last three decades, the Rashtriya Swayam Sevak Sangh (RSS) has been the main driving force behind the so-called Hindu revivalism. Some Hindu revivalist leaders believed that the interests of the Hindu founder had his doubts whether the Congress, which included Muslims, could bring about the desired revival of *"Hindu Rashtra"*.

The RSS was established in 1925 with the objective of training a group of Hindu youths who, on the basis of their character-building experience in the organisation, would work to unite the Hindu community so that India could again become an "Independent" country and a creative society. Its founder was convinced that a fundamental change in social attitudes was a necessary precondition for a revived India.

The two leaders of RSS, during the pre-independence period - its founder, Keshave Baliram Hedgewar (1925-1940) and Madhav Sadashiv Golwalker (1940-1973) - laid a firm foundation, supervising the training of the full-time workers who thereafter spread the organisation outward from its original base in eastern Maharashtra. This is proof enough the RSS was conceived and evolved as a semi-fascist organisation.

Linked to the RSS in India are several affiliated organisations, referred to in the RSS literature as the *'Parivar'* working in politics, in social welfare, in the media, among students, industrial workers and Hindu religious outfits and groups. If the BJP - and in the past the Jana Sangh - was the political platform of the RSS, the Vishwa Hindu Parishad was the ideological platform for Hindu revivalism. The pattern of the RSS organisation has resulted in a high degree of loyalty on the part of its cadre. The recruitment process employed by the 'Parivar' organisations has enabled the RSS to remain insulated from the day-to-day role as a controlling body which functions through various instruments in almost all walks of life.

The farsighted leadership of the RSS adopted a cautious, non-confrontational approach towards the political authority to reduce the chances of governmental restrictions in the post-independence period. After independence in 1947, however, the RSS came under political attack of the government. Though Gandhiji's assassination isolated the RSS from the national mainstream, the RSS leadership did not dilute its operations. The RSS was banned twice - first in 1948 after Gandhiji's assassination and again in 1975.

Till the sixties, the RSS could not integrate itself into the national mainstream. In the post-Nehru period when the Congress mass influence declined, the RSS and its political wing, the Jana Sangh, began to grow in strength. The main reason for this was that in a number of states, coalition governments were formed between 1967 and 1969, in which the Jana Sangh shared power with the non-Congress political formations, including the Indian Left. Blind anti-Congressism prompted certain secular forces to make common cause with the Jana Sangh. The formation of the Janata Dal government at the Centre gave a new credibility to the RSS and the Jana Sangh, though, later, this government disintegrated on the controversy over "dual" membership - one of the RSS and the other of the Janata Dal.

Jana Sangh merged into a new governing party, the Janata Party, and former Jana Sangh leaders were included in the national cabinet and served as Chief Ministers in several states during the 27 month period that the Janata Party remained in power, never before had RSS worked so closely with such a broad spectrum of groups, many of which had previously demanded curbs on its activities.

After the defeat of the Congress in 1989, and the formation of the Janata Dal government headed by V.P. Singh at the Centre a new phase began in the evolution of the RSS. The V.P. Singh government depended for its existence on two crutches - one of the BJP and the other of the Left Front; of the two the BJP was the stronger. Naturally, the RSS and the BJP began asserting themselves in shaping the policies and finally, as was expected, a break took place between the BJP and the Janata Dal.

Now, this Hindu revivalist force is far more self-confident about its place in the Indian society than at any time since India's independence. The unprecedented growth of the RSS and its affiliates may also be traced to the upsurge of militancy among a section of the Hindus. The main reason for this was that the Indian political forces, including Congressmen, the non-Congress formations and the Indian Left, grossly under-estimated the potential of the rise of Hindu revivalism in the Indian society.

As a result, many Hindus came to believe that the Congress and the Indian Left were "Pampering" the Muslims for political gain. The government's decision in March, 1986 to enact a legislation negating a court order that did not adhere to the traditional Islamic law on the question of alimony, was seen as one such favouritism.

In the eighties, Hindu militancy as represented by the RSS became more active than ever before because at a number of places temples used as mosques were restored. The RSS and its 'Parivar' had been in the thick of many of these activities.

Of a far-reaching significance is the fact that the various front organisations of the *'Parvar'* are controlled by the RSS cardre. The front organisations have a highly centralized authority structure, very similar to the RSS. All of them recruit their cadre largely from the RSS. And the RSS-trained cadres occupy main organizational positions. Thus, the RSS plays a key role in moulding the policies, ideology and orientation of the various front organisations of the 'Parivar'.

In recent years, the RSS has changed its tactics. RSS leaders have come to realise that close association with the political power evokes envy and opposition, which complicate their efforts from a long-term point of view. With the massive increase in its influence, the RSS leadership now controls these organisations from behind, though most of the front leaders had undergone RSS training some time or the other.

Thus training is carried out in the RSS *'Shakhas'* which meet daily ostensibly to teach character-building exercises to the 'Swayam Sevaks.' The founders of the RSS had devised a training system which was intended to establish what is described as the "Saffron Brotherhood". The RSS training ideally starts at the pre-adolescence stage and ideological training takes place at a time when the youth generally work out in their own experiences, satisfying a relationship between themselves and the society. This is the period when the individual is particularly susceptible to ideological brainwash. He seeks a person, a cause, to which he can give uncompromising obedience. The RSS appeals to this impulse by advocating sacrifice of the self for the *Hindu Rashtra,* and this impulse is expressed organizationally in the RSS and reverence for the RSS leaders. The society envisaged is not the one that objectively exists, but the one which is perceived by the RSS ideology.

However, the various movements sponsored by the RSS are religious in character. Religion is only a signboard.

What, for example, have the campaigns of the RSS-sponsored Vishwa Hindu Parishad got to do with the religious beliefs of the Hindus? There does not, and cannot, exist any threat to their religion and culture in a secular state, 80 per cent of whose population is Hindu. And yet, the RSS and the VHP are trying to convince the lay Hindus that they are "under siege" and that there is an international conspiracy to reduce their number through conversion! The whole propaganda is to intensify a perception of threat among the majority community with a view to inciting aggressive hatred against the adherents of other religions. The high watermark of this demagogy is the assertion that India should be declared a Hindu state because then alone would secularism, democracy and non-alignment be safe.

One is reminded of the Nazi propaganda which made the Germans believe that extermination of the Jews was essential to protect the German race and the nation; that the German race provided the only guarantee for civilised existence of mankind; and that Germany had the divine mission to rule and civilise the rest of the world.

The Zionist Jews who today dominate Israel are inspired by similar feelings of being the "chosen people" of God. So are the followers of the Ikhwan, whose Indian form is Jamaat-e-Islami:

they declare themselves the "Party of God-Hizb-e-Allah". They do not confine themselves to the propagation of mere faith; according to the Ikhwan belief, "Islam considers the enforcement of law and order as important as propaganda and precept", and insist that "God prevents and stops through state power what the *Quran* cannot accomplish". It is interesting to note, that these movements accept and admire each other despite their apparent contradictions. All of them hold fascism and racism in high regard. This is what Golwalkar had said about Nazi Germany in 1938 : "German racial pride has now become the topic of the day. To keep up the purity of the race and its culture, Germany shocked the world by her purging the country of the Semitic race - the Jews. Race pride at its highest has also manifested here. Germany has also shown how well-nigh impossible it is for races and cultures, having differences going to the rot, to be assimilated into one united whole, a good lesson for us in Hindustan to learn and profit by."

The RSS leaders are not generally known for commenting on events beyond India's borders. As a rule they avoid making international sympathies and possible contacts known to public, because they are extra careful about the veneer that they have no links outside India. If and when they choose to make an exception to this rule, it is obviously under compulsion of circumstances, but are indeed flashes that expose reality.

Nearly three decades back, the then RSS chief, Golwalkar, had sent a message to US President Johnson extending support to his Vietnam policy. That was the time when the US Administration had been totally isolated in the region; and opposition to the escalation of aggression in Vietnam was growing even within the USA. Golwalkar had then written that in the worldwide confrontation between *Dharma and Adharma the USA was leading the forces of Dharma.*

For the Zionists, the RSS has had as much admiration as for Hitler's Nazi Germany. In his first book, *"We and Our Nationhood Defined"*, Golwalkar has paid glowing tributes to the race spirit, both of the Nazi Germany and the Zionist Jews. That was the time when the Indian National movement was opposing fascism and condemning the induction of Jews into Palestine "under British bayonets".

These facts underline the political character of the RSS. Both Mahatma Gandhi and Jawaharlal Nehru were aware of this fact.

Gandhiji even refused to give RSS a good chit when somebody praised the discipline and hard work of the RSS men and pointed out that those qualities were found in Hitler's Nazis too. Jawaharlal Nehru, when repeatedly pressed by Golwalkar for an interview, informed the latter that it was no use because what the RSS people said was not the same as what they did. That is why various attempts by the RSS to secure entry into the Congress did not succeed.

As early as on September 10, 1949, in a letter to Mohan Lal Saxena, Jawaharlal Nehru had warned the nation, "All of us seem to be getting infected with refugee mentality, or worse still, the RSS mentality. That is a curious finale to our careers". This warning by Jawaharlal was given after the assassination of Gandhiji when the RSS-engineered tension in the country had led to a serious communal situation.

Though the first ban on the RSS was lifted in 1949, the ban had been a serious setback to the RSS. Its dreams of playing a major role in independent India were shattered as has been the case after the Ayodhya tragedy. The RSS leadership then had come under heavy attack both from within and without. The RSS was treated as a pariah organisation and the leadership was ridiculed in the press and by politicians. Its membership dropped and the number of *pracharaks* too decreased. Morale within the organisation was at an all-time low.

Between the lifting of the ban in 1949 and 1953, Golwalkar was confronted by an organisation beset by internal division. However, in 1952 the RSS leadership again became active and started agitation against cow slaughter. This enabled the RSS to partially rehabilitate itself. At the grass-root level, the agitation depended heavily on RSS volunteers. Nevertheless, till the early fifties, the RSS remained in a bad shape. It was faced with serious financial problems because it could not pay off.

Loans arranged during the ban. In fact, at one stage Golwalkar seriously considered selling off the RSS headquarters in Nagpur to raise money. It was not until 1956 that the RSS w as able to pay back its debts.

Given the continuing problems in the mid-1950s, the central leadership decided that a further consolidation was needed. Eknath Ranade, appointed general-secretary in 1956, ruled that the RSS could not afford to *loan pracharaks* to the affiliates when its own work continued to languish. The RSS would devote its resources almost exclusively to character-building. This policy came as a blow to the affiliates and their leaders lobbied against it. Some activist *pracharaks,* such as the Deoras brothers withdrew from RSS work.

The consolidation phase ended in 1962. Two years earlier, Golwalkar had called an assembly of full-time workers at Indore to review the future orientation to the RSS. For the first time, *pracharaks* working in the affiliates strongly recommended that the RSS should again allow some of its own full-time workers to work for the affiliates. They pointed out that the future of the affiliates would be bleak unless they could get the help of RSS *pracharaks.* Their arguments had the desired impact. Ranade, assigned to a long-term project aimed at popularising the revivalist message of Swami Vivekananda, was replaced in 1962 by Prabhakar Balwant Dani, who held the position between 1946-56, and who was more sympathetic to the activists' views. After 1962, RSS workers were again allowed to shift to the affiliates. Perhaps the most prominent on this score were the Deoras brothers. Balasaheb was appointed assistant general secretary, and Bhanrao was given the position of northern zonal *Pracharak.*

The main reason for the 1962 change in the policy was that following the Sino-Indian border conflict, the Congress received a serious setback and for the first time direct political attacks on Jawaharlal Nehru had began. Since then, the RSS and its various front organisations have been expanding their influence.

Far-sighted as the RSS leaders were in the sixties, they evolved a well-designed policy of "mind management." In the initial stages they created an informal communication system based on verbal messages carried by RSS cadres. The RSS in this period, created trusts for publication of newspapers and journals. The publication, *Organiser,* was started on July 3, 1947, a month after Lord Mountbatten announced the decision to partition the country. Later, weeklies *Panchjanya* in Hindi and *Rashtra-Shakti* in Marathi started their publications. In 1970, the *Hindustan Samachar* News Agency with a network of over 1000 correspondents began to function. By the 70's the RSS and its front organisation had nearly 41 newspapers and journals in the country. After the emergency period (1975-1977) the RSS newspapers experienced an upward surge in circulation.

Though the Vidyarthi Parishad was started in 1948, it was in the 50s and the 60s that it became an important factor in the youth movement, particularly in Delhi, Punjab, Uttar Pradesh, Madhya Pradesh and Maharashtra. By the early 1970s, the Vidyarthi Parishad had become a significant force in various Indian universities. In mid-seventies, it had a membership of 1.6 lakhs in 790 branches. In the 1974-75 agitation in Bihar and Gujarat, the Vidyarthi Parishad was most active. In Bihar for instance, the Vidyarthi Parishad fully backed the students' agitations behind Jai Prakash Narayan.

Surprisingly in the 50s, the RSS worked out a plan to penetrate the working class movement. In the sixties, the RSS-led Mazdoor Sangh became another important organ. Following the 1977 electoral victory of the Janata alliance, the influence of the RSS in the working class movement began to increase rapidly. The Bharatiya Mazdoor Sangh, according to its claims, has 1725 unions with a total membership of 18.79 lakhs. According to its claims it has already become the second biggest trade union organisation in the country.

However, the most important component of the multifaceted activities of the RSS was that it began to organise Hindus on a religious basis. In 1964, it established the Vishwa Hindu Parishad with three main objectives.

1. To consolidate and strengthen the Hindu society.
2. To protect and spread Hindu values, ethical and spiritual, and to make them relevant in contemporary society; and
3. To establish and strengthen the links among Hindus living in different countries.

Till the early 70s, the VHP concentrated its resources in the Hindi-speaking belt with the main focus on the tribal people. It was in the early 80s that the VHP started organising the Hindus at the national plane. A month-long *'Ekatmata Yagna'* was organised all over the country to raise resources for its activities. According to an estimate of the RSS leaders, 60 million people participated in this *'Yagna'*, with the various processions converging on Nagpur, the headquarters of the RSS. The processions were accompanied by portraits of 'Bharat Mata' and large urns containing water from the Ganga river. The Ganga water was distributed among the Hindu temples for use in the worship of the temple gods.

It was after this success that the VHP, in the late 1983, became an active participant in the campaign to restore the birthplace of Lord Rama, and with this began the Ram Janmabhoomi-Babri Masjid controversy. In its campaign to get the Ram Janmabhoomi at Ayodhya converted into a temple, the February 1986 court decision permitting the performance of *'pooja'* at the Ram Janmabhoomi gave the VHP new credibility. In this movement the VHP received help from the Hindu religious establishments, including the four *Shankarcharyas.* The VHP then decided to raise Rs. 250 million for building this temple, and simultaneously raised the demand for conversion of two other historic sites in Uttar Pradesh Krishna Janmabhoomi, the birthplace of Krishna at Mathura, and the Kashi Vishwanath Temple at Varanasi. In addition, the VHP identified 25 other mosques to be converted. Since then, the cleavage between the Hindus and the Muslims had been widening which reached its climax on December 6, 1992. But there is much more to it than meets the eye.

In 1970, RSS members residing in the United States met in New York City to form the Vishwa Hindu Parishad of the United States of America. The American and Canadian units of the VHP published a bi-monthly magazine. These two units have been organizing camps in various parts of America and Canada and several RSS leaders from India have been regularly touring these countries. Besides the US and Canada, the VHP has spread to other countries, especially England and several East African and South Asian countries. In Great Britain the VHP now claims 14 branches.

This amply shows that the Vidyarthi Parishad, the Mazdoor Sangh, the VHP, the BJP and other front organisations are run exclusively by the RSS. From all angles, the "Saffron Brotherhood", namely the RSS, has emerged as an important force in India, and has been pushing forward to build a theocratic state by demolishing the secular edifice built over the last one century - during the freedom struggle and in the post-independence period.

The defence of India's secular edifice has both regional and international significance. India's size and geography is such that what happens to this ancient nation will have a chain reaction in the entire Asia-Pacific region. Indian nation state based on secularism has been a model for this region, for that matter for the entire developing world. What happens to India and in India can change the course of history in the coming decades. In this sense all the liberal democrats throughout the world should realise that by encouraging communal, revivalist and terrorist forces, they are only destabilising the entire region. This study clearly shows that in the beginning of 21st century, the main contradiction in India is between Hindu revivalism and secularism, though casteist, regional and parochial parties too are growing in strength.

References

Writings and speeches of Dr. Ambedkar, 1925-1936, Vol. 4, Bangalore, 1979, p. 62.

1. Speech at Patna, 30 April 1959, the Hindu, 2 May, 1959.
2. Abdullah to Ayub, 1 September, 1967, pp. 81-82.
3. S. Gopal, Jawaharlal Nehru, A Biography Vol. III, p. 281.

20

India's Relations with Russia Rooted in History

V.D. Chopra

India in the early 21st century has become a focus of international attention more than ever before. Last over six decades, since India became politically independent, have witnessed tremendous changes in the socio-economic base of the country and thereupon in its political structure - political system and political parties. In fact, the last over 55 years will go down in the history of India as an era of change - change hitherto unprecedented in scale and depth. This has altered the entire course of the history of the Indian people because they have not only become masters of their destiny but have already begun to play a significant role, influencing world events and moulding world-situation. It is, therefore, but natural that every major power in the world should have started watching India from close quarters.

India is the seventh largest country in the world and next to China has the highest population on our planet. It is well marked off from the rest of Asia by mountains and seas, which give the country a distinct geographical identity. Bounded by the great Himalayas in the north, it stretches southwards and at the Tropic of Cancer, shrinks off into the Indian Ocean.

Such a vast country and that too being so densely populated and lying entirely in the northern hemisphere, obviously has a strategic position in the geopolity of the present-day world. A casual look at India's geographical location on the world map immediately brings home the fact of her enviable importance. The Himalayas and other lofty mountain ranges of Muztagh Ata, Aghil and Kunlun to the north of Kashmir and south-eastern portion of Zanskar mountains to the east of Himachal Pradesh from India's northern boundary. She is adjoined in the north by China, Nepal and Bhutan. A series of mountain ranges in the east separate India from

Myanmar. Also in the east, lies Bangladesh, bounded by the Indian States of West Bengal, Assam, Meghalaya, Tripura and Mizoram. In the northwest, Afghanistan and Pakistan border on India. South of the Tropic of Cancer, the country tapers off into the Indian Ocean between the Arabian Sea on the West and the Bay of Bengal on the East. The Gulf of Mannar and the Palk Strait separate India from Sri Lanka. The Andaman and Nicobar Islands in the Bay of Bengal and Lakshadweep in the Arabian Sea are parts of the territory of India.

Geopolitical location and its population apart, one thing that stands out clearly and unmistakably is that long before most parts of the world had embarked upon the path of civilisation, India could already boast of culture and progress with millennia of human endeavour behind it. Perhaps these civilisations flourished in the third millennium before Christ. The mystery of the ancient Indian culture remains a mystery even today because the distinction between 'history' and 'pre-history' is peculiarly elusive in her case. None can fully reconstruct the story of the culture that once thrived in this great country. Though writing was known and employed in India in the third and second millennia B.C., the exclusive script has yet to be deciphered in a meaningful way. It is recognised fact, however, that along with Persia, Mesopotamia, and Egypt, India was one of the most important centres on the globe where the civilisation-processes were initiated and matured.

No wonder then, India and its cultural achievements have started shaping the evolution of human thought, even during the unrecorded periods of history, by forging contacts with other areas and people.

Mohenjo-Daro and Harappa are outstanding examples of what was once Indus Valley Civilisation. That this civilisation takes its rank with the great ages of the Valleys of the Nile, the Tigris and the Euphrates, and had witnessed the rise of the ancient civilisations of Egypt, Assyria and Babylonia are indisputable facts. Its people knew the art of laying out towns and claimed a highly developed culture. Cotton and woollen fabrics were in common use; ornaments were worn both by men and women; polished pottery was produced; the sculptor's technique was fashioned. The carpenter, mason, blacksmith, goldsmith, jeweller, stonecutter and the ivory worker had flourishing trade and religion with its system of rituals prevailed. The Indus Valley civilisation is believed to be older than the culture of the Vedic age. While the Vedic Aryans were rural, the people of this valley possessed the amenities of developed town-life. Some hold that they were the same as the Sumerians, while others opine that they were in fact the Dravidians who at one time inhabited the whole of India, including the modern Punjab, the Sind and Baluchistan and had even migrated to Mesopotamia. The Dravidian language is still spoken by the Brahui people of Baluchistan and this further lends support to the original view. But Mohenjo-Daro and Harappa maintain a serene silence, like the inscrutable Sphinx, at the labours of the scholars. Darkness envelopes several succeeding centuries.

The most remarkable of the epic poems of ancient India are the Ramayana and Mahabharata, which were written down far later, between the fourth century B.C. and the fourth century A.D. However, the main subject matter of these poems and many of the stories that went into their making undoubtedly stem from the first half of the first millennium B.C.

Both the Ramayana and the Mahabharata are extremely well integrated works, no mosaics consisting of a variety of texts, but unified works, each being a compositional whole. The authorship of the Mahabharata is traditionally ascribed to Vyasa and that of the Ramayana to the poet Valmiki, but nothing definite is known about these poets or seers *(rishis)*.

These poems are veritable encyclopaedias of ancient India. They contain most interesting and informative material on various aspects of social and cultural life, political organisation and philosophical systems of the ancient Indians. It would be no exaggeration to say that these poems have been unrivalled in popularity in India. But what is most significant is that in olden times and in the Middle Ages they were famed far beyond India's frontier—in Eastern and Southern Asia and in the Far and Middle East. Translations of the Mahabharata and the Ramayana into a number of European languages were widely acclaimed. Many outstanding figures in the history of Western and Oriental culture, like Beethovan, Heine, Rodin, Gandhi, Tagore and Nehru drew inspiration from them.

It would be true to say that even in the earlier periods, India maintained close links with neighbouring and distant countries. These contacts were developed and consolidated over the centuries and Indian culture penetrated other ethno-cultural zones and a process of mutual cultural enrichment ensued.

The earliest and deepest of these cultural ties were those linking India and Iran, for they can be traced as far back as the Neolithic times. The ancient Indians and Iranians were closely related people, ethnically as well as linguistically. The period of particularly close Indo-lranian ties began after the formation of the Achaemenid Empire when certain areas of Northwestern India were integrated with that empire. Achaemenid-culture (architecture and sculpture) made a great impact on the development of Indian art during the Mauryan age. Buddhism spread to Iran from India and many Indian scientific achievements and works of art became known there.

Recent excavations made by Soviet archaeologists in Central Asia show that there existed direct links between the southern parts of Central Asia and India as early as the Harappan age and these became particularly deeper in the Kushana period. Central Asian influence took birth in India as the Kushana and the Shakas extended their sway while Buddhism and other aspects of India's religion, culture and philosophy spread to Central Asia in turn.

Judging by the inscription found in Central Asia, a large number of monasteries had been built during the Kushana and Gupta periods. The most striking demonstration of this is provided by the Buddhist monasteries at Kara-Tepeh (near Termez, in the first century A.D.) and in Ajina-Tepeh (Southern Tajikistan, seventh century A.D.).

In the earlier centuries A.D., trade links between India and China grew apace; these were established by way of the Great Silk Route and also by sea. Indian embassies and Buddhist missions were sent to China. In the third century A.D., Buddhist monasteries appeared in China and translations of Buddhist writings into Chinese were undertaken.

Indian culture exercised a strong influence on literature, architecture and religion of a large number of countries. At a very early stage, India began trading with many countries of South-East Asia and later Indian settlements appeared in some of them. The settlers popularised the Sanskrit language in these regions and enriched them with the many achievements of Indian culture.

At the time of the Harappan civilisation, trade and cultural ties were established with the Sumerians. Later, the Indians engaged in overseas trade with Arabia and Africa and consolidated links with countries bordering the Mediterranean, particularly with

Egypt.

A new era in relations between India and the west began after the campaign of Alexander the Great, when the Greeks came to acquire first-hand knowledge of India and her culture. During the Kushana period ties between India and Rome grew stronger; Indian embassies bearing rich gifts were sent to Rome and the Romans set up trading centers in Southern India.

The influence of ancient Greece and Rome made itself felt particularly deep when Indo-Greek states were established in North-Western India, and then later in the Kushana period. It was reflected in the art of the period (Gandhara Sculpture), in science and philosophy. Certain Indian astronomical treatises dating from the early centuries A.D. indicate that Indian scholars were acquainted with the work of Alexandrian astronomers and one of the siddhantas (astronomical treatises) actually came to be known as the Romakasiddhanta (the Roman siddhanta).

It would be relevant to stress that many crucial questions concerning the universe, man and Nature were posed and solved through mutual exchanges by Indian and classical thinkers. This interplay points to the underlying pattern of cultural advance shaped by the processes of historical development in the ancient period. While maintaining and consolidating trade and cultural links with other lands and people over the centuries, India did not fail to preserve her own essential and distinctive culture, philosophy, traditions and social and political institutions. At the same time, she gave to the world freely and generously. The contribution of ancient India to the common heritage of mankind is truly immense.

> *"A blind reverence for the past is bad so also is a contempt for it, no future can be founded on either of these. The present and the future inevitably grow out of the past and bear its stamp, and to forget this is to build without foundations and to cut off the roots of national growth."*
>
> ***Jawaharlal Nehru***

Jawaharlal Nehru underlined this in his book, "Discovery of India" in the context of role of nationalism. But he also said that "group memory of past achievements, traditions and experiences" is one of the most powerful forces that influence people. Thus when we say that India's relations with the other countries, particularly with Russia are rooted in history, one obviously recalls memory of past relations to mind. Though one need not go into detail here, there is sufficient proof that cultural and economic relations between India and Russia and with Central Asia go back of thousands of years. A large number of Buddhist architectural complexes, worship places and monasteries dating back to the period ranging from the first century A.D. to the Islamic Middle Ages have been discovered in the Central Asian Republics -Uzbekistan, Tajikistan, Turkmenia and Kirghizia. This evidence also shows that the Kushan Empire extended to the southern regions of what is now Central Asia. At the time of famous Kushan King Kanishka and his successors, Buddhism spilled over from Hindustan to the north of Hindu-Kush.

This would mean that as neighbours, people of Russia and Central Asia have not been only known to each other but have long been making cultural and economic exchanges. A thirteenth century book in Russian is aptly entitled "The Story of India, the Richi". In the last quarter of the eighteenth century Gerasim Stepanovich Lebedev, a Russian musician and dramatist made his way to India. He not only learnt Sanskrit and Bengali but also wrote plays in Bengali.

In fact, there are historians who contend that the Aryan tribes originally inhabited the region that comprises the present Tajik, Kirghizian and Uzbek Republics. They gradually moved across to present Iran, India and Europe. Alexander's route of conquests lay across Uzbekistan. Later, the Kushans too came from the same region of Central Asia. Kanishka's empire covered a good part of North India, Pakistan, Afghanistan and extended well into Tajikistan, Kirghizia and Uzbekistan.

The sweep of Changez Khan and massive Arab invasions followed by Timur's conquests destroyed the Buddhist culture in these parts. Buddhism had also spread to some tribes residing in Siberia. They received it from Tibet, Ladakh and Mongolia. Ulan-Ude, the capital of Buriat, is a small 'autonomous region' situated on the bank of Baykal Lake, on the border of Mongolia. Even today the people there are mostly Buddhists and have much in common with their co-religionists in the Ladakh area.

The whirlwind of Changez Khan swept through many a land. His thrust covered a vast area including Northern India, which suffered calamities of plunder and loot along with the people of Central Asia. Timur made Samarkand his seat of power and was buried there after his death. His mausoleum is a beautiful piece of architecture and Humayun's tomb and Shah Jahan's Taj Mahal were probably inspired by this design.

From the fifteenth century, European imperialism was spreading its tentacles in many directions. While India was subjugated finally by the British, the Czar's empire extended to Turkestan. From then on inter-relations between India and Russia were excluded to a large degree by European politics. The mighty powers of Europe had their own wars and peace treaties in a series of changing fortunes. But by the middle of the 19th century, the British Empire had consolidated itself and incorporated the Punjab, extending its rule right up to Khyber. This brought Russia and Britain face to face in open hostility, which continued till the First World War.

This notwithstanding, it appears that from the middle of the 18th century onward, interest of Russian scholars in Indian literature in most of the languages, apart from Sanskrit, kept on steadily increasing. As early as in 1851, a chair of Oriental languages was created in Moscow University and in 1855 a chair of Sanskrit was established at St. Petersburg. Progressive intellectuals and political leaders must have watched with interest India's first War of Independence in 1857. More significantly, a Russian scholar, Ivan Pavlovich Minaev, came to visit India a number of times.

Similarly trade between India and Russia has a history going back many centuries. In the Middle Ages, Indian pepper, ginger, products of sandalwood and handloom were known well to the Russians. It is likely that for centuries, the overland trade between India, Central Asia, Russia and beyond used to be largely in Indian hands. In the capital of Azerbaijan, Baku the great oil city on the Caspian Sea—a historical monument, a temple of fire worshippers was established hundreds of years ago by Indian merchants who had gone there to develop commerce between the two countries. Again in this city, particularly on the banks of the Caspian Sea, at least two "Sarais"— inns built by Indian traders—exist even now and one of these sarais is still known as the "Multani Sarai". Fortunately, the original architecture and the interior decoration of these sarais has been kept intact. One of them is in use as a tourist resort.

It is against this historical background that the real impact of the October Revolution on India's freedom struggle should be analysed.

21

Impact of Developments in Russia on Indian National Movement

V.D. Chopra

It may look too sweeping a statement but there is ample evidence to the effect that when the Russian people were fighting tyrannical and despotic rule of the Czars and the Indian people were engaged in a bitter struggle against British imperialism, the people of these two countries had developed a peculiar type of emotional attachment with each other, primarily because of their cause being similar.

That explains that even in the 19th century, Indian and Russian progressive circles took keen interest in each other's affairs. The forward-looking Russians closely watched the various anti-imperialist movements in the last century and particularly India's first War of Independence in 1857 attracted their attention the most. They in fact were disappointed when the widespread risings in 1857—which the British rulers dubbed as "mutiny"—were brutally crushed. However, the Russian scholars continued to take interest in India, notable amongst them was Ivan Pavlovich Minaev, Professor of Comparative Grammar at St. Petersburg University, who paid three visits to India between 1874 and 1886. He was present as an observer at the founding of the Indian National Congress in 1885. He described this event as a significant attempt for "the development of the feeling of nationalism in India, for the unification of India".

After the Russians moved into Central Asia, the British were all the time apprehensive of Czarist invasion of India. The British used every means to stem the expansion of Russian power in areas in proximity or adjacent to India and often used it as a pretext for regular invasion or intervention as in Afghanistan. However, the people of India did not subscribe to this bogey of the Russian threat. On the other hand, a feeling started growing in India that the

Russians would help India in throwing off the British colonial yoke. The Indian National Congress refused to accept Russian threat as real and consistently opposed excessive military expenditure by the British in pursuance of their "forward" policy.

In 1905, Bal Gangadhar Tilak approached the Russian Consulate and made enquires whether it would be possible for Indians to attend Russian military schools for training so that they could organise Indian patriotic forces against the British. Tilak in his speeches often admired the Russian people's rising against the Czar and advocated similar methods of defiance by the Indian masses.

Mahatma Gandhi was greatly impressed by the Russian thinkers and writers. His correspondence with Leo Tolstoy is well known. He was also an admirer of Maxim Gorky who, nevertheless, advocated methods quite different from those of Leo Tolstoy. He wrote about Gorky in 1905: "Without caring to make money, he writes with such vehemence and bitterness that authorities keep a stern eye on him. He has also been in jail in the service of the people and considers imprisonment as an honour. It is said that there is no other writer in Europe who is as great a champion of people's rights as Maxim Gorky". Mahatma Gandhi was enthused by the First Russian Revolution in 1905. He said: "We too can resort to the Russian remedy against tyranny. The movement in Bengal for the use of Swadeshi goods is much like the Russian movement. Our shackles will break this very day, if the people of India become united and patient, love their country and think of the well-being of their motherland disregarding their self interest ..... . We also can show the same strength that the Russian people have done".

Mahatma Gandhi prophetically declared: "If the Russian people succeed, the revolution in Russia will be regarded as the greatest victory, the greatest event of the present century".

On the other hand, Russian leaders evinced keen interest in India's struggle for independence. On the conviction of Tilak, Lenin wrote: "But the popular India is beginning to stand up in defence of her writers and political leaders. At the infamous sentence pronounced by the British jackals on the Indian democrat Tilak - he was sentenced to long term of exile—a question in the British House of Commons the other day revealed that the Indian Jurors had declared for acquittal and that the verdict had been passed by the vote of the British Jurors—this reprisal against the democrat by the lackeys of the moneybags evoked street demonstrations and a strike in Bombay".

Similarly, Gorky wrote to Shyamji Krishna Varma on 20th October 1912, asking him to send "an article for the *Russian Review* that could give to the Russian democracy the knowledge of the Indian movement for liberty and justice". He said: "We must let know one people to the other that everybody who thirsts for justice, who desires to live in accordance with the intellect, should understand their unity, the unity of their aims, their spirit and would be united in one and invincible strength which will conquer finally all the evil of the world".

With his usual insight, Lenin along with other socialist revolutionaries was quick to recognise that the struggle of the Indian and other colonial peoples against their imperialist masters was a necessary part of the growth of socialism in the world.

It is significant to mention in this connection that by 1905 the situation in India had ripened for a new stage of freedom struggle and a modern method was evolved, the weapon of economic boycott, in place of the earlier technique of protests based on religious and other compulsions.

The advance of freedom movement in India during 1905-1907 was in fact, a part of the wave of the world advance of the progressive forces, following the defeat of Czarism at the hands of Japan, the first victory in modern times of an Asian nation over a European power. This led to a far reaching and lasting effect on the consciousness of the Indian people. The initial success of the First Russian Revolution further strengthened the resolve of the Indian people to do or die. Against this background the national ferment against the British rule typified by the general strike of Bombay textile workers in 1905 - the first political action of the Indian working class - needs to be understood.

The events of the First World War, the unbridled exploitation of the Indian people and the October Revolution of 1917 unleashed unprecedented mass movements for national freedom in the post war period. Just as the awakening of 1905 was generated by the world situation at large, even more so was the birth of the mass movements in India which shook the foundations of the British rule in the years succeeding 1917.

This correlation of the development of the struggle in India and the world struggle is of special importance, in view of the subjective and isolationist explanations frequently trotted out by the traditional schools of Indian political thought for interpreting mass movements simply in terms of personalities or particular groups. The bias has by no means lost its hold even today.

There is no doubt that the transformation of the political movement in India from relatively restricted sections of the population to the broad masses of the people took place in the years following 1917. And this transformation was not limited to India alone!

The World War, in the wake of the defeat of Russian Czarism by Japan a decade earlier, completed the shattering of the myth of the invincibility of Western imperialism in the eye of the Asiatic people. The spectacle of the internecine conflicts of the imperialist powers and the emergence of the Soviet Union as the first socialist state in the world aroused renewed hopes in the breast of millions of subject people that the hour of collapse of the existing empires was approaching. This made a far deeper impact on the minds of the Indian people and their leaders than perhaps anywhere else. The news of the February Revolution and the overthrow of the Czar, which had come to India through the British press, spurred the Indian leaders to a greater activity for they had always regarded the Russian autocracy as a phenomenon on par with British despotism in India. A brochure published in 1917 by the Home Rule Committee and given the symbolic title "Lessons from Russia" (Home Rule Series—23) contained an appeal to the educated classes to expound to the masses of the Indian people the significance and implications of the liberation movement in Russia. The victorious revolution in Russia had truly inspired Indian nationalists to intensify their liberation struggle. Allahabad newspaper *Abhydaya* (24th March 1917) made a striking comment: "Russian revolution convinces us that there is no power in the world which an animating and life giving nationalism could not have overcome".

As the revolutionary events in Russia progressed, the British rulers and the mass media controlled by them embarked on a campaign of anti-Sovietism. However, despite all these measures of the colonial administration, the fact of the October Revolution could neither be suppressed nor denied its pull in India. "The revolution in Russia and its beginning was regarded in India as a triumph over despotism............ It has given an impetus to Indian political aspirations", confessed the Secretary of State for India, sadly though.

The demolished soldiers in India, particularly the Punjabi soldiers, returning from the battlefields of Europe and the Middle East, at the end of the War, carried the heroic story of Russian Revolution to their villages and those others who had seen action in Turkestan, Central Asia and the territories bordering on the Caspian Sea literally set the Indian hearts aflame.

It is not without significance to recall that the most influential of the national political organisations, the Indian National Congress, acclaimed the October Revolution, even though a section of leaders did not support its socio-political programme. Inaugurating the session of the Indian National Congress in 1917, Annie Besant said: "The Russian Revolution and the probable rise of a Russian Republic in Europe and Asia, have all entirely changed the conditions existing before in India".

The impact of the October Revolution on India was phenomenal. It had three distinct dimensions - stimulating the consciousness of the Indian people, widening the basis of the national movement and above all, hastening the evolutionary process of the Indian Left movement, particularly the communist movement.

This epoch making Revolution, besides shaping world events, gave a radical turn to relations between the British colonial rulers and the Indian people. The most noticeable aspect of this change was the raising of the all-important question of national self-determination and the resolve of the people to fight for it with spirit and courage. If some of the language papers editorially commenting on this Revolution hailed it as the harbinger of the dawn of a new era, national leaders of all political hues welcomed the new developments in Russia. Mahatma Gandhi, for instance, said that "Bolshevik ideals sanctified by the sacrifice of such master spirits as Lenin cannot go in vain".

Within the national movement, radicals probably had a clearer understanding about the international significance of this Revolution, a significance, which was further, heightened by Lenin's breathtaking Declaration of the Rights of the People of Russia. It was, therefore, most natural that a section of the leadership of the Indian national movement should defend and stand up for the Revolution. Bal Gangadhar Tilak's newspaper *Kesari* spoke up for Lenin in a forthright editorial underlining the fact that the Russian people were solidly behind him and the Revolution.

This being the situation, the British rulers shrewd as they were, rightly gauged the new temper of the people and started readjusting their strategy in India. Within five months of the fall of Czarism, the British Government hastened to issue a notification, known as Montague Declaration, and proclaimed the aims of British rule in India to be "gradual development of self governing institutions with a view to the progressive realisation of Responsible Government in India as an integral part of the British Empire" and promised suitable and speedy steps in this direction. The hasty character of this declaration was evident from the fact that real work began slowly and haltingly to concretise what was intended to be done, in producing what came to be known as Montague—Chelmsford Report, only a year later. It is noteworthy again that the entire move was directed to creating a division among the leaders of the national movement. Nevertheless, the reaction of the national movement and the way the British rulers started changing their tactics were unmistakable proofs of the fact of the Russian Revolution and of its indelible imprint on the Indian mind.

Much of the interest of the Indian nationalists in the far-reaching developments in Russia after the October Revolution must be seen against the background of the then nationalist aspirations of the Indian people—the success of the Revolution, the withdrawal of Russia from the War and Lenin's policy proclamation about the radicalising influence on Indian thinking and actions.

The Russian Revolution had taken place precisely at a time when the Indian freedom movement had begun to acquire the status of a defined struggle. It is also understandable that at this stage the mass sympathy for the Russian Revolution was generally articulated by the leaders of the middle classes, they being the main instruments of the developing national movement. Hence, these were the people who were most influenced by the Russian Revolution. But as the efforts of the Soviet people for building a socialist society began to unfold themselves and as the Indian national movement started broadening its mass base, the convergence of interest of the Soviet Union and the aspirations of the colonial and semi-colonial people against imperialism came to be widely accepted by the leading forces and personalities of the national movement in our country.

In November 1927, Jawaharlal Nehru with his father Motilal Nehru attended the tenth anniversary of the Russian Revolution in Moscow. On his return, Jawaharlal Nehru wrote: "Our work in

India will be easier, if Russians succeeded in the fight against poverty and illiteracy".

In 1936, while presiding over Lucknow session of the Indian National Congress, he said: "If the future is full of hope, it is largely because of Soviet Russia and what it had done. This new civilisation will spread to other lands and put an end to the wars and conflicts which capitalism feeds".

Jawaharlal Nehru, in fact on the basis of this penetrating analysis of the achievements of the socialist society, was one of the first leaders of the anti-colonialist movement who came to the conclusion that the movement towards socialism was a specific need for countries struggling for national independence. Again and again he declared that the only road of rapid development of the countries struggling for independence was through socialism. His mind was made up: "Are we to follow the English, French and the American way?" It was in this context that he firmly rejected that the developing countries could not tread on the capitalist path. "Have we time of 100 or 150 years to reach our destination?" he asked and came to the conclusion that it was impossible because "we will perish in the process".

It is axiomatic to say that in popularising socialism and lauding the achievements of the Soviet Union as a socialist state, Jawaharlal Nehru made a memorable contribution.

Scientific socialism attracted Jawaharlal Nehru not simply as a theory. The reason for its appeal was that Jawaharlal Nehru was intellectually moved and attracted by the colossal and unprecedented experiment in revolutionary changes, which were taking place before his very eyes. "While rest of the world was in the grip of depression and going backward in some ways, in the Soviet country a great new world was being built before our eyes", he said. But he did not rest at that. He opined: "We thought of the United States of America and even of some eastern countries which were forging ahead. But most of all we had the example of the Soviet Union, which in two brief decades, full of war and civil strife and in face of what appeared to be insurmountable difficulties, had made tremendous progress. Some were attracted to communism, others were not, but all were fascinated by the advance of the Soviet Union in education and culture and medical care and physical fitness and in the solution of the problem of nationalities—by the amazing and prodigious effort to create a new world out of the dregs of the old".

This attitude of Jawaharlal Nehru led to a radical shift in the Indian democratic thinking, shaped as it had been by the influence of Russian Revolution and the achievements of socialism in the USSR.

Rabindranath Tagore was also greatly impressed by the Soviet Union in the brief span of a decade. In the words of Jawaharlal Nehru, "Even Rabindranath Tagore, highly individualistic as he was and not attracted towards some aspects of the communistic system, became an admirer of this new civilisation and contrasted it with the present conditions in his own country".

"In Russia at last", wrote Tagore from Moscow on the 20th September 1930: "whichever way I look, I am filled with wonder. It is unlike any other country. It is radically different. From top to bottom they are rousing everybody up without distinction.

"Throughout the ages, civilised communities have contained groups of nameless people. They are the majority, the beasts of burden, who have no time to become men. They grow up on the leavings of society's wealth, with the least food, least clothes and least education, and serve the rest. They toil most, yet theirs is the largest measure of indignity. At the least excuse they starve and are humiliated by their superiors. They are like a lamp stand bearing the lamp of civilisation on their heads: people above receive light while they are smeared with the trickling oil".

Tagore further enlarged upon the subject, in his "Letter from Russia", that "for the first time since the dawn of history the entire society, and not merely the upper portion thereof, was being illuminated by the light of civilisation".

There was no doubt that the great poet was swept off his feet by "the complete disappearance of the vulgar conceit of wealth" and by provision of "equal opportunities for the entire people without any manner of discrimination". He acknowledged that without a visit to Soviet Union "my life's pilgrimage would have remained incomplete". Tagore's "Letters from Russia" were understandably proscribed by the British.

Similarly during his last years, Iqbal, another great poet turned more and more towards socialism. The stupendous progress and success of the Soviet experiment had awed him—a fact which is vividly reflected in his poetry of the last few years of his life.

Again, when Hitler invaded the Soviet Union in 1941, the Congress Working Committee in its meeting in Bardoli in December

1941, expressed sympathy and concern for Russia. The resolution passed in the presence of Mahatma Gandhi read: "The Soviet Union has stood for certain human cultural and social values which are of great importance to the growth and progress of humanity. The Working Committee considers that it would be a tragedy if the cataclysm of war involved the destruction of this endeavour and achievement".

It is plain that the leaders of the national movement and the intellectuals continued to draw inspiration from the Soviet Union and took keener and keener interest in developments there. Jawaharlal Nehru aptly gave expression to that universal sentiment, when he said: "the presence and example of the Soviets was a bright and heartening phenomenon in a dark and dismal world".

The impact of the Russian Revolution on Indian national movement and social thought would remain incomplete without a passing reference about the rise of working class movement and the communist movement. During 1905-1909 there was a notable advance in the working class movement, parallel to the militant national movement. But after the Russian Revolution, the working class movement in India received a fresh stimulus. The strike movement, which began in 1918, engulfed the country in 1919 and 1920. These were the objective conditions in which Indian trade unionism was born, the Indian Trade Union Congress having been founded in 1920.

Despite all obstacles and initial confusion, if was after the Russian Revolution, individuals and groups in their search for building a socialist society and bringing about a synthesis between national independence and socialism, were attracted towards socialism and communism, from at least four directions.

First, there were national revolutionaries, operating from abroad in countries like Germany, the USA, Turkey and Afghanistan, who were drawn towards socialism and communism.

Secondly, national revolutionaries from the Pan-Islamic Khilafat movement came under the influence of Russian Revolution and later applied themselves to the building up of socialist and communist movements in India.

Thirdly, national revolutionaries of the Ghadar Party organised among the Punjabi emigrant labour, particularly among the Punjabi Sikhs, were inspired by the communist ideology.

Fourthly, radical minded revolutionaries in India from practically all the streams of anti-imperialist movement, the Akalis, the leaders of the Khilafat movement and elements of the younger generation of Congressmen turned to scientific socialism.

These communist groups or their representatives came together at the first Indian Communist Conference at Kanpur towards the end of December 1925 and founded the Communist Party of India (CPI).

Without going into the various phases of the history of the Indian communist movement, it must be recorded, all the same, that the Russian Revolution, its success and achievements created a tremendous enthusiasm among the national revolutionaries both in India and abroad, more specifically among those who were working in India. This laid the basis for the development of the left and the communist movement in India. Jawaharlal Nehru was keenly alive to the seminal importance of the Russian Revolution and shared this faith with other national revolutionaries, past and present. The Communist Party of India too has acknowledged this fact, though naturally in a different form: "The Communist Party of India arose in the course of our liberation struggle as a result of Indian revolutionaries who under the inspiration of the Great October Revolution were seeking paths of achieving national independence". *(Preamble* to the *Party Constitution* adopted at its Amritsar Congress in April 1958).

Thus, the Russian Revolution laid the foundation for the building and expansion of new kind of ties between the Indian people and the people of USSR. These friendly relations naturally entered a new phase after India became an independent and sovereign state in 1947.

Appendix

Joint Statement on the Outcome of the Official Visit of H.E. Mr. Vladimir V. Putin, President of the Russian Federation to the Republic of India

1. The President of the Russian Federation, H.E. Mr. Vladimir V. Putin, paid an official visit to the Republic of India on January 25-26, 2007 at the invitation of the Prime Minister of the Republic of India Dr. Manmohan Singh. President Vladimir Putin is the first Russian Head of State who is participating as the Chief Guest at the celebrations on the occasion of the Republic Day. Besides a high level official delegation, President Putin was accompanied by a group of top Russian businessmen and industrialists representing diverse areas.

2. During his stay in New Delhi, President Vladimir Putin met the President of India, Dr. A.P.J. Abdul Kalam and the Prime Minister of India, Dr. Manmohan Singh. The Chairperson of the United Progressive Alliance, Mrs. Sonia Gandhi called on President Vladimir Putin. President Vladimir Putin also participated in a business meeting attended by high level representatives from the trade and industrial circles of India and Russia.

3. The Prime Minister of India and the President of the Russian Federation recalled with satisfaction their meeting in July 2006 on the sidelines of the G-8 Summit in St. Petersburg where the Russian Presidency had invited India as an outreach country. The two leaders discussed a broad range of issues relating to bilateral cooperation and exchanged views on important regional and international issues of mutual interest and concern. The talks were held in the traditionally warm and cordial atmosphere that is

characteristic of the longstanding India-Russia friendship. They noted with particular interest that this visit took place in the year when the two sides were actively preparing to jointly commemorate the 60th anniversary (on April 13, 2007) of the establishment of diplomatic relations between India and the Russian Federation. They expressed satisfaction that, despite many momentous developments affecting global geopolitical situation over the last several decades, India and Russia have consistently remained close and friendly partners, with a continued commitment at the highest political level to further consolidate their ties. The following documents were signed at the conclusion of the talks between the Prime Minister of India and the President of the Russian Federation-Programme of Cultural Exchanges between the Government of the Republic of India and the Government of the Russian Federation for the Years 2007-2009;

— Protocol between the Government of the Republic of India and the Government of the Russian Federation on holding Year of Russia in India in the year 2008 and Year of India in Russia in the year 2009;
— Agreement between the Government of the Republic of India and the Government of the Russian Federation on the access of the Indian Party to navigation signals of the Russian Global Navigation Satellite System GLONASS for peaceful purposes;
— Agreement between the Government of the Republic of India and the Government of the Russian Federation on access of the Indian Party to a part of the Russian Global Navigation Satellite System GLONASS radio frequency spectrum;
— Agreement between the Indian Space Research Organization and the Federal Space Agency on cooperation in the joint satellite project 'YOUTHSAT';
— Memorandum of Intent between the Department of Atomic Energy, the Government of the Republic of India and Federal Atomic Energy Agency, the Russian Federation on development of cooperation in the construction of additional nuclear power plant units at Kudankulam site as well as in the construction of Russian design nuclear power plants at new sites in the Republic of India;
— Also the following were adopted:

— Joint Statement by the Prime Minister of the Republic of India and the President of the Russian Federation on cooperation in the field of peaceful uses of atomic energy;
— Plan of major events to commemorate the 60th Anniversary of the establishment of diplomatic relations between the Republic of India and the Russian Federation (April 13, 2007).

4. The Sides stress that durable, friendly and mutually beneficial relations between the two countries are based on deep mutual confidence and understanding. The strategic partnership between India and Russia has served not only the long-term national interests of both countries but has also effectively contributed to stability and security in Asia and the world in general. The two countries hold identical or similar views on most international issues. The Prime Minister of India and the President of the Russian Federation highly value the successful practice of holding annual summits that have played a key role in consistently adding greater strategic content to the wide-ranging cooperation between the two countries. These Summits encourage intensive contacts between India and Russia at all levels with a view to further intensifying bilateral cooperation.
5. During the talks, the two Sides reviewed the implementation of the decisions taken during the India-Russia Summit in December 2005. While expressing satisfaction at the ongoing multifaceted cooperation, the Sides support its further development, particularly in priority spheres such as high technologies, telecommunications, outer space, metallurgy, energy, nuclear power and military and technical cooperation.
6. The Sides reaffirm their intention to intensify efforts to further develop and diversify their trade and economic cooperation. Noting that the Indian-Russian Inter-Governmental Commission on Trade, Economic, Scientific, Technological and Cultural Cooperation provides an important mechanism for the development of trade and economic ties, the Sides stress the need to pay particular attention to the further promotion of bilateral trade and investment, including in energy, technology and knowledge-intensive economic sectors.
7. The Sides express satisfaction over the signing in February 2006 of the India-Russia Protocol on completion of

negotiations on Russia's accession to the WTO. Particular importance is attached to the setting up of a Joint Study Group (JSG) in 2006 to work out practical recommendations aimed at effectively tapping the opportunities available in both countries to substantially raise their bilateral trade and economic cooperation. As an immediate step, the Sides support early finalization of a result-oriented programme of action by the JSG to increase their bilateral trade to $ US 10 billion by 2010.

8. The Sides advocate every possible effort to expand mutually beneficial contacts between the business communities of the two countries. They welcome the initiatives taken in this direction by the industrial and business associations of India and Russia, aimed at strengthening the important role played by the Joint Business Council. The Sides also agree to take steps to remove the existing barriers impeding the promotion of bilateral trade.

9. The Sides appreciate the establishment of the Indo-Russian Forum for Trade and Investment, co-chaired by the Minister of Commerce and Industry of India and the Minister of Economic Development and Trade of the Russian Federation. They are optimistic that its first meeting in India in February 2007 at which a large number of top businessmen from both sides are preparing to participate will yield positive results.

10. Noting the vital role played by energy in economic growth, the Sides attach particular importance to energy security issues. They endorse the concept of 'energy security' envisaging an acceptable balance between security of demand and security of supply. In view of their corresponding resources, needs, capabilities and potential, the Sides agree to further enhance direct dialogue between their oil and gas companies aimed at concluding concrete and mutually beneficial commercial agreements for joint work in all segments of oil and gas cooperation in India, Russia and third countries. The arrival of the first shipment of oil to India from Sakhalin-1 in early December 2006 as well as the signing on January 25, 2007 of an MoU between ONGC and Rosneft oil company setting up two Joint Working Groups - one each for upstream and downstream activities - demonstrate the viability of future India-Russia cooperation

in the entire hydrocarbon value chain. The Sides also expressed satisfaction at the progress in the ongoing construction of two nuclear power plants in Kudankulam (India) with Russian participation.

11. The Sides note with satisfaction that the progressive expansion of their traditionally important cooperation in the field of peaceful uses of outer space is based on deep mutual trust and high capabilities of the two countries in this sphere. In this context, they particularly welcome the signing of additional bilateral agreements during the present visit to jointly implement wide-ranging cooperation in the Russian Global Navigation Satellite System GLONASS. They also express satisfaction at the signing of a bilateral document to jointly develop and launch a Youth Satellite for educational purposes.

12. Military-technical cooperation between India and Russia has traditionally remained a major pillar of the bilateral strategic partnership. The Sides note with satisfaction that mutually beneficial interaction in the field of defence has steadily progressed from a buyer-seller format to also include joint research and development, manufacturing and marketing, regular service to service interaction and joint exercises. As a leading example of their shared potential in high technological collaboration, the India-Russia joint venture to manufacture BrahMos missile, which is expanding in scope, has led the way to further such joint projects. The Sides note with satisfaction the in-principle decision to jointly develop a new Multi-Role Transport Aircraft.

13. India and Russia, while recognizing vast possibilities offered by rapid development and mass use of information and communication technologies, systems and utilities, including internet, express their concern that along with the gains, new threats of use of information technologies have emerged, which are incompatible with the goals of ensuring international stability and security both in civil and military spheres. The Sides express their readiness to continue bilateral India-Russia dialogue and intensify joint efforts directed at strengthening national and international information security, including combating criminal and terrorist activities.

14. The Sides recall with satisfaction their wide-ranging bilateral cooperation in the field of science and technology that has been successfully and jointly steered and conducted in the framework of the Integrated Long Term Programme (ILTP). They affirm to jointly commemorate the 20th anniversary (on July 3, 2007) of the establishment of the ILTP. As a major initiative, the Sides welcome the decision to set up an India-Russia Technology Centre in Moscow to facilitate and channelize commercial /industrial applications of new jointly developed technologies. The Sides recognize that this new facet to S&T cooperation would also provide a stimulant effect to the overall scope of joint work. The Signing of the relevant Joint Work Document would enable the Centre to begin concrete work.
15. The Sides have agreed to continue work on the North-South international transport corridor project, in the interests of further development of trade and economic cooperation between India and Russia.
16. Cultural cooperation and people to people contacts have traditionally played an important role in promoting greater understanding and closer friendship between India and Russia. In this context, the Sides welcome the signing of the bilateral Cultural Exchange Programme and the Protocol to celebrate 2008 as the Year of Russia in India and 2009 as the Year of India in Russia. The Sides appreciate ongoing joint efforts aimed at development of partnership relations between institutions of the two countries in the fields of culture, Indian and Russian studies and languages. They agree to consider new mechanisms, including financial, to accelerate this trend through greater interaction between Indian and Russian scholars.
17. The Sides will work towards the establishment of a multipolar world order based on the principles of the rule of law, sovereign equality, territorial integrity and noninterference in internal affairs of States. Activities aimed at strengthening a central coordinating role of the United Nations in maintaining peace and security, and at increasing the efficiency and authority of the UN, form important elements of India-Russia cooperation at the international level. India and Russia stress the need to implement the process of UN reform, so as to reflect contemporary realities.

In this context, the Russian Federation reiterates once again that it regards India as an influential and major member of the international community. The Russian Federation reaffirms its support to India as a deserving and strong candidate for the permanent membership in an expanded UN Security Council.

18. India and Russia strongly condemn terrorism in all its forms and manifestations. Both Sides reaffirm that terrorism is one of the gravest threats to international peace and security, and that there can be no justification for any act of terrorism, irrespective of motivations, wherever and by whosoever committed. They are also convinced that terrorism cannot and should not be associated with any nationality, religious, cultural or ethnic group. The Sides affirm that bilateral cooperation in counter-terrorism is an important dimension of their strategic partnership. They agree to consolidate joint efforts in suppressing financing of international terrorism and fighting illicit drug trafficking.

19. The Sides reiterate their intention to continue comprehensive long-term international cooperation to combat terrorism and to address other new challenges and threats, acting on the basis of international law under the UN auspices as well as within other relevant international organizations of which India and Russia are members. They oppose double standards in combating this phenomenon. They will cooperate to implement the United Nations Global Counter-Terrorism Strategy and to ensure an early entry into force of the International Convention for the Suppression of Acts of Nuclear Terrorism. Both Sides affirm their strong interest in promptly reaching an agreement on the draft Comprehensive Convention against International Terrorism submitted by India.

20. The Sides note with concern the risk posed by the spread of terrorist ideologies and express their determination to counter this threat basing these efforts on UNSC resolution 1624, including through enhancing, in every possible way, dialogue among civilizations and cultures.

21. The Sides are interested in strengthening bilateral and multilateral interaction in Central Asia, which would contribute to enhanced stability and security in the region,

including through closer and mutually beneficial cooperation with individual countries in the region based on shared interests and mutual respect. India and Russia advocate the development of practical cooperation among all partner countries of the Shanghai Cooperation Organization.

22. The Sides are concerned about the continuing deterioration of the situation in Afghanistan and the growing terrorist threat posed by the Taliban and other extremist forces. India and Russia will continue to participate in the post-war recovery in Afghanistan and are interested in strengthening its statehood and in the re-emergence of that country as a peaceful, democratic, independent and prosperous state.

23. The Sides are convinced that an effective solution to the Iranian nuclear issue is best found through political and diplomatic efforts. In this regard the unanimous adoption of the UN Security Council Resolution 1737 is significant. It underscores the need for more active and transparent cooperation of Iran with the IAEA in order to resolve outstanding verification issues. They agreed that implementation of the Resolution should facilitate resumption of negotiations for a long-term comprehensive agreement, which would allow for the development of relations and cooperation with Iran based on mutual respect and the establishment of international confidence in the exclusively peaceful nature of Iran's nuclear programme.

24. The Sides call for ensuring peace and security on the Korean Peninsula, maintaining it free from nuclear weapons and addressing the nuclear problem through the six-party talks based on the Joint Statement of September 19, 2005.

25. The Sides reaffirm their commitment to securing a comprehensive, lasting and just settlement of the Arab-Israeli conflict on a firm international legal basis, i.e. relevant UNSC resolutions, the Madrid Principles and the Road Map. They also support the Arab Peace Initiative, adopted in Beirut in 2002. They condemn violence by all sides and call for negotiated solutions. They advocate the active support of the international community, the Quartet and regional players for efforts aimed at normalizing the situation in West Asia and Middle East, and resuming dialogue on all tracks;

the Palestinian, the Lebanese and the Syrian, for comprehensive and durable peace in the region.

26. The Sides express concern over the continuing deterioration of the situation in Iraq. They believe that a return to peace, stability and progress in Iraq can only be achieved through reconciliation and a broad internal dialogue between all ethnic and religious groups and political forces of the country. India and Russia believe that the developments in Iraq indicate the need for collective international efforts aimed towards an early normalization of the situation in the country.

27. The Sides call for expansion of cooperation within the China-Russia-India trilateral format. The first trilateral summit-level meeting, which took place in July 2006 in the outreach format of the G8 events in St. Petersburg, gave a fresh impetus to enhancing multifaceted interaction among the three states. The trilateral interaction promotes the development of mutually beneficial economic cooperation among India, Russia and China, enhances international accord in the field of countering new challenges and threats, especially in the fight against terrorism, and contributes to strengthening peace and stability in Asia and throughout the world.

28. The Sides reaffirm their strong commitment to strengthening their relations in every possible way, and express their conviction that the strategic partnership contributes to the development of mutually beneficial and comprehensive bilateral cooperation, and serves the cause of peace, security, stability and sustainable development at the regional and global levels.

29. The President of the Russian Federation invited the Prime Minister of the Republic of India to visit Russia at a mutually convenient time for the next annual Summit. The invitation was gladly accepted.

New Delhi,

25 January 2007.

INDEX

S